ILLUSTRATED HISTORY OF ENGLISH LITERATURE

VOLUME TWO

I. A scene from Gay's *The Beggar's Opera* by William Hogarth

ILLUSTRATED HISTORY
OF ENGLISH LITERATURE

VOLUME TWO

BEN JONSON TO SAMUEL JOHNSON

by

A. C. WARD

ILLUSTRATIONS COLLECTED BY
ELIZABETH WILLIAMS

LONGMANS

LONGMANS GREEN AND CO LTD
48 Grosvenor Street, London W.1

*Associated companies, branches and representatives
throughout the world*

First published 1954
Sixth impression by photolithography 1968

Permission has been given for this book to be transcribed into Braille

PRINTED IN GREAT BRITAIN
BY LOWE AND BRYDONE (PRINTERS) LIMITED
LONDON, N.W.10

THE AUTHOR TO THE READER

My governing convictions as a writer on literature are set out in the introductory pages to volume one of this work. I need now refer only to my first principle that books are to be enjoyed and that the permanent benefits of reading come through enjoyment. This is a hard saying to those who hold that the study of literature should be undertaken or imposed as an academic exercise in mental discipline. The evidence of the ages nevertheless supports my contention, for literary master-pieces reach classic rank by virtue of the pleasure given by them to generations of readers. From that pleasure—whether it be spiritual, rational, emotional, æsthetic, or at best a unifica-tion of all these—mental discipline grows more potently than from unready and laborious application.

Those who read (I trust with enjoyment) both this volume and its earlier companion, will observe that whereas volume one is concerned with a mainly amateur literature, the present book surveys a period in which authorship became an established profession, though the gifted amateur writer did not disappear. The eighteenth century saw the old printer-publisher-book-seller more and more displaced by the men who made pub-lishing a specialized business and brought the Book Trade into being, a process traced in chapter V below. The coming of the book trade created a growing market which led the new race of publishers to commission or employ authors to write books to order as a commercial supplementation of such works as originated in natural creative talent. Thereupon a multitude of lesser writers appeared, producing books which, however unimportant intrinsically, became characteristic features of the broadened literary landscape. While the consequent obligation to place a number of mediocre publications in their historical setting has compelled me to refer to certain writers that I would contentedly have passed by, I have endeavoured to do justice to them with a minimum interruption of the main narrative. Eighteenth-century literature was not poor in giants, but it was also exceptionally prolific of compulsive midgets.

A. C. W.

August 1954

CONTENTS

ILLUSTRATIONS

Colour Plates

Monochrome Plates

CHAPTER I

EARLY STUART DRAMA

Ben Jonson

OF the classic English playwrights, after Shakespeare, Ben Jonson is most praised but also least loved. More effective on the stage than in print, he has yet been in recent generations a scholars' dramatist rather than an actors', a paradox arising from two major inadequacies in Jonson's work. His plays are fundamentally uninteresting to the general reader because the text is fundamentally undramatic and therefore provides few aids to the process of mental visualization essential for intelligent play-reading. And while stage production of Jonson may effect the required visualization, it offers little reward to modern actors since the characters have no depth and no life of their own: almost everything depends upon the actors' capacity for invention, yet where that capacity is sufficient the result is less rewarding than might be expected, for the invention needed in acting Jonson has to be in an alien mode outside the range of our contemporary experience. The jealousy of Othello is in kind, even though not in degree, the desolating passion of everyone who has experienced love and doubt of the beloved, and it consequently strikes to the roots of human nature; but the jealousy of Kitely in Jonson's *Every Man in his Humour* is hardly more than a cerebral perturbation. What he utters (II, iii) is a recital of the universal experience of jealousy, but his speeches carry no emotional overtones or undertones and therefore do not trouble the blood of readers, actors, or spectators.

> A new disease? I know not, new, or old,
> But it may well be call'd poore mortalls plague:
> For, like a pestilence, it doth infect
> The houses of the braine. First, it begins
> Solely to worke upon the phantasie,
> Filling her seat with such pestiferous aire,
> As soone corrupts the judgement; and from thence
> Sends like contagion to the memorie:
> Still each to other giving the infection. . . .

The deficiencies we observe in Jonson are not in truth deficiencies at all, but the outcome of a principle of deliberate
excision. Jonson did not fail in what he set out to do: on the
contrary he did supremely well exactly what he intended. Our
dissatisfaction comes from the fact that the product of his
intention is now tasteless except to the drily intellectualized
palate.

By the year of Queen Elizabeth's death, 1603, five notable
plays by Jonson had been staged: *Every Man in his Humour* at the
Curtain in 1598; *Every Man out of his Humour* at the Globe in
1599; *Cynthia's Revels* (1600) and *The Poetaster* (1601) by The
Children of the Chapel;[1] and the first of his extant tragedies
Sejanus at the Globe in 1603. The chronological distribution
of Jonson's plays between Elizabeth's and James I's reigns is
unimportant, for in his practice as a playwright he was anti-
Elizabethan and he belongs in spirit and temper to seventeenth-
not sixteenth-century literature.

Christened Benjamin but always called by the diminutive,
Ben Jonson was born, probably at Westminster, in 1572,
shortly before the death of his father, a cleric. Educated at
Westminster School, Jonson was there the pupil of the eminent
antiquary William Camden. After leaving school he worked for
his stepfather, a master bricklayer, and later served as a volun-
teer in Flanders, having married about 1592. By 1597 he was
working for the theatre manager Henslowe as actor and playwright. His earliest plays have disappeared, but in 1598
Francis Meres named him in *Palladis Tamia*[2] as one of the six
leading writers of tragedy. The year 1598 saw not only the
production of *Every Man in his Humour* (with Shakespeare in
the cast), but also Jonson's bare escape from execution for
murder when he killed Gabriel Spencer, a fellow actor, in a
duel. For this, Jonson was branded and imprisoned and his
property confiscated. While serving the sentence he joined the
Roman Catholic Church but returned to the Anglican communion after twelve years. He died in 1637 and was buried in
Westminster Abbey.

With the *Masque of Blackness* (1605) he began the long series

---

[1] See Vol. I of the present work (cited hereafter as Ward: I), p. 182.
[2] See Ward: I, 168.

of Court entertainments for which Inigo Jones designed the stage sets until Jonson quarrelled with him in 1630. With *Volpone* (acted at the Globe and at Oxford and Cambridge in 1606), *Epicœne, or the Silent Woman* (1609), *The Alchemist* (1610), and *Bartholomew Fair* (1614) Jonson reached his highest level and, except for *The Staple of News* (1625), nothing of later date advanced his reputation as a serious playwright.

The Masque as a genre is not easy to define. It embodied elements of comedy, pastoral, morality, ballet, opera, and spectacle, and was rarely more than light amusement for amateur performers at Court and in noble houses. Jonson adopted the form from other writers of masques (among whom Beaumont, Fletcher, Middleton, Chapman, and finally Milton, were the chief) but he elaborated it with an innovation of his own, the anti-masque, which introduced a somewhat more serious note—of grotesque fantasy, or of satire which looked back to the comedies of Aristophanes. The uncertainty of definition is shown by the inability of literary historians to decide whether Milton's *Comus* should be labelled masque or pastoral drama.

It has been said above that Jonson succeeded well in his deliberate aim to bring about a revolution in the writing of plays and to reform the stage. He had the temperament of a classicist who abhors whatever is immoderate and disorderly, and his personal affection for Shakespeare was far from making him a wholehearted admirer of Shakespeare's work. While he no doubt allowed that in their kind his friend's plays were unequalled, he disliked the kind and considered Shakespeare a slapdash undisciplined writer, as we know from Jonson's scornful rejoinder to another contemporary's admiring assertion that Shakespeare never 'blotted a line', i.e. never revised. What Jonson set out to do was to write plays in a manner that would certainly have been approved by Sir Philip Sidney, who died twelve years before a player delivered from the stage of the Curtain Theatre in 1598 the manifesto of the reformed drama. This manifesto was the Prologue to *Every Man in his Humour* and its complaint against the loosely-constructed, wide-ranging Elizabethan romantic plays is in substance identical with Sidney's complaint in the *Apologie for Poetrie*.[1] With his belief in

[1] See Ward: I, 165–7.

the validity, indeed the inviolability, of the classical unities of
time and place, Jonson thought it ridiculous or worse

> To make a child, now swadled, to proceede
> Man, and then shoote up, in one beard, and weede,
> Past three score yeeres: or, with three rustie swords,
> And helpe of some few foot-and-halfe-foote words,
> Fight over *Yorke* and *Lancasters* long jarres:
> And in the tyring-house bring wounds to scarres.
> He rather prayes, you will be pleas'd to see
> One such, to day, as other playes should be.
> Where neither *Chorus* wafts you ore the seas;
> Nor creaking throne comes downe, the boyes to please;
> Nor nimble squibbe is seene, to make afear'd
> The gentlewomen; nor roul'd bullet heard
> To say, it thunders; nor tempestuous drumme
> Rumbles, to tell you when the storme doth come.

So much, then, of what Jonson thought plays should not be
and of what his own play would not do. At this point he turns
from negative to positive. His play is to present

> . . . deedes, and language, such as men doe use

and

> . . . persons, such as *Comœdie* would chuse,
> When she would shew an Image of the times,
> And sport with humane follies, not with crimes.

But human follies can become crimes, Jonson goes on to suggest,
if they remain uncorrected 'when we know th'are ill'. Comedy,
in his view, could be the great corrective of human follies. If
the follies are laughed at, he tells his audience,

> . . . there's hope left, then,
> You, that have so grac'd monsters, may like men.

As was to appear, the laughter encouraged by Jonson would be
the wry laughter of ridicule, the edged laughter of satire, the sour
laughter of disgust—never the kindly compassionate laughter
of understanding. The high praise often given to his powers
of characterization, his solid building-up of character, rarely
takes note of the deficiency which destroys absolutely what he
has constructed so painstakingly—namely the almost total lack
of humanity in his characters. Nothing in literature is more

ironical than that the man who wrote at the beginning of his career

> You, that have so grac'd monsters, may like men

spent that career principally in the creation of monsters, comic monsters at best, repulsive monsters at worst, bloodless monsters always—for the ichor in their veins carries not red and white corpuscles but only 'humours'. Jonson was the virtual inventor of the Comedy of Humours, a 'humour' being 'some individual passion or propensity' or an obsession of some kind. In *Every Man in his Humour*, the 'humour' of old Knowell is an overdone concern for his son's moral welfare; that of Kitely, unfounded jealousy; that of Bobadil, a ridiculous boastful pretence of prowess and courage. The gulf between Jonson and Shakespeare may be gauged from Bobadil, who is often regarded as the Jonsonian counterpart of Falstaff. The account given in *Henry IV* (I, II, iv) by Falstaff of his fight at Gadshill—

> . . . a hundred upon poor four of us. . . . I am a rogue, if I were not at half-sword with a dozen of them two hours together. I have 'scaped by miracle. I am eight times thrust through the doublet, four through the hose, my buckler cut through and through, my sword hack'd like a handsaw—*ecce signum!* I never dealt better since I was a man: all would not do. A plague of all cowards!—

is living comedy; Bobadil's boast (IV, vii)—

> . . . They have assaulted me some three, four, five, six of them together, as I have walk'd alone in divers 'skirts i' the town, as Turnbull, Whitechapel, Shoreditch, which were then my quarters, and since upon the Exchange, at my lodging, and at my ordinary: where I have driven them afore me the whole length of a street, in the open view of all our gallants, pitying to hurt them, believe me. . . . By myself I could have slain them all, but I delight not in murder.—

seems a plagiarism, but whether it is or not it lacks comedic energy. Shakespeare's characters always *give* to the actor, whereas it is the actor who has always to give to Jonson's characters, for as conceived by the author their temperature is usually subnormal.

While the Elizabethan romantic drama was a breakaway from the old Morality plays the Comedy of Humours was an extension from them. Its purpose was a moral one, and Jonson forestalled Hogarth by doing in literature what the eighteenth-century painter was to do still more sombrely in line and colour. The Comedy of Manners, of which Sheridan became the great master in the next century, has been considered the lineal descendant of the Jonsonian Comedy of Humours, but its ancestry is not patently evident there and Sheridan was very little touched by the curmudgeonly view of mankind that runs through much of Jonson's work. It was in the English novel rather than in the drama that the Jonsonian mood lingered. Smollett had something of Jonson's temper, and Bobadil was one of Dickens's favourite characters. For humoristic writing prose narrative is a more appropriate medium than the acted drama: it allows space for development and embellishment and for analysis of personality and motive. A novelist's description of Bobadil would make effective play with his fantastic attire and accoutrements; while in a novel Volpone could be shown in earlier stages of development and thus be made less inexplicable and monstrous. It is not perhaps off the mark to suggest that Jonson strayed into the wrong vocation through his early association with the theatre, which may have been entirely fortuitous, for we know nothing of the circumstances in which it began. Despite the endeavours of scholars, commentators, and actors, the English have steadfastly refused—or have pointedly neglected—to take Jonson to their hearts, except as the author of a few fine lyrics.

If one writer more than any other is in the direct line from Jonson, it is Swift, whose virulent detestation of humanity in *Gulliver's Travels* and in his pamphlets matches the mood of *Volpone, or The Fox*. In that play Jonson dredged the sewers of base conduct with brilliant skill to which admiration cannot justly be denied any more than to a feat of sanitation in a plague-infected city. Volpone, a wealthy childless Venetian, feigns to be dying and connives with Mosca, his hanger-on, to trick certain persons into believing that his fortune will be theirs if they bring gifts. One of these human ghouls (Corvino, a merchant) is apprised that his only hope of ingratiating himself is to offer his own young wife Celia as a means of reviving

Volpone temporarily. When Corvino falls into the trap, Volpone throws off the pretence of mortal sickness and attempts to outrage Celia. The tables are turned when Mosca blackmails Volpone and one of the cheated would-be heirs accuses him to the Senate. Mosca is sent to the galleys, while Volpone's property is confiscated and he is condemned to rigorous punishment. Celia is almost alone among Jonson's characters in being drawn with humanity and compassion, though even she is more given to rhetoric than to the language of natural emotion. In his Prologue to the play Jonson speaks of himself as a provider of 'quick comedy refined', but *Volpone* is, rather, a nightmarish dance of death, with its horrors aggravated by the mopping and mowing antics of Volpone's creatures, Castrone the eunuch, Nano the dwarf, and Androgyno the hermaphrodite.

The Alchemist is saturated with roguery less vile in kind, and it belongs to the conny-catching[1] type of writing which had hitherto been confined to Elizabethan pamphlets and pamphlet-novels. It is as near to true comedy as Jonson ever got and has welcome passages of almost irresponsible fun. In Tribulation Wholesome and Ananias, Jonson presented two of those satirical portraits of hypocritical Puritans which culminated in Zeal-of-the-land Busy in *Bartholomew Fair*, the nearest now to a popular play among Jonson's writings. A brawling, sprawling piece, it rambles and ambles among the booths and stalls of the fair, and, before the end, has drained and exhausted its substance. But some of the characters are more than types or 'humours': Ursula the pig-woman would be a worthy companion for Chaucer's Wife of Bath and Shakespeare's Mistress Quickly, though neither could match the virtuosity of Ursula's language.

From the pig-woman's scurrility to Jonson's graceful and tender lyrics and elegies is so astonishing a leap that it is difficult to believe that the same man wrote both, until the tenderness of the poems is seen to be more in appearance than in reality, and to come more from the skill of the poet than from the feeling of the man. This is true even of his most 'moving' poem, the 'Epitaph on Salathiel Pavy, a Child of Queen Elizabeth's Chapel', the 12-year-old boy actor:

[1] See Ward: I, 153.

Weepe with me all you that read
   This little storie:
And know, for whom a teare you shed,
   Death's selfe is sorry.

.   .   .   .

Yeeres he numbred scarse thirteene
   When *Fates* turn'd cruell,
Yet three fill'd *Zodiackes* had he beene
   The stages jewell: . . .

The simulation of feeling is perfect, but it is simulation
nevertheless, with the mind dwelling on Death as a personifica-
tion and on far-fetched images, while the heart is obscured.
Yet, for all that, English poetry would be without something
precious if it did not possess that epitaph and such of Jonson's
songs as 'Drink to me only with thine eyes', 'Still to be neat,
still to be drest', 'See the Chariot at hand here of Love', and
'Come my Celia, let us prove', as well as this stanza from the
ode to the memory of Sir Lucius Cary and Sir Henry Morison:

It is not growing like a tree
   In bulke, doth make man better bee;
Or standing long an Oake, three hundred yeare,
To fall a logge at last, dry, bald, and seare:
   A Lillie of a Day
   Is fairer farre, in May,
Although it fall, and die that night;
It was the Plant, and flower of light.
In small proportions, we just beautie see;
And in short measures, life may perfect bee.

The first folio edition of Jonson's works (1616), contained
plays, masques, and poems. The second folio, published
posthumously in 1640, added some previously unprinted
material: *Underwoods*, a gathering of poems including the verses
on Shakespeare; and *Timber, or Discoveries made upon Men and
Matters*, a sort of Commonplace Book such as the studious
compile from miscellaneous thoughts, observations, and
quotations. *Timber* was much praised in the nineteenth century
for the striking quality of many of its thoughts and for its supposed originality. It is now known that the bulk of its contents
was taken from Latin authors, classical and modern, whose
works furnished the staple of Jonson's reading.

Beaumont and Fletcher

Many attempts have been made to untwine the collaborative works of John Fletcher (1579–1625) and Francis Beaumont (1584–1616), but for general purposes it is enough to know that for some ten years (*c.* 1606–16) they produced a sequence of plays to which Beaumont's contribution may have been principally plot-material, since his contemporaries had so high an opinion of him in that connection that Jonson was said by Dryden to have consulted Beaumont about the plots of his own plays.

Fletcher was born at Rye in Sussex and educated at Cambridge; Beaumont came from Grace-Dieu, Leicestershire, and went to Oxford before entering the Middle Temple. Beaumont was buried in Westminster Abbey, and Fletcher (who died of the plague) in St. Saviour's, Southwark (now Southwark Cathedral). Of their conjoint plays the best are *The Knight of the Burning Pestle* (1609), *Phylaster* (1611), and *The Maid's Tragedy* (1611). Beaumont may have written *The·Woman-Hater* (1607) alone, and Fletcher was himself a prolific playwright on his own account, as well as in collaboration with others than Beaumont—Middleton, Massinger, etc. Fletcher's *The Faithful Shepherdess* (before 1610) and *The Wild Goose Chase* (1621) are the outstanding works from his own pen.

The Knight of the Burning Pestle, a good-tempered and still very amusing tilt at the contemporary craze for romances of knight-errantry, is one of the very few lesser Jacobean plays which stand up well to revival on the modern stage. A play within a play, it has an Induction with gentlemen spectators seated on the stage and, below, citizens and artisans, including a master grocer and his wife with their apprentice, Ralph. The grocer interrupts the speaker of the Prologue to insist that instead of performing a new play called *The London Merchant*, which he objects to as probably girding at citizens like himself, they shall do one of the old plays dealing with Dick Whittington, or Sir Thomas Gresham, or 'The Story of Queen Eleanor, with the Rearing of London Bridge upon Woolsacks'. The grocer's wife also intervenes to demand that Ralph shall take the chief part, and it is agreed that the play shall be *The Grocer's Honour*, though they accept the Prologue-speaker's suggestion that it should be called *The Knight of the Burning Pestle*. Ralph appears

as the Grocer-Errant, carrying a shield bearing a Burning
Pestle as device. The play proceeds (with numerous interrup-
tions from the grocer's wife), and with its deliberate absurdities
a kind of 'straight' plot is interwoven concerning another
apprentice, Jasper, in love with his master's daughter, Luce,
whom he abducts just before she is to be married to a gentleman
rival, Humphrey. This also turns to burlesque when Luce,
having been brought back by her father and Humphrey, is
recovered by Jasper who has had himself carried to her home
in a coffin; Luce takes his place in the coffin and is thus conveyed to his father's house, he himself in the meantime frighten-
ing Luce's father into benevolence towards them by pretending
to be a ghost.

If *The Knight of the Burning Pestle* has but small importance
as literature, it has some significance as an early piece of that
pure nonsense which the English delight in. The play is, at
the least, good farce and among farces is distinguished by its
survival for over three hundred years. Most farces perish in
early infancy.

The Maid's Tragedy shows that these successful makers of
nonsense had little tragic sense. Evadne, debauched by the
King of Rhodes, becomes his mistress and is married by his
command to Amintor a gentleman of the Court, who was
betrothed to Aspatia the chamberlain's daughter. On the marriage night Evadne, withholding herself from Amintor, reveals
to him her illicit relationship with the king. Her brother later
discovers from Amintor his sister's shame and incites Evadne
to kill the king. Her hope that Amintor will now accept her
as his wife having been destroyed, she kills herself. Aspatia
also dies after a duel which, while disguised as her own brother,
she forces upon Amintor, who stabs himself after her death.
Preposterous though the story may be in outline it rises to
dignity through the quality of the blank verse, which captures
and sustains interest and, notwithstanding a melodramatic
bent, has some emotional conviction.

Phylaster, or Love Lies a-Bleeding, altogether lighter in tone and
an attractive specimen of the contemporary romantic drama, is
based on a false accusation that Arethusa, daughter of the King
of Sicily, has taken as lover her young page Bellario, assigned
to her service by her betrothed, Phylaster, heir to the throne.

The accusation is credited by Phylaster until it is revealed that
Bellario is really Euphrasia (the daughter of a Sicilian lord),
who has adopted male disguise in order to be a near servant
of Phylaster himself. *The Faithful Shepherdess* (before 1610) stands
only below Ben Jonson's *The Sad Shepherd* (unfinished) and
Milton's *Comus* among plays of the pastoral-masque type. The
light enchantment of Fletcher's rhyming verse provides the
main attraction of the piece, and in its whole context the sometimes cloying sweetness of the lines is palatably assimilated.

Chapman; Massinger; Heywood; Marston

No greater fame has been conferred by proxy than that
given to George Chapman (*c.* 1559–1634) by Keats's sonnet
'On first looking into Chapman's Homer'. The translation
that enraptured Keats has been superseded from generation
to generation by others, and such direct fame as belongs to
Chapman comes from his repute as a dramatist. Of his many
plays, only *Bussy D'Ambois* (1604) now receives much attention, and that almost wholly from students. Yet it is a powerful
work, in verse that is often majestic in its expression of the
darker passions—lust and hatred and revenge. A drama of
blood and terror, it would be a tragedy of high rank if the
characters moved by inner laws of their own nature rather than
by manipulation at the will of their creator. Bussy D'Ambois,
brought to the Court of Henry III of France by Monsieur, the
king's brother, incenses the courtiers by his insolent pride and
in a multiple duel kills three of his enemies. He seduces Tamyra,
the Count of Montsurry's wife, and by insolent ambition stirs
the hatred of his patron as well as of the Duke of Guise. They
and Montsurry (who calls him 'Fortune's proud mushroom
shot up in a night') plot Bussy's death, and Tamyra is forced
by torture to entice her lover fatally into the trap laid for him.
Incidental to the main plot are magical contrivances engineered
by a pandering Friar who summons Behemoth from hell to
inform Bussy of the plotters' movements. The verse has its
finest moments in the full account given by the messenger
Nuntius of the fight between D'Ambois and the three courtiers
and in the terrible scene (V, i) between Montsurry and Tamyra,
with the husband in a madness of jealousy and hate and the

wife in a frenzy of terror and remorse. Montsurry's speeches burst from him like a tempest:

> Who shall remove the mountain from my breast,
> Stand the opening furnace of my thoughts,
> And set fit outcries for a soul in hell?
> For now it nothing fits my woes to speak
> But thunder, or to take into my throat
> The trump of Heaven, with whose determinate blasts
> The winds shall burst, and the devouring seas
> Be drunk up in his sounds; that my hot woes
> (Vented enough) I might convert to vapour,
> Ascending from my infamy unseen,
> Shorten the world, preventing the last breath
> That kills the living, and regenerates death.

From the dramatic writings of Philip Massinger (1583–1640) one comedy, *A New Way to Pay Old Debts* (before 1626), and one tragedy, *The Roman Actor* (*c.* 1626), continue to be read, but the giant passions with which he and most of his contemporaries charged their plays are no longer to the taste of audiences, and occasional passages of impressive verse rhetoric do not counterbalance the extravagances of emotion and the excessive violence of action which are the marks of stage drama in decline. *A New Way to Pay Old Debts* has in Sir Giles Overreach, however, a character that has continued to attract leading actors, the nephew (Frank Wellborn) whom he tries to swindle of his property is a sympathetic prodigal, and Margaret (Overreach's daughter) has some gallant lines in reply to her father's demand that she should go to all lengths to capture Lord Lovell as husband. But the play tends to lose its own thread in complicated intrigue, and the final plunge of Overreach from villainy into insanity is too easy and mechanical a resolution. The theme of *The Roman Actor*, drawn from the life of the Emperor Domitian, treats of his taking by force as empress the wife of Lamia, a senator. She falls in love with Paris, a tragic actor, whereupon Domitian contrives to kill him in an acted scene from a play called 'The False Servant' and condemns her also, but before the decree can be carried out she procures the emperor's assassination. Paris's defence (I, iii) of the stage as a mirror of correction for the abuses and vices of the age no

doubt expressed Massinger's own views, for he was among
the contemporary playwrights who used the stage as an
occasional political platform. Though the characters in *The
Roman Actor* have no interior vitality the verse is at times so
excellently wrought that semblances of individuality are
momentarily given to them.

While the early Stuart tragedies of blood carried on the
Marlowean drama, sporadic attempts were being continued
simultaneously to establish the domestic tragedy, of which
the anonymous *Arden of Feversham* [1] had been a tentative
specimen, and *A New Way to Pay Old Debts* a later example.
Between these two came *A Woman Killed with Kindness* (1603) by
Thomas Heywood (died *c*. 1650), whose two hundred or more
other plays included *The Fair Maid of the West* (published 1631),
one of the first English plays with a nautical atmosphere. *A
Woman Killed with Kindness* is notable for its attempt to introduce
into domestic tragedy a civilizing note, for here no blood is
shed either by the deceived husband or by the illicit lovers.
When Frankford discovers his wife's unfaithfulness with his
friend Wendoll, he is restrained by a maidservant from
injuring him (IV, v):

> I thank thee, maid; thou, like the angel's hand,
> Hast stay'd me from a bloody sacrifice.

He dismisses Wendoll with:

> Go, villain, and my wrongs sit on thy soul
> As heavy as this grief doth upon mine!

In an affecting scene with his wife, Nan, whom he confronts
with her two infants, he pronounces her punishment: for the
rest of her life she is to live apart in his 'manor seven mile off'
and never again see either husband or children. She justly
and without intentional irony answers, 'A mild sentence'.
Nevertheless she pines away and dies; her husband composes
her epitaph; and Wendoll, deciding to go abroad, looks forward
to reforming and getting a Court post when he returns. All this
is essentially undramatic—and to the risible almost ludicrously
comic—yet the play does distil some however limited tragic

---

[1] See Ward: I, 193; *and below*, pp. 201–2.

feeling from character alone, though the characterization is mostly embryonic, Nan's reception of Wendoll's advances being a muddled piece of writing with no motive beyond the author's impatience to get the plot moving. It is Heywood's 'feeling' for truth in human character, more than any ability to present it clearly, that raises his play above the average of the period: this feeling is gropingly presented in Wendoll's soliloquizing at the opening of the seduction scene (II, iii) that he is damned by his desires yet unable to escape his soul's self-destruction.

From being one of the firebrands of 'the war of the theatres' —perhaps the noisiest of the many literary quarrels of the age— in which his principal opponent was Ben Jonson his erstwhile friend, John Marston (?1575–1634) became an inconspicuous country clergyman after 1607. He now belongs almost exclusively to the pages of literary history, since his plays have had no modern stage currency, and he wrote of himself 'hungry Oblivion devour me quick'. Nevertheless, he stands on the high road of English comedy, and such plays as *The Malcontent* (1604) and *The Dutch Courtezan* (1605) merit more attention than they have received in recent times. It is for his part (with Jonson and Chapman) in *Eastward Ho!* (published 1605) that he is most remembered. This farcical comedy gained some notoriety from the fact that the three collaborators were imprisoned on account of a passage which was held to libel the Scots, but its later reputation depends upon its interest as a roistering play of London merchant life and manners.

Tourneur, Webster, Ford, and Others

Before the tragedy of blood and horror became finally exhausted as a scarifying type of stage entertainment, it produced two remarkable playwrights of whose personal lives little or nothing is known. Cyril Tourneur (or Turner) (?1575–1626) is generally supposed to have written both *The Revenger's Tragedy* (published 1607) and *The Atheist's Tragedy* (published 1611), though the former bears no author's name. These embrace almost every major crime of which men and women are capable, and in this respect they are tediously overwrought and enfeebled by their own excess. But however unbelieving and inattentive an eye may be turned upon the welter of vileness and crime, it is impossible to remain unaffected by the balefully fascinating atmosphere which Tourneur creates, yet does not consistently maintain. The characters are seen as through a drifting lurid fog which magnifies and distorts. Most of Tourneur's creations, male and female, are moral and spiritual cripples, and as a writer he was himself crippled. Since his plays communicate horror but neither terror nor pity they fail as tragedies. They do not purge but only constipate the emotions.

John Webster (?1580–?1625) is known to have been a freeman of the Merchant Taylors Company, but beyond that the records are as silent on him as they are on Tourneur. He collaborated with Dekker, Heywood, and others, but his lasting fame comes from his own two tragedies, *The White Devil* (*c.* 1608) and *The Duchess of Malfi* (before 1614). The theme of the former differs little from the familiar adultery-murder-revenge type, and although the plot of the other is less hackneyed, more complex, and more original, Webster might have had little after-fame but for his intermittent power as a poet. Aided by verbal eloquence and resource, scenes in *The White Devil* that would fail through melodramatic extravagance or inadequate stagecraft become dramatically impressive: as in Vittoria Corombona's insolent defiance of her accusers when she is on trial for murder and adultery (III, i), Brachiano's death scene (V, iii), and the last scene (V, vi) in which Flamineo (Vittoria's brother) tricks his sister and her maid into thinking they are to rid themselves of him with pistols which he knows are unloaded. The strangest feature of the play is Cornelia's mad scene (V, iv) after her young son Marcello has been killed by his brother, Flamineo, for it comes near to parody of Ophelia's mad scene in *Hamlet*, though its comparative flatness can be judged from the last line and a half of these three:

> There's rosemary for you;—and rue for you;—
> Heart's-ease for you; I pray make much of it:
> I have left more for myself.

This scene includes the song—'Call for the robin redbreast and the wren' that Charles Lamb admired so warmly.

In *The Duchess of Malfi* the widowed Duchess marries secretly Antonio, the steward of her household, against the injunction of her brothers Duke Ferdinand of Calabria and the Cardinal to preserve the honour of their blood by remaining unwed. Having bribed Bosola, another of the Duchess's gentlemen servants, to spy on her, they learn through him of her marriage. Antonio is forced into exile with one of the three children the Duchess has borne to him, and she is imprisoned in the palace. The torments devised for her include a visit from a body of madmen who sing, talk, and dance crazily before her as a prelude to the dreadful but dramatically magnificent scene in which Bosola brings in executioners who strangle her, her waiting-woman Cariola, and her other two children. When Ferdinand comes to the room where she lies dead he speaks Webster's one immortal line: 'Cover her face; mine eyes dazzle: she died young.' After that great scene, the last act is hardly more than a prolonged anti-climax, in which Ferdinand becomes insane before being killed by Bosola, who is himself at the same time fatally wounded by Ferdinand. Julia, the Cardinal's mistress, is poisoned lest she betray his part in the Duchess's murder; Antonio, mistaken for an assassin, is killed by Bosola, and the Cardinal also dies at Bosola's hand. Webster moves with natural ease from prose to verse as the mood of the drama requires and is effective in both. While it cannot be claimed that the action is the inevitable outcome of the interplay of character and circumstance, the Duchess, Antonio, Bosola, and the two brothers have some genuine animation which makes their behaviour appear to be guided more by intelligible motives from within than by arbitrary dictation from the author. In spite of manifest shortcomings *The Duchess of Malfi* is the only post-Elizabethan tragedy which can be judged by Shakespearean standards.

With a single exception the remaining playwrights of the period need only be named: Thomas Middleton (?1570–1627) for *A Trick to Catch the Old One* (1608), *A Mad World, my Masters* (1608), *A Chaste Maid in Cheapside* (1630), and *The Witch* (before 1627; first published 1778); William Rowley (?1585–?1642), *All's Lost by Lust* (1622); Nathan Field (1587–1633), *A Woman's a Weathercock* (1612); John Day (*fl.* 1606), *The Parliament of Bees*

(?1607); James Shirley (1596–1666), *The Maid's Revenge* (1626) and *Hyde Park* (1632).

John Ford (*fl.* 1639) collaborated with Dekker and Rowley in *The Witch of Edmonton* (?1623), a domestic tragedy. *'Tis Pity She's a Whore* (published 1633) is outstanding among his own gloomily impressive plays. Annabella marries Soranzo to cover her incestuous love for her brother Giovanni, who later stabs her to forestall Soranzo's intention of killing her after a public denunciation at a banquet arranged for the purpose. Giovanni goes to the banquet, fights and slays Soranzo, and is then himself killed by Soranzo's servant. Without mitigating the naked passions and lusts which tear at the vitals of the brother and sister and her husband, Ford imparts some tragic dignity to the whole play through blank verse which serves its exacting purpose fully without ever rising to the level of great poetry.

Ford stretched the moral limits of stage representation to the utmost, however forbidding he made the enormities of his sinners appear. While in general the Puritan enemies of the theatre had little firsthand knowledge of the institution they denounced, such plays as Ford's gave understandable cause for attack. The Puritan campaign against the stage began early in the last quarter of the sixteenth century and a running fire of pamphlets was kept up until the theatres were closed by parliamentary decree in 1642 on the ground that public stage-plays did not well agree with the calamities and humiliations of the times. The immediate reason may have been no less political than moral and religious, since the theatres were places of public assembly managed by persons whose sympathies were doubtless Royalist and anti-Cromwellian. Nevertheless, Puritan animosity was whipped-up and sustained by their own pamphleteers, among the most influential being, in addition to Stephen Gosson,[1] Philip Stubbes—who included in *The Anatomy of Abuses* (1583) a short but violent diatribe on the wickedness of stage-plays—and William Prynne, whose huge *Histriomastix* (1632) was more of a compendium of earlier Puritan anti-theatrical writings than a record of personal observation, for Prynne was no playgoer and was comprehensively ignorant of what he condemned. His monster pamphlet did not go

[1] Author of *The Schoole of Abuse* (1578). See Ward: I, 164–5.

C

unheeded, however, in the campaign to discredit the stage. It also had unanticipated consequences for its author, who was pilloried, imprisoned, fined £5,000, branded on both cheeks, and cropped of his ears, mainly because he had called women actors (a scandalizing novelty then) 'notorious whores' at the very moment when (quite possibly unknown to Prynne) Queen Henrietta Maria and her ladies were rehearsing a play for performance at Court.

CHAPTER II

EARLY STUART VERSE AND PROSE

HISTORIANS no less than artists function by imposing order upon their material, but in so doing the historian achieves clarity at the cost of some sacrifice of proportion and accuracy. Focused through time and distance which smooth away uneven contours of the past, earlier ages often appear to us in an over-simplified aspect. While it may be pleasing to see the Elizabethan period as an era of sweetness and light from which there was an extreme reaction in the seventeenth century, there was in truth no singleness of mood among the Elizabethans, and their literature shows some early signs of the dark serpentine probings of mind and heart and spirit which engaged those successors in the next century who are lumped together as 'Metaphysicals'. When used of this particular body of literature the word Metaphysical needs the capital initial, since few great writers' works of any time or country are entirely devoid of a metaphysical (beyond-the-physical: i.e. philosophical or spiritual) quality. Where the seventeenth-century Metaphysicals differed was in finding a verbal style and a literary technique identical with their involuted and convoluted mental and spiritual processes: the instrument and what it uttered became one.

The foregoing preamble is necessary in a survey of seventeenth-century literature, for not everything metaphysical in that century was also Metaphysical. Those to whom the distinctive label can be attached are discussed below (p. 27 ff.).

Perhaps more than for any earlier time it is essential to consider the literature of this period in relation to the contemporary affairs and events which were its background and often its originating impulse. But the religious and political turmoil which claims so much attention in histories of the seventeenth century was scarcely more important in shaping the literature than was the advancement of science, with which at that time philosophy was still linked. Francis Bacon's influence as a

scientific thinker (he was also an amateur experimenter) has
been permanent and universal, and his great importance as the
innovator of modern ways of thinking in displacement of the
medieval ways into which he was born is well recognized. But
whereas Bacon's works are accepted as an indispensable part of
literature, a much narrower view is taken of other seventeenth-
century scientific writings whose effect on contemporary and
later authors has been equally important, even if less often
declared. The establishment of the Royal Society for Improving
Natural Knowledge[1] (projected 1645; founded 1660; incorporated by royal charter 1662) represented the culmination of
the investigating trend encouraged by Bacon's *The Advancement of Learning*, a trend which in its own field was as important
as the Elizabethan voyages of exploration, while it marked
even more directly than the fifteenth—sixteenth century
Revival of Learning the birth of the modern mind. To the
Royal Society we are largely indebted for orderly English
prose—it imposed upon its members the duty of 'a close, naked,
natural way of speaking; positive expressions, clear senses, a
native easiness'—and its laudable aims in that respect were
furthered by its enrolling, then, not only scientists but also men
of letters. Abraham Cowley (*see below*, p. 35) was one of
its leading founders, while John Evelyn (p. 79) and John
Dryden (p. 70 ff.) were among the writers who became members.
As will be seen, Dryden brought about the great revolution in
English prose that made it both a fine and responsive literary
instrument and a thoroughly efficient everyday tool. The
impact of pure science on pure literature was not to become
evident until the early eighteenth century, when the researches
and discoveries of Sir Isaac Newton (1642–1727) began to
work upon the poetic imagination of writers,[2] particularly
through his treatise on *Opticks* (1704).

In a history of English literature it is necessary to distinguish between works in the native language and those
written in Latin by English authors: the latter are outside the
main stream of our literature, however much they may have

[1] The present 'Royal Society', which confers its Fellowship (F.R.S.) as
the highest mark of distinction available to scientists only.

[2] See Marjorie Hope Nicholson: *Newton Demands the Muse* (Princeton
University Press, 1946) and Douglas Bush: *Science and English Poetry* (Oxford
University Press, New York, 1950).

moulded thought. Only the few of Bacon's writings which were originally in English qualify for attention here; while, vitally important though they are in the history of ideas and human enlightenment, neither William Harvey's truly epoch-making treatise on the circulation of the blood, *Exercitatio Anatomica de Motu Cordis et Sanguinis in Animalibus* (1616; published 1628), nor Sir Isaac Newton's incomparable work on motion and gravitation, *Philosophiæ Naturalis Principia Mathematica* (1687), belongs to *English* literature.

Francis Bacon

Many of the plays dealt with in the preceding chapter and in volume one were performed or published, or both, after James I had succeeded Elizabeth in 1603. The first non-dramatic work of real importance to appear in the new reign was Bacon's philosophical treatise, *The Advancement of Learning* (1605).

Francis Bacon (1561–1626) has been much beset by detrac-tors, adulators, and apologists through more than three centuries, without a final clear judgement of his character being reached. He was born at York House, London, the second of two sons of Sir Nicholas Bacon (Lord Keeper of the Great Seal under Elizabeth) and his second wife, sister-in-law of Lord Burghley, the Queen's chief minister. Francis took to the Law after leaving Trinity College, Cambridge, and was ad-mitted to Gray's Inn. In 1576–9 he served the English embassy in France, became a barrister in 1582, and M.P. for Melcombe Regis in 1584 and later for other constituencies. As a parlia-mentarian he was both assiduous and judicial-minded, and his moral courage was evident in his speaking against certain proposals favoured by Elizabeth, whose ill-will—and the indifference or worse shown by his relatives at Court—frus-trated his ambitions. Though he was befriended by the Earl of Essex, he took an active part in securing his benefactor's conviction after Essex's plot against the Queen in 1601, and this has been interpreted as evidence of treachery. A fairer interpretation may be that Bacon believed Essex guilty of a grave crime against the nation and would not subordinate justice to personal sentiment. After James's accession Bacon's expectations of high office were at length fulfilled. He was appointed Solicitor-General in 1607 (the year following his marriage), Attorney-General 1613, Lord Keeper 1617, Lord Chancellor 1618. Knighted unillustriously among a horde of some three hundred others in the accession honours of 1603, he was subsequently well compensated by being made Baron Verulam (1618) and Viscount St. Albans (1621). In 1621 he crashed. Accused of bribery, he was condemned by the House of Lords after confessing to corruption and neglect. It is disingenuous to plead that bribery was common form at the time; and that Bacon did not allow the acceptance of gifts from interested parties to influence his legal decisions—his own plea, which seems little better than an admission that he took money under false pretences. The heavy penalties imposed upon him (to be stripped of all his appointments, imprisoned in the Tower of London during the King's pleasure, fined £40,000, excluded from Court, and barred from Parliament) were all quickly relaxed, though he never again sat as an M.P. He retired to the family estate at Gorhambury, near St. Albans, Hertfordshire, and devoted the remaining five years of his life to philosophical study and writing. He fell a victim to his own passion for experimental observation, dying in London of a chill after leaving his carriage on a winter day to investigate the preservative action of snow.

Bacon's writings are classed under three heads: philosophical, literary, legal, though all are in some measure philosophical and none is unliterary. His philosophical system stands by the principle of the fundamental unity of knowledge: he claimed in a letter written in his early thirties to Burghley, 'I have taken all knowledge to be my province', while he referred elsewhere to 'one universal science, by the name of *Philosophia Prima*'. He planned a vast work, *Instauratio Magna*, the Great Instauration or Renewal of the sciences, of which only fragments were written. His most important single book was the *Novum Organum* ('New Instrument for the Interpretation of Nature and the Discovery of Truth') (1620), in Latin. It advocated induction from experience, though Bacon never completely severed himself from medieval authoritarianism—subservience to scholastic and hierarchic dogma—in spite of the anti-Aristotelian views he adopted while at Cambridge. In theory at least, however, he revolted from the abstractions to which the scholastics adhered, and advocated processes of rational inquiry adjusted to the observable facts of the natural world. Bacon was nevertheless aware that the human mind is an imperfect and fallible instrument, subject to delusions which he named Idols, i.e. false images. He enumerated four main classes of these: *Idols of the Tribe*—errors natural to humanity and leading to the tyranny of preconceptions; *Idols of the Cave*—errors arising from the circumstances and disposition of individual persons; *Idols of the Market Place*—errors due to the pretences and confusions to which social groups are prone; *Idols of the Theatre*—errors proceeding from false philosophies which, like stage-plays, deal with unreality. This sapient diagnosis of human error was not matched by an equivalent ability to frame a corrective philosophy; for this, as a critic has said, Bacon did not know enough. Nevertheless he pointed a way which others could take, and the experimental scientists of later generations have been in a large measure the heirs of his speculative mind.

The Advancement of Learning, written in a stately processional English with great nobility of movement, begins with a flattering address to King James which is made almost believable by the sheer impressiveness of the language. Book I discusses the Dignity of Learning and the errors which beset it; Book II gives a Survey of Learning, with a wealth of instances impossible to summarize, though note may be taken of the brief but eloquent tribute to Elizabeth's achievements as Queen (Book I, vii, 9). Bacon begins the last paragraph of his book: 'Thus have I made as it were a small globe of the intellectual world, as truly and faithfully as I could discover. . . .' We might say, rather, that he carried out a 'beautiful' dissection of the body of knowledge, cutting through the integument and exposing cleanly the veins and sinews of universal learning: history, poetry, philosophy (physic, metaphysic, mathematic), human nature, business, government, divinity. Though Bacon's method in the book is general and analytical, his purpose is not wholly impractical or unconstructive. It is a work for philosophic-minded readers, who will discover in it not only a dissection of the body of knowledge but also a directive map of the functionally articulated intellectual organism of man.

So far as his æsthetic rank in English literature is concerned, the rest of Bacon's work is subsidiary to his *Essays*, which contain more wisdom than any other writer has concentrated in so small a compass with so much strength and grace of style. Montaigne's *Essays* first appeared in France in 1580, and the first English translation (by John Florio) in 1603. Bacon issued his *Essays* originally in 1597, but that volume contained only ten very short pieces, as compared with thirty-eight amplified essays in the 1612 edition, and fifty-eight in the final edition of 1625. Whether or to what extent Bacon was moved by Montaigne's example to take up the essay form has been much discussed, though the question is of no great moment, for the two writers have little in common. Montaigne's style is discursive and familiar, Bacon's compressed and severe; Montaigne reflects and gossips at large with no more urgent motive than the pleasure of reflecting and gossiping, whereas Bacon uses the word 'essay' in its basic sense of an 'assay' or test or trial or attempt. Bacon's primary intention in the essays was to try out his thoughts on particular topics, and it must have been to some extent accidental that what began as (and in the 1597 edition still was) a kind of notebook, turned into a set of miniature masterpieces, ranging over Love, Revenge, Truth, Atheism, Friendship, Suspicion, Parents and Children, Seditions and Troubles, Beauty, Studies, Riches, Youth and Age, Gardens, Death, and much else. While they are notable as a mine of aphorisms and wise saws—'Men fear death as children fear to go in the dark'; 'Reuenge is a kinde of Wilde Iustice'; 'God *Almightie* first Planted a *Garden*. And indeed, it is the Purest of Humane pleasure'; '*Studies* serue for Delight'; 'Reading maketh a Full Man; Conference a Ready Man; And Writing an Exact Man': to give a very few—these *Essayes or Counsels, Civill and Morall* do not lack beauty when the subject warrants and allows. The essay *Of Gardens* is largely a catalogue of plants and trees, fruit and blossom, yet more also:

And because, the *Breath* of Flowers, is farre Sweeter in the Aire, (whence it comes and Goes, like the Warbling of Musick) then [than] in the hand, therfore nothing is more fit for that delight, then to know, what be the *Flowers*, and *Plants*, that doe best perfume the Aire. Roses Damask & Red, are fast flowers of their Smels; So that; you may walke by a whole Row of them, and finde Nothing of their Sweetnesse; Yea though it be, in a Mornings Dew. . . . That, which aboue all Others, yeelds the *Sweetest*

Smell in the *Aire*, is the Violet; Specially the White-double-Violet, which comes twice a Yeare; About the middle of *Aprill*, and about *Bartholomew-tide*. Next to that is, the Muske-Rose. Then the Strawberry-Leaues dying, which [yeeld] a most Excellent Cordiall Smell. Then the Flower of the Vines; It is a little dust, like the dust of a Bent, which growes vpon the Cluster, in the First comming forth.

If Sir Thomas More had not introduced a new kind of book into English literature with *Utopia* and given rise to later 'Utopian romances', less might have been heard of Bacon's unfinished *New Atlantis*, which may owe little or nothing to More but is of the Utopian genre. It is so burdened and weakened by an excess of picturesque trappings and ceremonial mumbo-jumbo, and shows Bacon so obsessed by a lust for scientific experimentation, that if the book had been completed it is likely that New Atlantis would have been inhabited by an abomination of synthetic animal and vegetable monsters.

The King James Bible, 1611
The long-familiar title, Authorized Version, is now inseparable from the English translation of the Bible published in 1611, though it was not specifically authorized to be read in churches, as Coverdale's 1539 version (known as the Great Bible) was. The omission had no derogatory significance, however, and it was well understood from the moment of its conception that this new English rendering was to supersede all others for use in public worship. In its origins it was one more manifestation of the English belief in compromise as the infallible national solvent, a belief which was in this instance to be magnificently justified. From the year of its publication until to-day, notwithstanding profound differences on points of doctrine and Church government among the several denominations, the Authorized Version has been accepted as The English Bible by an overwhelming majority of Protestants throughout the British Commonwealth, and its influence on English literature has been continuous. The Revised Version published in the 1880s was based upon more reliable texts in the original languages than were available to the King James translators and it was in that sense more 'accurate'; but it totally failed to displace the Authorized Version.

In 1604 James I summoned at Hampton Court Palace a conference of High Church and Low Church divines, purposing to reconcile the doctrinal antagonisms of the conflicting sects. The Puritan John Reynolds, President of Corpus Christi College, Oxford, proposed that a committee be set up to produce an improved translation of the Bible. James readily concurred and a company of forty-seven scholars was assembled to undertake the work. Six groups were constituted, two meeting at Oxford (Isaiah to Malachi; Gospels, Acts, and Apocalypse), two at Cambridge (Chronicles to Song of Solomon; Apocrypha), and two in the Jerusalem Chamber at Westminster (Genesis to Kings; Epistles). Their terms of reference instructed them to follow as far as possible the Bishops' Bible of 1568. They wrote, in the preface ('The Translators to the Reader'): '. . . we never thought from the beginning, that we should need to make a new translation, nor yet to make of a bad one a good one, . . . but to make a good one better, or out of many good ones one principal good one. . . .' As it proved, they were much indebted to Tindale and in no small degree to Coverdale and also to Wiclif and those who had worked with him. They did, in fact, examine carefully all earlier translations of the Old and New Testaments.

When the beauty and dignity and fitness of their language in the translation is considered (and the credit for this must go more to them than to any forerunner) their achievement seems little short of a miracle. Among the translators only one (Lancelot Andrewes, bishop in turn of Chichester, Ely, and Winchester) has an independent literary reputation—for his *Sermons*, and for the *Private Devotions* in Latin; and inasmuch as the work of the several groups was subjected to final revision by a central committee appointed from their whole number, it would not have been surprising if the approved version had been uninspired, characterless, and flat. It is, moreover, a curious fact that their 'Epistle Dedicatory to King James' is almost ridiculously flamboyant and 'The Translators to the Reader' for the most part ponderously self-conscious.

Obviously the translators developed a collaborative genius which none possessed as an individual prose-writer; the genius was exclusive to their great main undertaking and forsook them when they turned to the lesser tasks of flattering the King and explaining themselves to readers. 'But they had, so to speak, a collective ear and taste and, above all, they had intense and reverent zeal . . . the fundamental fact for them and their readers was the infinite importance to every individual soul of God's revelation of the way of life and salvation. . . . Like earlier translators, these men were raised above themselves by the consciousness of their responsibility for making the divine word clear and persuasive to "the very vulgar".'[1]

The Metaphysicals

The term 'Metaphysical poetry' as commonly used of a part of seventeenth-century literature is too limited, for Metaphysical characteristics appear also in prose writings of the period. Donne's prose no less than his verse is Metaphysical; so also, in style and in matter, is Burton's *Anatomy of Melancholy*. The Melancholick element [2] in one or other of its numerous aspects is as familiar and recurrent in seventeenth-century literature as the Fantastick—which Burton embraced with total devotion. These two elements, the Melancholick in matter and manner and the Fantastick in form and style, are persistent among the Metaphysicals, who cannot, however, be confined within a simple definition.

Samuel Johnson established the term, in the essay on Abraham Cowley written in 1777 and published as one of his *Lives of the Poets* in 1779. Johnson wrote:

> . . . About the beginning of the seventeenth century appeared a race of writers that may be termed the metaphysical poets; . . . The metaphysical poets were men of learning, and to show their learning was their whole endeavour; but, unluckily resolving to shew it in rhyme, instead of writing poetry, they only wrote verses, and very often such verses as stood the trial of the finger better than of the ear; for the modulation was so imperfect, that they were only found to be verses by counting the syllables.

Perceptive and independent though Johnson often was as a critic, in many respects he remained a typical child of the age, swayed by its tastes and prejudices, and sharing the common eighteenth-century desire for correctness in literature and art.

[1] Douglas Bush: *English Literature in the Earlier Seventeenth Century 1600–1660* (Oxford History of English Literature, vol. V. Clarendon Press, 1945).
[2] See below, p. 212 ff., on the eighteenth-century cult of melancholy.

But although the Metaphysicals were not greatly to his liking and he too hastily committed himself to absurdities in judging them, Johnson nevertheless detected certain of their qualities with unsurpassed acuteness. He wrote of their 'discovery of occult resemblances in things apparently unlike', a discovery which has since become an important source of the twentieth-century's eagerness to find likeness in many apparently unlike things, either through the psychologists' principle of 'free association' or through profound and obscure channels of symbolism. Johnson thought the Metaphysicals perversely strange and strained: 'The most heterogeneous ideas are yoked by violence together; nature and art are ransacked for illus-trations, comparisons, and allusions; . . . Their wish was only to say what had never been said before.' While he dis-trusted and in a measure resented their unusualness of themes and treatment—'Those writers who lay on the watch for novelty could have little hope of greatness; for great things cannot have escaped former observation.'—he did not fail to notice (however paradoxically) that beneath the superficial novelty lay a fundamental originality:

> . . . if they frequently threw away their wit upon false conceits, they likewise sometimes struck out unexpected truth: if their conceits were far-fetched, they were often worth the carriage. To write on their plan, it was at least necessary to read and think. No man could be born a metaphysical poet, nor assume the dignity of a writer, by descriptions copied from descriptions, by imitations borrowed from imitations, by traditional imagery, and hereditary similes, by readiness of rhyme, and volubility of syllables.

Johnson conceded, then, that they were original, that they were honest thinkers, and that at least sometimes they lighted upon truth; but he denied that they experienced genuine feelings: 'Their courtship was void of fondness, and their lamentation of sorrow.' It was here that Johnson went seriously astray in his assessment of the Metaphysicals, failing to com-prehend that beyond fondness lie the torments of love and beyond sorrow the agonies of grief. 'Their attempts,' he said truly, 'were always analytick; they broke every image into fragments: and could no more represent, by their slender conceits and laboured particularities, the prospects of nature, or the scenes of life, than he, who dissects a sun-beam with a prism, can exhibit the wide effulgence of a summer noon.' What was hidden from him was the significance of their breaking every image: they broke not only poetical images but also the universe and life itself into fragments; their passion for analysis arose from an absolute incapacity to see nature only in terms of 'the wide effulgence of a summer noon', or religion as a polite observance of conventional rites, or love as a comfortable affection. They were always aware of the Life beyond life—of the agony of dissolution, of death and burial and the descent into hell, preluding spiritual rebirth; they saw all things under an aspect of the divine purpose in Christ. Though immortality might be their confident hope and expectation, they were still possessed if not obsessed by a consciousness of mortality and by an often morbid determination to find reality only through a denial of appearance. At its worst (or perhaps, rather, at its stupidest) this determination resulted in a fixed mawkish disgust which is itself only the other side of sentimentality. At its best the haunting awareness of mortality is often expressed by the Metaphysicals in unforgettably vivid imagery, as in Donne's line—'a bracelet of bright haire about the bone'. Or in Andrew Marvell's 'To his Coy Mistress':

> But at my back I alwaies hear
> Times winged Charriot hurrying near:
> And yonder all before us lye
> Desarts of vast Eternitie.
> Thy Beauty shall no more be found;
> Nor, in thy marble Vault, shall sound
> My ecchoing Song: then Worms shall try
> That long preserv'd Virginity:
> And your quaint Honour turn to dust;
> And into ashes all my Lust.
> The Grave's a fine and private place,
> But none I think do there embrace.

or, with a curious humour, in Burton:

> . . . But be she fair indeed, golden haired, . . . a pure sanguine complexion, little mouth, coral lips, white teeth, soft and plump neck, body, hands, feet, all fair and lovely to behold, composed of all graces, elegancies, an absolute piece: . . . after she hath been married a small while, and the black ox hath trodden upon

her toe, she will be so much altered, and wax out of favour, thou wilt not know her. One grows too fat, another too lean, etc.; modest Matilda, pretty pleasing Peg, sweet-singing Susan, mincing merry Moll, dainty dancing Doll, neat Nancy, jolly Joan, nimble Nell, kissing Kate, bouncing Bess with Black eyes, fair Phyllis with fine white hands, fiddling Frank, tall Tib, slender Sib, etc., will quickly lose their grace, grow fulsome, stale, sad, heavy, dull sour, and all at last out of fashion.[1]

These are for most tastes more agreeably sane than the passage quoted by Burton from St. Chrysostom:

'When thou seest a fair and beautiful person . . . bethink with thyself that it is but earth thou lovest, a mere excrement which so vexeth thee, which thou so admirest, and thy raging soul will be at rest. Take her skin from her face, and thou shalt see all loathesomeness under it, that beauty is a superficial skin and bones, nerves, sinews; suppose her sick, now rivelled, hoary-headed, hollow cheeked, old; within she is full of filthy phlegm, stinking, putrid excremental stuff: snot and snivel in her nostrils, spittle in her mouth, water in her eyes, what filth in her brains,' etc.

The Metaphysicals never attain so repulsive an ecstasy of disgust, though they escape it not through sensual optimism but only through art. Whatever torments of passion—either erotic or spiritual—they experienced took on beauty in their verse and prose, for the seventeenth century created most of the English prose which can be said to possess inherent beauty.

While there is little or no sensual optimism in the writings of the Metaphysicals, there is considerable sensuality, frequently disillusioned and not seldom bitter. The bridge between the typical Elizabethan and the typical Metaphysical may be found in the torment of the 'dark lady' sonnets, in which Shakespeare's mood is akin to Donne's, though Donne was more apt to burst through the covers, as he does in the first line of 'The Canonization': 'For Godsake hold your tongue, and let me love'.

This passionately un-urbane, harsh, hard-surfaced, granite-textured writing is one important aspect of the Metaphysical style as it appears, most notably, in Donne and Burton—as if with a gesture of dismissal to mere smoothness and eloquence.

[1] *The Anatomy of Melancholy*: Part 3, Section 2, Member 5, Subsection 3.

Some few tricks of typographical lay-out were carried over from the Emblem writers,[1] as in George Herbert's 'Easter Wings' and 'The Altar':

> A broken Altar, Lord, thy servant reares
> Made of a heart, and cimented with teares.
> Whose parts are, as thy hand did frame;
> No workemans toole hath touch'd the same.
> A heart alone
> Is such a stone,
> As nothing, but
> Thy power doth cut.
> Wherefore each part
> Of my hard heart
> Meets in this frame
> To praise thy Name.
> That, if I chance to hold my peace,
> These stones to praise thee may not cease.
> O lett thy blessed sacrifice be mine,
> And sanctify this Altar to be thine.

Another leading Metaphysical characteristic consists not so much in the pursuit of far-fetched 'conceits' or comparisons as in the determination to drain from every chosen image its last vestiges of significance. Thus in Marvell's 'On a Drop of Dew' the minute object begins elaborately as

> . . . the Orient Dew,
> Shed from the Bosom of the Morn
> Into the blowing Roses,

passes in the space of a score of lines into a symbol of

> . . . the Soul, that Drop, that Ray
> Of the clear Fountain of Eternal Day,

and twenty lines later reaches its apotheosis:

> Such did the Manna's sacred Dew destil;
> White, and intire, though congeal'd and chill.
> Congeal'd on Earth; but does, dissolving, run
> Into the Glories of th' Almighty Sun.

The oddities of the Metaphysical writers are easier to isolate than the excellences are to assess, since their value lies not so

[1] See Ward: I, 142–3.

much in perceptible beauty and power to engage the mind as in an inexhaustible depth which makes a great deal of poetry in other modes seem stale and unrewarding. It was for a long time damaging to their reputation that extravagances are far more obvious than virtues; but, unless the judgement of twentieth-century poets and critics and others is desperately at fault, the Metaphysicals are now established as a major force in English literature.

Johnson's observations on the Metaphysical poets were focused principally upon Cowley, whom he regarded, however, as a follower of Donne and Ben Jonson, and his illustrative quotations are drawn almost without exception from Cowley and Donne. Sir Herbert Grierson's representative anthology [1] includes poems by twenty-seven writers, of whom ten call for individual notice: Donne, Cowley, and Marvell as dissimilar Metaphysicals; Crashaw, Vaughan, and Herbert as religious poets in a larger sense; Carew, Lovelace, and Suckling as representative of the group called Cavalier poets. Milton wrote no more than two or three Metaphysical poems, though he wrote nothing that was not metaphysical.

The work of John Donne (1576–1631) splits into the youthful profane poems and the later sacred writings, both poetry and prose. Born in London, he was the son of an ironmonger who had married the daughter of John Heywood, nephew-in-law of Sir Thomas More and author of *The Four P's* [2] and other Interludes. When he was eleven Donne went to Oxford for three years and then to Trinity College, Cambridge, from 1587 to *c.* 1590. He was admitted to Lincoln's Inn as a law student in 1592, but afterwards went abroad, part of the time on foreign service with the Earl of Essex, and in 1597 with the expedition to the Azores. In 1598 he became secretary to Sir Thomas Egerton, Keeper of the Great Seal, until in 1601 he eloped with and married Anne More, Lady Egerton's young niece and daughter of Sir George More, Lieutenant of the Tower of London. As this was virtually abduction, Donne was sent to the Fleet Prison for some weeks and the marriage was not

[1] *Metaphysical Lyrics and Poems of the Seventeenth Century: Donne to Butler.* Selected and edited, with an Essay, by Herbert J. C. Grierson (Clarendon Press, 1921).

[2] See Ward: I, 175–7.

1. Title-page of Ben Jonson's *Workes*

2. Costume design by Inigo Jones for Queen Henrietta Maria as Chloris in Ben Jonson's *Chloridia*, 1631

3. Design by Inigo Jones for *The House of Fame* for Ben Jonson's *Masque of Queenes*, 1609

4. Scene from *Phylaster* by Beaumont and Fletcher

5. Scene from *The Maid's Tragedie* by Beaumont and Fletcher

6. Sir Francis Bacon after Paul van Somer

7. Part of letter from Sir Francis Bacon to the Lord Chancellor

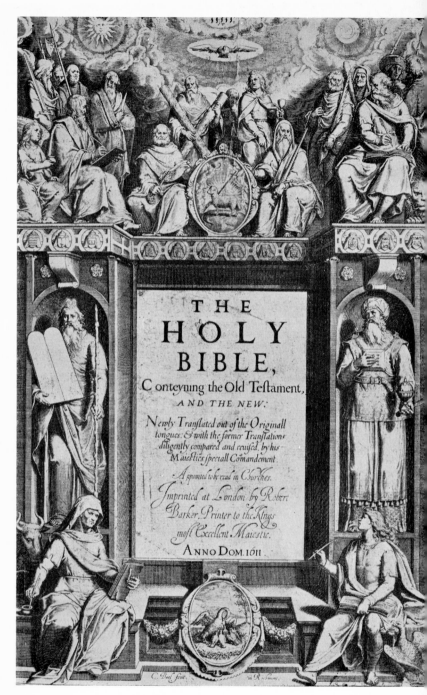

8. Title-page of King James' *Bible*

Tempora cinxit et Foliorum densior umbra:
Debetur Genio laurea Sylva tuo.
Tempora et Illa Tibi mollis redimiset Oliva;
Scilicet excludis Versibus Arma tuis.
Admisces Antiqua Novis, Jucunda Severis:
Hinc Juvenis discat, Foemina Virgo, Senex.
Ut solo minor es Phœbo, sic major es Unus
Omnibus, Ingenio, Mente, Lepore, Stylo.
W. Marshall Fecit.   scripsit I.H.C.W.M.

9. Robert Herrick from the
frontispiece to *Hesperides*

10. John Donne in his
shroud from the frontispiece
to *Death's Duell*

11. Title-page of *Steps to the Temple*
by Richard Crashaw

12. Title-page of *Religio Medici*
by Sir Thomas Browne

ratified until April 1602 after a law suit. Following further periods of secular employment and the writing of his *Songs and Sonets* and some prose, he travelled further on the Continent. After prolonged meditation Donne abandoned the Roman Catholic faith into which he was born and in 1615 took Orders in the Anglican Church. His high contemporary repute as a preacher has not dwindled, and his sermons are among the very few devotional compositions which are also durable prose. Donne's wife died in 1617; in 1621 he took office as Dean of St. Paul's (after holding livings in Kent) and was also appointed vicar of St. Dunstan-in-the-West, Fleet Street, in 1624. A serious illness in 1623 led to the writing of his *Devotions upon Emergent Occasions* (published 1624) which demonstrate 'the intense interest Donne took in the spectacle of mortality under the shadow of death, a vision that haunted him perpetually, and inspired the highest flights of his eloquence'.[1]

Izaak Walton tells [2] how Donne towards the end of his life was persuaded by his physician, Dr. Fox, to have his monument prepared. Donne sent for a carver to cut a board in the shape of an urn and of Donne's own height. He then employed a painter to depict him on the wood, acting as his own model in a winding-sheet 'so tyed with knots at his head and feet, and his hands so placed, as dead bodies are usually fitted to be shrowded and put into their Coffin, or grave. Upon this *Vrn* he thus stood with his eyes shut, and with so much of the sheet turned aside as might shew his lean, pale, and death-like face, which was purposely turned toward the East, from whence he expected the second coming of his and our Saviour Jesus.' This object stood beside Donne's bed until he died, when it was copied as an effigy in marble and placed in St. Paul's, where Donne was buried.

Walton also records that Donne, in his penitential years, deplored 'those pieces that had been loosely (God knows too loosely) scattered in his youth', namely the early love poems and other secular verses, which were nevertheless preserved in manuscript though not printed until after his death. Among

[1] *Complete Poetry and Selected Prose of John Donne*, edited by John Hayward (Nonesuch Press, London, 1929).
[2] In Walton's *Lives* (*see below*, pp. 77–8). This biographical study first appeared in 1640 as the introduction to *LXXX Sermons* by Donne.

those first poems, the manneristic aspect of the Metaphysical mode appears most startingly in the *Song* beginning:

> Goe, and catche a falling starre,
>   Get with child a mandrake roote,
> Tell me, where all past yeares are,
>   Or who cleft the Divels foot,
> Teache me to heare Mermaides singing,
>   Or to keep off envies stinging,
>   And finde
>   What winde
> Serves to advance an honest minde.

Donne's attitude towards the love of women was at that time by turns sensually amorous, cynical ('I can love any, so she be not true' [1]), and disillusioned; yet also sometimes melodious and often deeply moving, as in another *Song*:

> Sweetest love, I do not goe,
>   For wearinesse of thee,
> Nor in hope the world can show
>   A fitter Love for mee; . . .

In addition to the *Songs and Sonets*, Donne's poems include a series of Epigrams, twenty Elegies (love poems and hate poems, not true elegies, i.e. songs of lamentation), Epithalamions, Satires, Letters in Verse, Divine Poems, Holy Sonnets, and other pieces. Some of the worst failures as well as the master-pieces of Metaphysical poetry were written by Donne. His longest poems, *The First Anniversary* and *The Second Anniversary* (two of what were intended to be annual poems on the death of Elizabeth Drury, who died in 1610 aged fifteen) and *The Progress of the Soule* (in fifty-two ten-line stanzas, uncompleted), show that while Metaphysical ingenuities of thought and imagery and verbal dexterity can appear fresh and meaningful in lyrics and other short pieces, it baffles human skill to sustain a long poem on that model without its becoming ridiculously forced and tedious.

Something of Donne's effectiveness as a preacher may be gathered from Walton's description of his pulpit manner; of his eloquence much can be deduced from his printed sermons, which, however greatly they impress us as wonderful perform-ances in prose, are so intricate in expression that the assimila-

---

[1] 'The Indifferent.'

tive capacity of seventeenth-century congregations is as much to be admired as the sermons which carried some, Walton says, 'to Heaven in holy raptures' and enticed others 'to amend their lives'. That hearers would be rapt by the following (and there are many such passages) is easily believed:

> . . . Clocks and Sundials were but a late invention upon earth; but the Sun it self, and the earth it self, was but a late invention in heaven. God had been an infinite, a super-infinite, an unimaginable space, millions of millions of unimaginable spaces in heaven, before the Creation. And our afternoon shall be as long as Gods forenoon; for, as God never saw beginning, so we shall never see end; but they whom we tread upon now, and we whom others shall tread upon hereafter, shall meet at once, where, though we were dead, dead in our several houses, dead in a sinful *Egypt*, dead in our family, dead in our selves, dead in the Grave, yet we shall be received, with that consolation, and glorious consolation, you were dead, but are alive. . . .[1]

Abraham Cowley (1618–87), born in London and educated at Westminster School and Trinity College, Cambridge, first appeared in print with *Poetical Blossoms*, a volume published in 1603 when he was fifteen. This included two 'epical romances' and a pastoral drama. *The Cutter of Coleman Street*, an anti-Puritan comedy, came out in 1641. When the Civil War began in the next year, Cowley was forced to leave Cambridge, and from 1646 engaged in secretarial and diplomatic duties in France. Venturing to return to England as a royalist agent in 1655 he was imprisoned for a short term. After his release he qualified as a physician. The Restoration brought him substantial rewards, including the grant of an estate.

Cowley's most ambitious work, an epic with David as hero, the *Davideis* (1656) made no lasting impression. More attention has been given to his sequence of love poems *The Mistress* (1647), and he introduced into English the ode (based on Pindar's), a verse-form which was to be much used by later writers.[2] His poetry is little remembered, apart from a few

---

[1] From Sermon XXI (1625) in *XXVI Sermons* (1660).
[2] The Pindaric ode as loosely naturalized by English poets uses an elaborately patterned stanzaic form with intricate harmonies: e.g. Dryden's *Saint Cecilia's Day*. It was also imitated in more formal measures by Johnson and Gray.

Metaphysical pieces. There is no such depth of thought in Cowley as there is in Donne, and as a love poet he can seldom resist the impulse to sacrifice a promise of simplicity to mere cleverness and ingenuity: e.g.

> *Love* in her Sunny Eyes does basking play;
> *Love* walks the pleasant Mazes of her Hair; . . .[1]

A stalwart supporter of the parliamentarian cause, Andrew Marvell (1621–78) was a tutor in Cromwell's household and afterwards assistant to Milton when the latter served as Latin Secretary to the Council. He was born near Hull and educated at Hull Grammar School and Trinity College, Cambridge. He became a member of parliament and a fiery political controversialist against the ministry and the King after the Restoration, writing an important series of newsletters to his Hull constituents. *An Horatian Ode upon Cromwell's Return from Ireland; A Poem upon the Death of Oliver Cromwell;* and *Last Instructions to a Painter* (a satire on the conduct of the war against the Dutch) were among Marvell's larger performances in verse, but he is most esteemed for smaller pieces such as: 'Where the remote *Bermudas* ride' and 'To his Coy Mistress' (*see above*, p. 29)—the latter being one of the supreme English lyrics. Further study of Marvell, however, may lead to his rediscovery as a philosophical poet of higher rank than the familiar anthology poems might suggest.

George Herbert; Crashaw; Vaughan

It is difficult to discuss the Metaphysical poets without overstressing the freakish element in their works. Donne is a religious poet, one of the greatest; yet his religiousness is invariably thought of as secondary to his metaphysicalness. With Herbert, Crashaw, and Vaughan it is otherwise. They are in the main stream of English religious poetry and only incidentally Metaphysicals.

George Herbert (1593–1633), yet another poet-graduate of Trinity College, Cambridge, continued there as Public Orator (1619–27). He then entered the Church and in 1630 became Rector of Bemerton in Wiltshire for the short remainder

---

[1] Cowley's *Essays* are noticed below, p. 43.

of his life. Herbert's personality suffuses his writings and a reader's response to the poetry depends largely upon whether or not the personality is sympathetic. No doubt it is a fact that the contents of *The Temple* (1633), 'a collection of 160 poems of a religious character', are 'marked by quaint and ingenious imagery rather than exaltation, and occasionally marred by extravagant conceits and bathos'; yet it is also a fact that many lovers of poetry are exalted by at least a few of George Herbert's poems and that there is in *The Temple* a handful of pieces that English poetry could ill afford to lose, most notably 'The Pulley'; 'Easter' ('I gott mee flowrs to straw thy way'); 'The Elixir' with its immortal stanza:

> A servant with this clause
> Makes drudgery divine
> Who sweeps a roome, as for thy laws
> Makes that and th' action fine.

'The Collar', if only for its final lines:

> . . . But as I rav'd and grew more fierce and wilde
> At every word;
> Me thoughts I heard one calling, *Child!*
> And I reply'd, *My Lord.*

and 'Vertue' for the exquisite effect of the shortened last line in each of the four stanzas:

> Sweet day, so cool, so calm, so bright,
> The bridall of the earth and skie:
> The dew shall weep thy fall to night;
> For thou must die.

The son of a Puritan divine, Richard Crashaw (?1612–49) (educated at Charterhouse and Pembroke Hall, Cambridge, where he was a fellow of Peterhouse, 1637–43), joined the Roman Church and went to Paris. Through his friend Cowley and the patronage of Queen Henrietta Maria he became private secretary to Cardinal Palotto of Rome, and in his last year a sub-canon at Loretto, where he died. He was the most mystical and ecstatic among the English poets of the period, yet also one of the most mannered. His principal volume, *Steps to the Temple* (1646), comprises secular as well as sacred poems,

the former including 'Wishes. To his Supposed Mistresse' with
its much-quoted second line, 'That not impossible she'. This
pleasant piece in the manner of much of the Cavalier verse on
love themes is no more than a trifle among Crashaw's writings,
and it is through such poems as 'The Flaming Heart. Upon
the book and picture of the seraphicall saint Teresa' that
we experience the union of spiritual exaltation and Christian
humility which distinguishes his finest poetry. He is at his best
in the noble apostrophe to St. Teresa, 'usually expressed with a
Seraphim beside her':

> By all thy dowr of LIGHTS & FIRES;
> By all the eagle in thee, all the doue;
> By all thy liues & deaths of loue;
> By thy larg draughts of intellectuall day,
> And by thy thirsts of loue more large than they;
> By all thy brimfill'd Bowles of feirce desire
> By thy last Morning's draught of liquid fire;
> By the full kingdome of that finall kisse
> That seiz'd thy parting Soul, & seal'd thee his;
> By all the heau'ns thou hast in him
> (Fair sister of the SERAPHIM!)
> By all of HIM we haue in THEE;
> Leaue nothing of my SELF in me.
> Let me so read thy life, that I
> Vnto all life of mine may dy.

Like Herbert, Henry Vaughan (1622–95) was born in Wales.
Herbert came from Montgomeryshire, Vaughan from Breck-
nockshire, the district once inhabited by the Silures,[1] whence
Vaughan is called 'the Silurist'. From Jesus College, Oxford,
he went to London as a law student but by 1645 was a qualified physician: he passed his remaining fifty years practising
medicine, first in Brecknock and from 1650 in Newton-by-Usk.
Of his several works (among them a volume of secular *Poems*,
1646) the chief is *Silex Scintillans*, in two parts (1650; 1655) containing his best-known piece, the Ascension hymn 'They are
all gone into the world of light', and 'The World' which opens
with Vaughan's most impressive passage:

---

[1] A tribe of Ancient Britons who resisted the Roman invaders in the
Welsh marches.

I saw Eternity the other night
Like a great *Ring* of pure and endless light,
   All calm, as it was bright,
And round beneath it, Time in hours, days, years
   Driv'n by the spheres
Like a vast shadow mov'd, In which the world
   And all her train were hurl'd; . . .

Cavalier Poets

As with other literary labels, 'Cavalier Poets' is more convenient
than precise. It is used of those early seventeenth-century
verse-writers who sided with Charles against the Parliament
and whose poetry had a certain aristocratic grace, light-
heartedness, and (sometimes) charming triviality, at variance
with the sombre didacticism of the Puritan faction. It so
happens, however, that of the four who are considered the
principal 'Cavalier' poets, the most renowned (Herrick) was a
country parson, not a Cavalier gentleman; while the other three
(Carew, Suckling, and Lovelace)—who, though gallants all,
were far from being always lightheartedly graceful or trivially
charming—are ranked among the Metaphysicals. They lived
in a troubled and moody age, and their poetry mirrors the
age's fluctuating moods. Perhaps the only common quality of
the four is insubstantiality, for even when their themes were
serious they were more pleased to toss ideas into the air and
juggle with them than to settle to strenuous thought.

Among the 'Little Masters' in English poetry, Robert
Herrick (1591–1674) is unique in respect of the brevity and yet
the sufficiency of his best pieces. Neither his love poetry nor
his religious poetry touches either the depths or the heights;
nevertheless it often attains a miniature perfection within its
confined and unambitious limits. It is as impossible to wish
that Herrick had been capable of a *Paradise Lost* as to regret
that Jane Austen did not attempt a *Middlemarch*. *Hesperides: or
The Works both Humane and Divine of Robert Herrick Esq.* (1648)
comprises some 1,200 lyrics, epigrams, epitaphs, and other
brief pieces. *His Noble Numbers; or, his Pious Pieces*, though dated
1647, were bound up as an end-section to the *Hesperides* and

published at the same time. The *Noble Numbers* are consistently more or less pious, but are greatly outnumbered by the profane *Hesperides*, which has no governing mood and shifts capriciously from the pretty to the ugly, the dainty to the draggled, the amorous to the scurrilous. An ingenious prettiness and sweetness rather than beauty is the limit of Herrick's best, and it is not insignificant that he was apprenticed for ten years to his uncle, a London goldsmith, before he went to Cambridge (St. John's College and Trinity Hall). Herrick's art is akin to that of the goldsmith and jeweller, who does not aim to compete with the monumental sculptor. So far as any single note in his poetry

Cherrie-ripe.

CHerrie-Ripe, Ripe, Ripe, I cry,
   Full and faire ones ; come and buy :
If so be, you ask me where
They doe grow ? I answer, There,
Where my *Julia's* lips doe smile ;
There's the Land, or Cherry-Ile :
Whose Plantations fully show
All the yeere, where Cherries grow.

prevails, it is the note of playfully sensual pagan dalliance. 'Jocund his Muse was; but his life was chast' is Herrick's verdict upon himself in the last line of the *Hesperides*, and there is no reason to doubt that the verdict was just. In the remote Devonshire parsonage of Dean Prior where the Reverend Robert Herrick ministered for some thirty years in all (1629–1647; 1662–74) he delighted in pretty women as frankly as he did in pretty flowers:

> I sing of *Brooks*, of *Blossomes*, *Birds*, and *Bowers*:
> Of *April*, *May*, of *June*, and *July*-Flowers.
> I sing of *May-poles*, *Hock-carts*, *Wassails*, *Wakes*,
> Of *Bride-grooms*, *Brides*, and of their *Bridall-cakes*.
> I write of *Youth*, of *Love*, and have Accesse
> By these, to sing of cleanly-*Wantonnesse*. . . .

Certainly Herrick is cleanly in his wantonness, and grubby only in his satirical epigrams: the poems on Julia and others, dressed and undressed, are charming and minutely immortal, as also is one at least of the pious numbers, 'Another Grace for a Child':

> Here a little child I stand,
> Heaving up my either hand;
> Cold as Paddocks though they be,
> Here I lift them up to Thee,
> For a Benizon to fall
> On our meat, and on us all. *Amen.*

Thomas Carew (?1598–?1639), Sir John Suckling (1609–42), and Richard Lovelace (1618–58) were all of good families; the latter two were wealthy, but Carew's father was impoverished by a financial disaster. All three spent some time abroad, in France or Italy, and served the Stuart cause. They are fairly representative of the majority of gentlemen Cavalier poets, who were too often tediously sophisticated and academic. Apart from Carew's *A Rapture*[1]—often condemned in the past as licentious but accepted now as decently natural—these Cavalier poets' legacy to us is a few anthology pieces: e.g. Suckling's 'Why so pale and wan fond lover?', 'A Ballad upon a Wedding', 'Out upon it, I have lov'd Three whole days together'; Lovelace's 'To Lucasta, Going beyond the Seas', 'To Lucasta, Going to the Warres', 'To Althea from Prison'. Their inclination to strain after forced imagery is illustrated in Lovelace's poem apostrophizing 'Elinda's Glove' as 'Thou snowy Farme with thy five Tenements!'

The seventeenth century bred a very large number of lesser poets: Phineas Fletcher (1582–1650), who wrote a long and elaborate allegorical poem in ten books on the human body and mind, *The Purple Island* (1633); his brother Giles Fletcher (?1588–1623), author of *Christ's Victory and Triumph* (1610), known to Milton; William Drummond of Hawthornden (1585–1649); William Browne of Tavistock (?1590–?1645), *Britannia's Pastorals* (1613); Edmund Waller (1606–87), an extremely copious poet now remembered for two brief lyrics, 'Goe Lovely Rose, Tell her that wastes her time and me', and

---

[1] This poem by Carew, Herrick's *Description of a Woman*, and *A Song of Dalliance* by another Cavalier poet, William Cartwright (1611–43), denote the contemporary hankering for verse-descriptions detailing lovers' voyages of amorous exploration.

'On a Girdle'; Sir Henry Wotton (1568–1639), *Reliquiae Wottonianae* (1651) in which first appeared 'You meaner *Beauties* of the *Night*' (on Elizabeth of Bohemia), 'The Character of a Happy Life', 'On a *Bank* as I sate a *Fishing*'; and the poets included in George Saintsbury's *Minor . Poets of the Caroline Period*.[1]

Character Writers and Others

The beginnings of the novel as a literary form have been speculatively detected in different times and different places, from Hellenistic Greece to Elizabethan London. Some small credit as workers on the foundations of modern prose fiction must certainly be given to the men who wrote the seventeenth-century prose essays and sketches called *Characters*. Four writers, mainly, established and developed these interesting and often attractive pieces: Joseph Hall (1574–1656), Bishop of Exeter and later of Norwich; Sir Thomas Overbury (1581–1613), who was fated to be drawn into the orbit of Robert Carr (Earl of Somerset) and Frances Howard, at whose instigation he was slowly murdered by poison in the Tower of London; John Earle (?1601–65), Bishop of Salisbury; and Abraham Cowley. Hall deserves the largest share of the credit, for introducing in his *Characters of Virtues and Vices* (1608) a kind of composition originated by Theophrastus (*c*. 371–*c*. 287 B.C.), pupil, friend, and successor of Aristotle. The Characters written by Theophrastus draw upon contemporary life in Athens and present *types* of character to objectify some specific human vice or idiosyncrasy. Hall set the pattern for English writers of Characters, as the opening of 'The Busybody' is sufficient to show when compared with examples by others: 'His estate is too narrow for his mind, and therefore he is fain to make him-

---

[1] Saintsbury's three large volumes (Clarendon Press, 1921), embrace the works of William Chamberlayne, Edward Benlowes, Katherine Philips (called 'the Matchless Orinda' from her pen name), Patrick Hannay, Shakerley Marmion, Sir Francis Kynaston, John Hall, Sidney Godolphin, Philip Ayres, John Chalkhill, Patrick Carey, William Hammond, William Bosworth, John Cleveland, Thomas Stanley, Henry King, Thomas Flatman, Nathaniel Whiting. Their writings are complementary to those of Donne, Cowley, Marvell, Crashaw, and others discussed above, whose poetic excellence frequently overrides and obscures the handicaps of the mode. In the verse of the minors, the grotesque and many of the duller conceits of the Metaphysicals provoke æsthetic disgust in the reader.

self room in others' affairs; yet ever, in pretence of love.'
Overbury's 'A Fair and Happy Milkmaid'—from *Characters*
(1614)—begins: 'A fair and happy milkmaid is a country
wench that is so far from making herself beautiful by art, that
one look of ʌers is able to put all face physic out of countenance.'
John Earle's 'A Child'—*Micro-Cosmographie* (1628): 'A child is
a man in a small letter, yet the best copy of Adam before he
tasted of Eve, or the Apple; . . .' Cowley's 'Of Myself'—
Essays (published 1668): 'It is a hard and nice subject for a
man to write of himself; it grates his own heart to say anything
of disparagement and the reader's ears to hear anything of
praise for him.' Though the Characters are concerned more
with general types than with diverse individual men and
women, Cowley at least is concerned with a unique personality,
his own, and thus takes a step in the direction of one of the
essential features of the English novel-to-be, *characterization*.
The next stage of progress was to be reached in the eighteenth-
century periodical essay which, in the hands of Addison,
Steele, and others, produced Sir Roger de Coverley, Mr.
Bickerstaff, and that semi-detached assemblage of more or less
individualized and fictionalized characters who needed only to
be provided with an interacting relationship and a plot or
situation in order to make the novel as we know it. But a
century was to go by before Richardson and Fielding showed
the way.

Next after, or perhaps alongside, Robert Burton's *Anatomy
of Melancholy* stand the works of Sir Thomas Browne (1605–82)
as the most remarkable prose writings in the Metaphysical
manner. Both Burton (1577–1640) and Browne had command of abundant stores of rare and curious knowledge
which they presented, however, very differently. Burton collected like a magpie and displayed his treasures of learning in a
literary mosaic where each fragment settles beside its neighbour
fragments until a wonderful vast pattern develops from what
seemed madly crazed.

Burton was a divine with philosophical, psychological,
mathematical, and comprehensive pharmaceutical leanings.
Sir Thomas Browne was a physician by profession and something of an antiquarian by temperament, but it is impossible

to define the bounds of his intellectual interests. Born in London, the son of a merchant, he had his general education at Winchester and Oxford, afterwards studying medicine at Leyden and elsewhere abroad. He settled in practice at Norwich in 1637 and remained there. His masterpiece *Religio Medici* came out in 1642, followed by *Pseudodoxia Epidemica: Enquiries into Vulgar Errors* (1646), *Hydriotaphia, or Urn Burial* (1658)—inspired by the finding of some Roman sepulchral urns in Norfolk—*The Garden of Cyrus* (1658), and *Christian Morals* (posthumously, 1716). To say that *Religio Medici* is an exposition of the author's Christian faith is to say next to nothing. Indeed, the reader's interest in Browne's subject-matter is perpetually subordinate to the fascination of his style. His prose is not 'good' prose, if information, argument, or description is the proper aim and chief end of prose. The prose of Sir Thomas Browne acts upon our senses as an incantation before it informs our thinking part. He catches our ear with some magical phrase and we read on, more bewitched than instructed. It was, to put it lightly, a miraculously happy accident that this Norwich physician, crammed with precious yet mostly useless erudition, should have written just then a prose which gives pure pleasure, for within a generation English prose became utilitarian and not again, outside poetry, would there be such verbal spells as Browne's: 'This [prayer] is the Dormative I take to bedward; I need no other Laudanum than this to make me sleep; after which I close mine eyes in security, content to take my leave of the Sun, and sleep unto the Resurrection.'—*Religio Medici*. 'Look not for Whales in the Euxine Sea, or expect great matters where they are not to be found.'—*Christian Morals*. 'What song the Syrens sang, or what name Achilles assumed when he hid himself among women, though puzzling questions are not beyond all conjecture.' 'But the iniquity of oblivion blindly scattereth her poppy. . . .'—*Hydriotaphia*. 'Nor will the sweetest delight of gardens afford much comfort in sleep; wherein the dulness of that sense shakes hands with delectable odours; and though in the bed of Cleopatra, can hardly with any delight raise up the ghost of a rose.'—*The Garden of Cyrus*.

No immutable boundary-line can be drawn between writings which belong solely to the history of ideas and those which may properly be taken into a history of literature; but since some boundary has to be fixed, otherwise histories of literature would be compelled to admit every book, the word 'literature' may be confined to works which please by their manner (style) as well as serving for mental, spiritual, emotional, or imaginative enlightenment. Many books momentous in their own day fall dead tomorrow; they were important but are not memorable. Literature can therefore be defined as permanently memorable and pleasurable writing, and this definition accounts well for the fact that from among the innumerable volumes on the political issues of the seventeenth century those which are literature fit into one very small shelf. The *Oceana* (1656) of James Harrington (1611–77) influenced political thinkers through several generations, and as serious fiction it belongs with More's *Utopia*. Yet as literature it has long since ceased to count. 'If *Oceana* is not now one of the living classics, probably the essential reason is that Harrington's Utopia is not only doctrinaire but somewhat drab and dusty; he wrote, not unnaturally, with a passion for external peace and order, but the greatest political thinkers have had a broader, more positive, and more humane vision of life.'[1] The *Leviathan* (1651) of Thomas Hobbes (1588–1679) stands in a literary half-world. Few could now read it for pleasure alone, but those who turn to it for what it is—one of the paramount masterpieces of political theory—will find no obstacle in Hobbe's style. Intended as an apologia for the Stuart conception of kingship, it was nevertheless interpreted by certain royalists as a defence of Cromwell's assumption of power. In the present century *Leviathan* is again much studied, since some part of it appears singularly appropriate to the state of a world seeking peace and security, and debating systems in which men 'conferr all their power and strength upon one Man, or upon one Assembly of men, that may reduce all their Wills, by plurality of voices, unto one Will: . . .'

Bookish people find themselves drawn to 'old Fuller' by affinity, for *The Holy State and the Profane State* (1642) and *The Worthies of England* (posthumously, 1662) by Thomas Fuller (1608–61), Chaplain-in-extraordinary to Charles II, have a

[1] Douglas Bush: see above, p. 27, n. 1.

seductive charm which comes from his combination of wit, glancing humour, anecdote, odd learning, innocence of manner (this may often be a subtly calculated flirtation with naivety), wisdom, sententiousness, urbanity—and boredom. A lamprey is 'A deformed fish, which for the many holes therein, one would conceive nature intended it rather for an instrument of music than for man's food.' 'Nunneries were good she-schools. . . . virginity is least kept where it is most constrained. . . .' '. . . as Hatto archbishop of Mentz is reported to have been eaten up by rats, so the vermin of taxes, if continuing, is likely to devour our nation.' Fuller's *Worthies*, published as a folio volume of more than a thousand pages, has been described as 'among other things a dictionary of national biography, a series of county histories, a topographical and historical gazetteer, a guide-book, and a dictionary of proverbs'. To gather material for it Fuller wandered through the length and breadth of the land, 'First, to gain some glory to God. Secondly, to preserve the memories of the dead. Thirdly, to present examples to the living. Fourthly, to entertain the reader with delight. And lastly, which I am not ashamed publicly to profess, to procure some honest profit to myself.' *The Holy and the Profane State* is mainly a book of good and bad Characters drawn from biblical, hagiographical, and historical sources and interspersed with generalized pieces ('The Good Husband', 'Of Anger', etc.)—all much after the style of the Characters of Theophrastus and Bishop Hall.

Jeremy Taylor (1613–67), Bishop of Dromore, wrote less engagingly than Fuller, but his *Holy Living* (1650) and *Holy Dying* (1651) are full of literary delight even for secular readers. Whatever his topic he may at any moment break into some such passage as: '. . . when the sun approaches towards the gates of the morning, he first opens a little eye of heaven, and sends away the spirits of darkness, and gives light to a cock, and calls up the lark to matins, and by and by gilds the fringes of a cloud, and peeps over the eastern hills. . . .' Taylor writes not only impressively but also with limpid beauty, and though his sentences are sometimes of astonishing length they are never tangled or obscure.

CHAPTER III

MILTON AND BUNYAN

ANY supposition that 'Cavalier literature' and 'Puritan litera-ture' can be neatly herded to right and to left according to either ideological or chronological grouping, cannot be sustained in relation to the writings of the Civil War and Commonwealth period. Verse and prose with more or less impassioned Puritan moral tendencies and partisan motives became familiar in Tudor days and grew in volume under the early Stuarts; and though the rule of Parliament and Cromwell after 1642 had some features of dictatorship, it did not impose upon imaginative literature the gyves of a paralysing totalitarianism. The publications records in the years before and after 1642 show little difference in general character, and a number of works already discussed in the preceding chapters on Early Stuart literature did not get into print until the 1640s and 1650s. In spite of the closing of the public theatres in 1642 plays continued to be printed, while 'private' performances kept the native dramatic impulse alive until the Restoration permitted it to burst again into liberty—and into licence. Moreover, when the 'Puritan' Parliament imposed licensing restrictions upon the press in 1644, it was the greatest of the Puritan writers, Milton, who produced almost immediately the greatest of all pleas for freedom of expression, the pamphlet *Areopagitica*.

Many seventeenth-century writers were men of affairs as well as men of letters, and very few went untouched by the religious and political hostilities of the age; but in so far as a distinctively Puritan literature is distinguishable at all, it consists of the works of Milton and Bunyan and, beyond them, of a body of only passingly important controversial pieces by authors now mostly forgotten. Throughout the century there was a marked lack of definition not only between parties but also between the fluctuating circumstances and allegiances of individual persons. Richard Baxter, whose *Saints' Everlasting Rest* (1650) is still cherished by Evangelicals as a Puritan masterpiece, was at one period a chaplain to the Parliamentary forces and later a chaplain to Charles II; and Dryden's political and theological divagations are notorious. What has been called 'the Puritan interregnum' was as much a time of uncertainty among many as of certainty among others: no party, no creed, had a monopoly of right thought and conviction; good men might understandably and honourably halt between two—or several —opinions, waver on occasion from one to another, and display inconsistencies shocking to rigidly indoctrinated modern minds. Counterbalancing the waverers were innumerable zealots, but all too few who, like Milton and Bunyan, attained certainty without brutal fanaticism.

John Milton

Whether Milton should be ranked third or fifth among the English poets—between Chaucer and Spenser, or below Wordsworth—is not a question to be settled dogmatically. Any answer is likely to depend more upon the temperament of the reader than upon abstract critical judgement, for the personality of the man is more omnipresent in Milton's poetry than that of most other poets in theirs, and to very many Milton is an unsympathetic character.

There is in Milton's poetry a more-than-human largeness of vision but a less-than-human capacity for normal feeling. This is no doubt due to the fact that, excepting Wordsworth, Milton is the only English writer who addressed himself solemnly and with magnificent deliberation to becoming a poet. Poetry was to him a duty and a dedication, and the time he spent at Horton when a young man was as much a retreat preparatory to solemn entry into an order—the sacred Order of Poetry— as any undertaken by a religious devotee. Though Wordsworth determined to be, as a poet, 'a teacher or nothing', he had human frailties and even sillinesses to which Milton seems to have been immune. But for his marriage muddle we might suppose that Milton was altogether free from human imperfection. We ought to admire him in proportion to his admirableness; yet it is only natural to reflect that we might find him more admirable if we were less continuously aware of the impulsion to admire.

John Milton was a Londoner, born in Bread Street, Cheapside —near where the Mermaid Tavern stood—on 9 December 1608, the son of a flourishing scrivener who was also an amateur composer of music. He went to St. Paul's School, only a hundred yards or so from his birthplace, until in 1625 he entered Christ's College, Cambridge, and remained there for seven years. It is known both from his own testimony and from external comment that he was a born student who devoted long hours to a single-minded determination to acquire learning. Even if there were no other evidence, we could hardly fail to deduce from his poetry that Milton was steeped in the kinds of knowledge most valued by seventeenth-century scholars. But he was not only an assiduous student. He was physically beautiful, though not tall; he valued exercise and was a proficient fencer; he was 'a virtuous and sober person', not unaware of his own virtues yet morally courageous. His nickname, The Lady of Christ's, was possibly both an acknowledgement of his exceptional character and conduct and a sly hit at his superior niceness of manner.

Before leaving Cambridge in 1632 at the age of twenty-three he had composed (in addition to Latin verse and prose) his earliest English poems: he was, indeed, only seventeen when 'On the Death of a Fair Infant dying of a Cough', a pretty and precocious piece, was written; and at twenty-one, on Christmas Day 1629, he started what was to become the first of his 'great' poems, the ode 'On the Morning of Christ's Nativity', in which prettiness is displaced by loveliness, and precociousness by an assured command not only of the seven-line stanza (ababbcc) of the introduction and of the different verse-form (aabccbdd) used in the hymn that follows it, but also of that conjoint classical and biblical learning which persisted throughout his poetry as one of its most striking and uncommon features. In this ode the Miltonic wealth of imagery also appears in early abundance, and it is particularly interesting, in view of the musical home atmosphere in which he grew up, to note the extent to which he employs aural epithets and images as well as visual ones. Yet Milton in the year he left Cambridge lamented in the sonnet 'On being arrived at twenty-three years of age', that his 'late spring no bud or blossom shew'th' and that, in comparison with others, 'inward ripeness' was

E

delayed in him. Nevertheless, he speaks of his being led by Time and the will of Heaven, and concludes:

> All is, if I have grace to use it so,
> As ever in my great Task-Master's eye.

At heart he had no meagre conceit of his own destiny.

By the end of the Cambridge period Milton's father had retired from London to settle at Horton, near Windsor, and there the son lived for some six years which appeared wantonly unproductive to relatives and friends. It had been Milton's intention earlier to enter the Church, but he had come to regard the ministry as a form of spiritual slavery and found it impossible to accept the oaths which holy Orders required of him. He therefore gave himself up to a period of further study and contemplation in the country home, at intervals visiting London in search of books or new knowledge. At length he overcame the objections which (as Milton's Latin poem *Ad Patrem* indicates) his father had registered in the belief that the young man was wasting his time and neglecting opportunities for a legal or a mercantile career. While at Horton Milton meditated possible subjects for the great poem which he was determined should be his life-work and his permanent legacy to mankind. He was drawn towards the story of Arthur as the ideal topic for a national epic, but it had the fatal drawback of being legend and not fact; and of being therefore, in Milton's eyes, unserviceable to the cause of Truth. His suspicion of anything rooted in fiction led his mind away from the Arthurian story, and his utter belief in the Bible as the Word of God (for his objection to entering the Church turned upon matters of ecclesiastical rule, not upon any doubt of Christianity) made it inevitable that only in the Scriptures would he discover a fit subject.

The Horton period also had positive results, for it was in those years that he wrote most of the poems by which he might have been entirely loved if his later and greater works had not overawed readers' affections with many signs of mental and spiritual gianthood. Although they were not published until 1645—modestly titled *Poems*—'L'Allegro', 'Il Penseroso',[1] and

[1] Throughout the nineteenth century, and for some time after, the belief that 'L'Allegro' and 'Il Penseroso' were written at Horton was accepted. The case for assigning them to the Cambridge period as academic 'poetical

'Arcades' were composed before Milton left Horton and England in the early part of 1638 for a tour of France, Italy, and Switzerland lasting until late summer in the following year. The masque *Comus* and the elegy *Lycidas*, also included in the 1645 volume and also written at Horton, had been published before, each separately, in 1637 and *c*. 1640. In this one book, therefore, issued when the author was thirty-six, the English language received a rarely equalled accession of great poems.

The jocund life and the meditative life surveyed in 'L'Allegro' and 'Il Penseroso' are both delightful yet both rational and restrained, and within the bounds of Milton's own capacity for jollity in the one mood and for melancholy in its opposite. Both poems are short (152 lines and 176 lines) but their scope is remarkable: personifications reminiscent of the later medieval English Moralities; a wealth of reference to Greek mythology; country pictures drawn from Milton's observations of nature by day and night whether in the garden and neighbourhood of Horton or elsewhere; echoes of romance and folk tales and of earlier poets' lines; exquisite felicities of phrasing—e.g. 'scatters the rear of darkness thin' for the imaginative impact of cock-crow at dawn; allusions to music; indoor pictures, in the study, by the fireside, and in church. Among lovers of poetry, probably a majority of the lines in the two poems are 'familiar quotations'; and phrases from them are used as proverbial sayings by many who have never knowingly heard a single line of Milton: 'the light fantastic toe', 'native wood-notes wild', 'the cricket on the hearth', 'a dim religious light'.

It has often been said that the major English elegies— Milton's *Lycidas*, Shelley's *Adonais*, Tennyson's *In Memoriam*, Matthew Arnold's *Thyrsis*—are too elaborate as poems to be effective as songs of mourning for lost friends. This comment mistakes the nature of Elegy, which, as a classical poetic kind, is an elaborate ceremonial ode designed to produce its effect at least as much by impressive dignity of language and form as by emotional content: the manner must be regarded as equal in importance to the matter. By this test *Lycidas* is beyond question

exercises' is presented by E. M. W. Tillyard in *The Miltonic Setting* (London, 1938). Internal evidence in criticism should be assessed with the same balance of attention and scepticism as circumstantial evidence receives in crime.

the greatest of English elegies, and is the only piece remembered from the volume by several hands published in 1638 in memory of a young Cambridge scholar, Edward King, drowned in the Irish Sea in the preceding year. Because of its classical allusions and Milton's deepened thought, *Lycidas* is a more difficult poem than 'L'Allegro' and 'Il Penseroso', and at least one reference —'that two-handed engine at the door Stands ready to smite once and smite no more'—has puzzled generations of students. Though Elegy is commonly pastoral in content, with the conventional rural setting and figures of shepherds and their like, Milton extends its scope, introducing into *Lycidas* references to Druids, and the famous passage beginning with a biblical allusion to 'The Pilot of the Galilean Lake' which attacks the established clergy of Milton's day and contains some of his most powerful denunciatory lines:

> Blind mouthes! that scarce themselves know how to hold
> A Sheep-hook, or have learn'd ought els the least
> That to the faithfull Herdmans art belongs!
> What recks it them? What need they? They are sped;
> And when they list, their lean and flashy songs
> Grate on their scrannel Pipes of wretched straw,
> The hungry Sheep look up, and are not fed,
> But swoln with wind, and the rank mist they draw,
> Rot inwardly, and foul contagion spread: . . .

But within a few lines this dark mood is compensated by a beautiful flower-piece:

> Bring the rathe Primrose that forsaken dies.
> The tufted Crow-toe, and pale Gessamine,
> The white Pink, and the Pansie freakt with jeat,
> The glowing Violet.
> The Musk-rose, and the well-attir'd Woodbine,
> With Cowslips wan that hang the pensive head,
> And every flower that sad embroidery wears:
> Bid *Amarantus* all his beauty shed,
> And Daffadillies fill their cups with tears,
> To strew the Laureat Herse where *Lycid* lies.

Comus was written for performance as a masque at Ludlow Castle, where it was acted in 1634 to music by Henry Lawes and by a company including Viscount Brackley (the Earl of Bridgewater's heir), Lady Alice Egerton, and her brother

Thomas Egerton. If a sense of proportion is to be kept in discussing *Comus*, the circumstances and character of Masque as a contemporary form of entertainment must be considered. Masques arose from the wish of amateur actors among the aristocracy to entertain their families and friends with a kind of play more refined than those seen in the public theatres. Since singing and performing on instruments were also polite amusements, music and drama became more or less equal partners in the Masque; while the widespread and prolonged affection for the arcadianism of a figmentary Golden Age accounts for the frequent choice of pastoral themes. It also became the fashion—no doubt as a carry-over from the earlier Moralities and Interludes—to centre the Masque upon some moral virtue. But, primarily, the Masque was for entertainment; and *Comus*, too, must be considered as an entertainment, not exclusively as a sermon. It has been said that Wordsworth found in stones the sermons he had previously hidden there. It is equally true that interpreters usually find in *Comus* what they set out to find—a mystical cult of Chastity, or a didactic apologue, or on the contrary an attack on Chastity, for there have been those who take Comus's remarkable speech on the error of Virginity as Milton's own opinion. It would be easier to uphold the view that Comus is deliberately falsifying the issue by attacking virginity (barrenness) whereas the real theme is chastity (which may be fully consistent with fruitfulness in marriage), if the Lady when answering Comus did not herself use the two words synonymously. Were a contemporary description of the first performance to be found, it would not be surprising to learn that *Comus* impressed the audience most by its own magics—the magic of poetry and the magic of Comus the enchanter who could work transformation scenes and other wonders by a wave of his charming-rod—and that the dogmas of the sheltered twenty-four-year-old Milton were not taken over-solemnly. The important thing in *Comus* is that the moral case is presented with a measure of dramatic detachment, and that the poetry given to Comus himself is as splendid as the rest.

During his continental tour in 1638–9 Milton was received in Paris by the·famous Dutch jurist Hugo Grotius, then serving as Swedish ambassador there. In Florence the young

Englishman read one of his Latin poems to the academy of letters, and called on Galileo the aged and then blind astronomer. He visited many other cities before returning to England, where he occupied lodgings close to St. Bride's church, Fleet Street, later taking a house in Aldersgate Street. He was soon absorbed by the political tumult which came to a head with the outbreak of civil war in 1642. For the twenty years from 1640 until the Restoration in 1660 Milton devoted himself to the composition of pamphlets upholding the presbyterian opponents of episcopal rule in the Church and on the political side giving general support to Parliament and the Commonwealth against monarchical rule. Much of what he wrote in prose at that time is tainted with the irrational excesses which beset propagandists, but in addition to the strictly political and religious works he produced his prose masterpiece *Areopagitica* (1644) and in the same year the tract *Of Education*. Even in a propaganda piece he might digress to autobiographical matters, as he does in the preamble to Book II of *The Reason of Church Government* (1641/2), in order to speak of his own early ideal view of the function of a poet, his conviction of the lasting worth of his own poetry, and of the duty of writing poetry in the native tongue. The Latin pamphlet *Defensio Secunda Pro Populo Anglicano* (1654) is valuable for the biographical sketch of himself and his opinions which Milton incorporated. The pamphlets on divorce have at times brought odium on his memory, inasmuch as the arguments in justification of divorce can be taken as special pleading occasioned by his own unfortunate first marriage to Mary Powell, whom he wed (1643) in Oxfordshire, his father's birth-county. Milton was then in his middle thirties, his wife only seventeen. The disparity in age and a probably still more marked temperamental disharmony are the most likely causes of the almost immediate rupture of the marriage, for the new Mary Milton returned to her family very soon after she was taken to London by her husband, and she did not go back to him until 1645, after the royalist Powells had become impoverished by the failure of their cause.

Milton's *Of Education* takes an independent line, running counter to educational methods of the time in the matter of language teaching, and commending a system of local academies 'at once both School and University' where studies, exercise, and diet would have equal attention. Whatever the interest and merit of this and other of his tracts and pamphlets, the *Areopagitica: A Speech for the Liberty of Unlicensed Printing* excels the rest, both as the classic defence of the freedom of the press, and as one of the most majestic prose works in English. Milton did not claim absolute liberty for the printed word: indeed (he wrote), 'I deny not, but that it is of greatest concernment in the Church and Commonwealth, to have a vigilant eye how Bookes demeane themselves as well as men; . . .' Directly after comes the great passage beginning: 'For Books are not absolutely dead things, but doe contain a potencie of life in them to be as active as that soule was whose progeny they are'; and ending: '. . . a good Booke is the pretious life-blood of a master spirit, imbalm'd and treasur'd up on purpose to a life beyond life. . . .' As always, Milton ranges wide in time and place and digs deep in his citation of authorities in support of his thesis, which he nevertheless advocates also with independent strength of argument that leads him to dwell weightily upon the imperative need to uphold Truth. Milton was, without apology and in the purest sense, a patriot, and in the *Areopagitica* are two noble passages in praise of his country:

> Lords and Commons of England, consider what Nation it is whereof ye are, and whereof ye are the governours: a Nation not slow and dull, but of a quick, ingenious, and piercing spirit, acute to invent, suttle and sinewy to discours, not beneath the reach of any point the highest that human capacity can soar to. . . .

. . . .

> . . . Methinks I see in my mind a noble and puissant Nation rousing herself like a strong man after sleep, and shaking her invincible locks: Methinks I see her as an Eagle muing her mighty youth, and kindling her undazl'd eyes at the full midday beam; purging and unscaling her long-abused sight at the fountain itself of heav'nly radiance; . . .

After Mary Milton returned to her husband in 1645 (the passage in Book X, lines 905–45, of *Paradise Lost* is thought to allude to the reconciliation) three daughters were born to them. She died in 1653/4. Milton married Katherine Woodcock in 1656 and, following her death in childbirth in the next year, took in 1663 a third wife, Elizabeth Minshull, who was only twenty-five to Milton's fifty-four. He predeceased her by fifty-three years. In the house in the Barbican, by London Wall, to which he moved in 1645, Milton set up an almost patriarchal establishment (his father and other relatives lived with him) and also a school taught by himself. When the Commonwealth was proclaimed in 1649, Milton became, until Charles II's return in 1660, Cromwell's Latin Secretary (Secretary for Foreign Tongues to the Council of State) with a lodging in Whitehall.

About 1652, when he was forty-four, Milton became blind and took Andrew Marvell (*see above*, p. 36) as assistant in the Secretaryship. During his prose period, it must have seemed that the gift of verse had all but left him, though of the dozen or so sonnets belonging to that period three, 'On the late Massacre in Piedmont', 'On his Blindness', and 'On his Deceased Wife' are among the best by English poets: in particular, the first-named shows that invective occasioned by the day's news can be transmuted into fine poetry.

When 1658 began, Milton was a blind State official in his fiftieth year, twice a widower, the author of a great deal of controversial prose which could not be expected long to survive the events which had inspired it, and of half a dozen excellent short poems and a masque. Yet before the end of the year, that ageing man whom life appeared to have discarded started on a work far greater than anything he had attempted before, a work that was to carry him to the pinnacle of fame. *Paradise Lost*, completed in 1664, came out in 1667, to be followed in 1671 by *Paradise Regained* and *Samson Agonistes* in one volume. Milton was then in his middle sixties, and he died three years later. There is no parallel in English literature to a poet's producing, as Milton produced, not only his own longest and greatest works in his fifties and sixties,[1] but works which are, moreover, supreme in their kind, for whether *Paradise Lost* is congenial or not to any individual reader its supremacy is beyond question. Its imaginative force is reflected in the remarkable fact that although Milton took up his sacred theme in all reverence and humility, his handling of the theme has so imposed a Miltonic mythology upon the biblical story that multitudes throughout several generations have grafted Milton

---

[1] Robert Bridges published *The Testament of Beauty* (1929) in his mid-eighties, but its quality has yet to be determined by time.

on to Genesis and mistakenly supposed that the exploits of the Miltonic Satan and his legions are a part of Holy Writ. In this way Milton has posthumously assumed the character and stature of a great master of fiction: his creative imagination dominated his theological intention to 'justifie the wayes of God to men'. Milton was possessed by a sublime spiritual arrogance which qualified him to create his Satan with so thorough an understanding of the Arch-rebel who sought to outface God, that a suspicion has lingered that Satan is the real hero of *Paradise Lost*. What can be asserted with less doubt is that Milton was a dormant playwright whose latent dramatic instinct compelled him to present the adversary's case as fairly as its opposite: hence Comus's dangerously powerful challenge to the Lady's testimony in behalf of chastity; hence, also, the masterly rhetoric of Satan.

The greatness of *Paradise Lost* is so overwhelming as to become its chief obstacle, for the poem in its entirety, in all its religious and philosophical and æsthetic implications, and in its total significance, can be comprehended by only a select minority. The speeches of Satan and the other fallen angels in the opening books are on the highest level of rhetoric that has been touched in English poetry: there is scarcely an amplifying adjective that could not justly be used to express its grandeur. These burning fountains of words deluge the mind and the terrible images of hell infest the imagination.

The astonishing power of visualization in *Paradise Lost* was the poet's compensation for physical blindness: the inward sight of imagination became intensified as his eyes dimmed and failed. Yet this intensification was also a distortion, or at least a limitation; the visualizing capacity of Milton's imagination was confined to an extremely narrow colour-range, predominantly black and red (the pitchy darkness of hell broken by leaping flames—'yet from those flames No light, but rather darkness visible'), gold ('The riches of Heav'ns pavement, trod'n gold'), and 'bright', a recurrent word, in e.g. Book III ('underneath a bright Sea flow'd', 'His back was turnd, but not his brightness hid', 'the Angel bright, Ere he drew nigh, his radiant visage turned'). The frequent mention of jewels and of flowers in the Paradise passages is unaccompanied by any sign that the poet could *see* those with his inward eye: only dark and bright—the brightness of fire, of gleaming metal, of divine radiance, of pure light—seem real.

In comparison with the terrific driving power of evil in the fallen angels and the horror of the regions of the damned, the landscape of the Garden of Eden, the love of Adam and Eve, and their disobedience and expulsion have diminished in impressiveness for those who reject not only Milton's views on the loving subjection of wives to husbands conscious of superiority, but who also reject the idea of the Temptation and the Fall. Nevertheless, the stretches in *Paradise Lost* dealing with these matters are the most beautiful in the poem, though the human relationships, however ardently expressed, remain emotionally unmoving and almost frigid, in the fashion characteristic of Milton. If he was ever a lover, he must have loved by the rule-book of duty and conscience; if he was amorous, as certain passages in his works portend, a touch of ice and acid, perhaps of gall, was also in his blood.

Paradise Regained (1671), on a superficial assessment, is in aim as well as in length a less ambitious work than its counterpart. Instead of setting out to justify God (as *Paradise Lost* does) by enlarging and adorning Genesis with a new mythology and all the resources of heroic poetry, it is confined to the temptation of Christ in the wilderness by a Satan who appears here as a smarmy insinuating hypocrite instead of as an evil hero defying God. The whole of *Paradise Regained* is played in a lower key. It has vast pretensions, however: 'to tell of deeds . . . unrecorded left through many an age'; to

> . . . sing
> Recovered Paradise to all mankind, . . .

To all mankind: no less. Moreover, whereas Milton in *Paradise Lost* takes advantage of the legitimate freedoms of the artist's creative imagination, in *Paradise Regained* he proposes less, yet demands more. While much of the narrative is a verse paraphrase of the relevant New Testament passages, there is also a venturesome pretence of entering into the mind of Christ, and a bold putting of Miltonic speeches into his mouth. Some parts of the poem resemble in technique the 'dramatic monologue' which Browning, long after, developed impressively and used with acute psychological penetration. Milton was more hampered than Browning in the use he could make of the dramatic monologue, however, for his choice of supernatural characters ruled out any possibility of indicating psychological development. It is, indeed, one of the limitations of Milton's major poems that the fate of the persons and personages in them is preordained and affords no scope for subtleties of characterization.

Samson Agonistes (1671), his final work, though it suffers from this same limitation, is lifted above the rhetorical plane by being, in a degree, a personal document: blind Samson a projection of blind Milton, and Samson's wretchedness in the land of the Philistines a figuration of Milton's in Restoration England. In more than a few respects *Samson Agonistes* is the greatest of Milton's works. It has the spiritual humility which elsewhere he so patently lacked; the verse is taut and genuinely tragic in tone and feeling, not voluminous, nor garrulous, nor orotund; the play has humanity as well as gravity and dignity. Though we know beforehand what the hero's fate is to be, quite as well as we know Adam's and Eve's, *Samson Agonistes* has enough dramatic tension to engage our interest as acutely as if Samson were an original character in a play on an original theme. It is also the only successful attempt, of the many that have been made, to imitate Greek tragedy in English. Milton declared in the preliminary note that the piece was not intended for the stage, yet it is effective and impressive when acted.

Miltonic verse requires close study if it is to be appreciated in proportion to its merits: in particular the fitness to its purpose of the freer and often intentionally broken rhythm in *Samson Agonistes* is in impressive contrast to the more regular heroic blank verse used for the *Paradises*, which is discussed briefly (and with scorn of rhyme) in the foreword to *Paradise Lost*.

The genius and the beauty of much of Milton's poetry might be ungrudgingly acknowledged far beyond the confines of the scholars' world if, first, common prejudice against Milton the man could be removed (prejudice arising mainly from his seemingly oriental notions of woman's subjection to man, which affected not only the unfledged Mary Powell—committed to him, it seems, on account of her family's indebtedness to the poet's father—but also his daughters, who were

devoted but sorely tried amanuenses to him in his blindness);
and if, secondly, the tendency of Milton enthusiasts to approach
him as half demi-god, half oracle, could give way to simple
acceptance of him as a human among humans and a poet
among poets.

Whatever rank readers may severally give to Milton, he is
at the very least a pre-eminent enricher of our language. Not
only phrases and simple lines but whole passages engrave the
memory. Nothing lovelier has been written than the description
of Dalila

> Like a stately Ship
> Of *Tarsus*, bound for th' Isles
> Of *Javan* or *Gadier*
> With all her bravery on, and tackle trim,
> Sails fill'd, and streamers waving
> Courted by all the winds that hold them play, . . .

while other passages in *Samson Agonistes* are no less fine though
more sombre:

> Nothing is here for tears, nothing to wail
> Or knock the breast, no weakness, no contempt,
> Dispraise, or blame, nothing but well or fair,
> And what may quiet us in a death so noble.

The preliminary note to *Paradise Lost* condemns rhyme as 'the
invention of a barbarous age, to set off wretched matter and
lame metre', yet Milton's last lines (in *Samson Agonistes*) are
in rhyming verse—and, with not unsuitable irony, are perhaps
more often quoted than anything else he wrote:

> All is best, though we oft doubt,
> What th' unsearchable dispose
> Of highest wisdom brings about,
> And ever best found in the close.
> Oft he seems to hide his face,
> But unexpectedly returns
> And to his faithful Champion hath in place
> Bore witness gloriously; whence *Gaza* mourns
> And all that band them to resist
> His uncontroulable intent,
> His servants he with new acquist
> Of true experience from this great event
> With peace and consolation hath dismist,
> And calm of mind all passion spent.

John Bunyan

Milton imposed invented characters and invented incidents upon biblical material; so did Bunyan. Milton set out to justify the ways of God to men in a very long poem which is an exacting mental and spiritual exercise; Bunyan's aim in *The Pilgrim's Progress*, a short prose work with occasional snatches of verse, was to lead men and women into God's way, the way of salvation, through a simple parable with homely characters and exciting events. As Puritans, though not Puritans of the same complexion, both Milton and Bunyan distrusted fiction; both, however, were masters of imaginative creation and invented narrative and were also, therefore, masters of the art of fiction. They took what they fully believed to be spiritual truth and subjected it to the expository treatment natural to men with the instincts of Christian teachers; but neither was a mere religious pedagogue or sermonizer; both were artists, and the artist instinct became the leading partner of the teacher instinct. *Paradise Lost* and *The Pilgrim's Progress* have survived while thousands of equally fervent religious works of the seventeenth century have long since perished, because both are, on different levels, masterpieces of literary art which please those whom they also teach and please no less those who ignore the teaching or suppose themselves to have outgrown it.

The Pilgrim's Progress has all the basic requirements of the traditional type of English novel: a good story, interesting (even though ready-made) characters, arresting conversation, vivid description, narrative that is always moving towards a definite end, and that evasive quality, 'literary style'—a subtle emanation from the writer's personality through verbal good manners and fitness in the choice and arrangement of words. Almost the only quality of a novel proper that is absent from *The Pilgrim's Progress* is imaginative development of character. Bunyan's characters belong to the long-established family which produced the medieval Morality plays. They are puppets with label-names; they play assigned parts leading to a pre-determined end; they are debarred from taking charge of the story and providing the author as well as the readers with dramatic surprises, as the characters in great novels do. It was by working within these limitations, however, that Bunyan triumphed so remarkably, for though each character is

proclaimed by its label-name, each has an extraordinary freshness and individual interest such as no earlier characters of the
Morality type possessed. Here, for the first time in English
imaginative prose, the characters possess the vital third
dimension: they have depth, they step away from the background. This new achievement is the hallmark of Bunyan's
great genius, which does not work through elaborate detailed
descriptions of the characters; sometimes it works without
appearing to work at all: 'a young woman, her name was
Dull'—we have not heard of Dull before that moment, we do
not hear of her again, nothing but those seven words are said
of her; yet somehow we know Dull for the rest of our lives and
meet her every day in twentieth-century England. Dull, dear
dumb Miss Dull, is an immortal in seven words.

Of the 'great' passages in *The Pilgrim's Progress* there is no
more need to write than there would be to point out that the
story of the Prodigal Son is in the New Testament. The Slough
of Despond, the Interpreter's House, the Palace Beautiful, the
Valley of Humiliation, Vanity Fair, the Delectable Mountains,
the Celestial City, Doubting Castle: these are embedded
lastingly in our national memory, and the names are household
words even to unfortunates who do not read *The Pilgrim's Progress*. Bunyan's literary tact and sense of style never forsook him
for a moment in his masterpiece: his personal names and place
names are always significant and always exactly right.

Not even Bunyan could keep dull patches out of this story
of 'the pilgrim's progress from this world to that which is to
come, delivered under the similitude of a dream', for the traditional dream-formula had long since lost vitality. That the dull
patches are so very few is due to Bunyan's instinct for illuminat-
ing words and phrases and to the fact that the book is continuously on the move: it is by nature as well as by name a
pilgrimage and therefore a progress: someone is on the way,
someone coming, someone going, someone meeting someone or
something else, nearly all the time:

> Now as Christian was walking solitarily by himself, he espied
> one afar off, come crossing over the field to meet him; and their
> hap was to meet just as they were crossing the way of each other.
> The gentleman's name was Mr. Worldly Wiseman: he dwelt in
> the town of Carnal Policy, a very great town, . . .

· · · · · ·

[Christian] went on, and Apollyon met him. Now the monster was hideous to behold; he was clothed with scales like a fish, and they are his pride; he had wings like a dragon, feet like a bear, and out of his belly came fire and smoke; and his mouth was as the mouth of a lion. When he was come up to Christian, he beheld him with a disdainful countenance, . . . [After the 'sore combat . . . for about half a day'] Apollyon spread forth his dragon's wings and sped him away, that Christian saw him no more.

Writing as he was for an unspecialized audience, and in particular for unlearned readers, Bunyan made *The Pilgrim's Progress* at least as much a tale of wonder—a Christian fairy-tale—as a parable. For generations of readers it lived as a hallowed fairy-tale, and did not relax its hold upon the national imagination until in the nineteenth century it was forcibly fed to children as 'a Sunday book'. Taken as what it is—a work of superb literary genius, an unsurpassed demonstration of the beauty of plain English, and the lonely instance of a Christian novel which, as literature, is not inferior to the great secular novels—*The Pilgrim's Progress* is as much a book for the twentieth century as it was for the seventeenth. It is like a landscape in which one is for ever pointing out fresh lovelinesses that come into sight and remain ineffaceable in memory, and many besides professing Christians would select as the finest single passage of English prose the description towards the end of *The Pilgrim's Progress* of the death of one of Bunyan's Christian heroes, Mr. Valiant-for-truth:

I am going to my Father's; and though with great difficulty I am got hither, yet now I do not repent me of all the trouble I have been at to arrive where I am. My sword I give to Him that shall succeed me in my pilgrimage, and my courage and skill to him that can get it. My marks and scars I carry with me, to be a witness for me, that I have fought His battles who will now be my rewarder. When the day that he must go hence was come, many accompanied him to the river side, into which as he went he said, *Death, where is thy sting?* And as he went down deeper, he said, *Grave, where is thy victory?* So he passed over, and all the trumpets sounded for him on the other side.

The usual description of Bunyan as 'a tinker' has too much encouraged the romantic notion that he was a divinely inspired ignoramus. He is more properly called a tinsmith, for that was the craft of his father in the village of Elstow, near Bedford, where John Bunyan (1628–88) was born and schooled and taught his trade. Shortly before his seventeenth birthday he enlisted or was conscripted into the parliamentarian army, where he served under a Puritan commander, Sir Samuel Luke, the Sir Samuel Hudibras of Butler's mock-heroic epic (*see below*, pp. 152–3). Bunyan's whole-hearted and single-minded study of his great source-book, the Bible, dated from the time he left the army in 1647, when he was nineteen. A few years later he became a local preacher in the Nonconformist fellowship of Bedford and its neighbourhood. The first of his sixty or so works was written in 1656 as a confutation of Quaker views, and apart from the four main books—*Grace Abounding to the Chief of Sinners* (1666), his spiritual autobiography; *The Pilgrim's Progress* (Part I 1678, Part II 1684), and *The Life and Death of Mr. Badman* (1680), and *The Holy War* (1682), both of which are also near-novels—his writings stand on much the same level as the bulk of the many forgotten polemical and disputatious works of the period. As an unlicensed preacher Bunyan was arrested at the Restoration and confined in Bedford gaol from 1660 until the promulgation of the Declaration of Indulgence by Charles II in 1672. He resumed preaching, but was again imprisoned for a short term when parliament repealed the Declaration in 1675. It was then, in the town gaol on Bedford bridge, that he began to write *The Pilgrim's Progress*, perhaps the greatest of the books which have been born in prison. After his release, the remainder of his life was devoted to preaching in London and elsewhere and to writing. His grave is in the Dissenters' burial ground, Bunhill Fields, London, where George Fox (leader of Bunyan's arch-opponents, the Quakers), Daniel Defoe, and William Blake also lie.

CHAPTER IV

DRYDEN AND HIS CONTEMPORARIES

JUST as there was no obvious revolutionary change in the general character of published books in the years on either side of 1642, 'Cavalier' writings appearing after the dethronement of Charles I as well as before, so also after the Restoration in 1660 'Puritan' works continued with little hindrance. Though Bunyan.was imprisoned for preaching he was not prohibited from publishing; nor do the authorities seem to have been dismayed by the printing in 1671 of Milton's *Samson Agonistes*, which could have been classed not unreasonably as subversive literature. Nevertheless, the Restoration brought with it a very different moral and mental atmosphere, quickly apparent in the licentiousness of stage plays and more gradually in the development of philosophical and scientific curiosity and inquiry. By 1700 literature presented a very different aspect from that of 1600. Elizabethan freshness and exuberance were gone; the Augustan mode of weighty deliberation was already on the way.

Among many new names in the publishing annals of the last thirty years of the seventeenth century, those of Dryden and Congreve are outstanding, though there were lesser writers (among them several whose works did not appear in print until the nineteenth and twentieth centuries: Pepys, Evelyn, Dorothy Osborne, Traherne) who have given much enduring pleasure. Isaac Newton has already been named (*above*, p. 20) as an influence on non-scientific writers, though his works are not directly a part of English literature; and John Locke (*see below*, pp. 80–1) is more important in the history of thought than in literature.

Restoration Drama

The Puritan closing of the theatres from 1642 was hardly more effective in suppressing the desire for stage plays than Prohibition in the United States was in suppressing the desire for alcohol some three centuries later. Not only were 'private' performances given in the houses of noblemen and others, but, also, means were found of getting round the law, sometimes with impunity, sometimes at the cost of imprisonment for the players. Much turned upon the interpretation of the phrase 'stage-plays shall cease and be forborne', and a type of dramatic representation called Droll Humours or Drolleries seems to have been, by official connivance, outside the formal category of 'stage-plays'. These pieces, performed on makeshift stages, were often abbreviated from standard works (e.g. *Bottom the Weaver* and *The Grave-Diggers* from Shakespeare), no doubt with liberties taken in the actual dialogue as well as in the addition of music and dancing.

The first to secure open relaxation of the ban was Sir William D'Avenant (1606–68), godson (or, possibly, illegitimate son) of Shakespeare, who became Charles I's Poet Laureate in 1638, wrote masques, and managed the King's Company of players before their disbandment. In 1656 he was permitted to produce at Rutland House an entertainment of combined music and declamation, consisting of rhetorical argument between two pairs of characters, and accompanied with music by Henry Lawes. There soon followed D'Avenant's *The Siege of Rhodes*, 'an heroic play' with 'musical recitative' by Charles Coleman and George Hudson. This was staged with the scenic trappings of a spectacle, and ranks as the first English opera. Having gained acceptance of this type of entertainment, D'Avenant forestalled the Restoration as far as the stage was concerned by establishing himself with other operas at the Cockpit in Drury Lane two years before the Commonwealth ended. Under the restored monarchy D'Avenant and Thomas Killigrew (1612–83) received the Royal Patent giving them a joint monopoly of theatrical performances. D'Avenant set up the Duke of York's Company at a playhouse in Lincoln's Inn Fields, and Killigrew revived the King's Company, which had no fixed location until it occupied the Theatre Royal, Drury Lane in 1663. There are many references to both these companies and their performances in Pepys's Diary.

As an author D'Avenant concerned himself largely with operatic (or, as the unfriendly thought, pantomimic) adaptations of Shakespeare, while Killigrew—a Court favourite with

both Charles I and Charles II—had written several tragi-
comedies before 1642 and *The Parson's Wedding*, revived in 1664
and described by Pepys (11 October) as 'a bawdy loose play
. . . acted by nothing but women at the King's house'.

Any detailed study of English drama in this period would
need to take account of the liberal borrowings from Spain and
France. Both countries had their greatest playwrights in the
seventeenth century, and English writers were very conscious
of foreign contemporaries'[1] works.

Considering the familiarity of the term 'Restoration Drama'
and the attention given to it by scholars and students, it is dis-
concerting to find that so few of the plays have genuine merit.
There is no play of the time which is good both in print and
on the stage, and a prejudiced critic (possibly even an objective
and dispassionate one) might convincingly maintain that none
is, from beginning to end, either good drama or good literature.
Those that act well in parts—such as *The Country Wife* (1675)
of William Wycherley (?1640–1716) and *The Relapse* (1697) of
Sir John Vanbrugh (1664–1726)—have boring patches during
performance and are negligible in print. Congreve, though
head and shoulders above the rest as a writer, is utterly de-
pendent upon the players' skill in performance; without an
actress of genius even *The Way of the World* (1700) is poor stuff
on the stage, and no play depends so much as this upon the
memorableness of a few lines. We wait all too long (until Act II,
Sc. iv) for the words that so magnificently herald Millamant's
entrance: 'Here she comes i'faith, full Sail, with her Fan
spread and Streamers out, and a Shoal of Fools for Tenders'.
It would perhaps be fair to say that it is the excellence of wit
in Millamant that makes her so exquisitely hard to act. She is
as near wit incarnate as a creature can hope to be, and that is
her weakness as a dramatic character; she lacks the grosser part
that makes a woman of flesh and blood. When Mirabell asks
on what conditions she will marry him, she finishes her catalogue with 'These Articles subscrib'd, if I continue to endure
you a little longer, I may by degrees dwindle into a Wife',
a magnificent but scarcely loving prospectus for young spouses.
At its rare best Restoration comedy is over-intellectualized;

[1] Lope de Vega (1562–1635) and Calderon (1600–81); Corneille
(1606–84), Molière (1622–73), and Racine (1639–99).

at its frequent worst it is either imbecile or bestial, for the constant harping on cuckoldry turns into the dreariest of all sexual jokes, æsthetically as well as ethically. It is, indeed, on æsthetic grounds that much of the Artificial Comedy of the Restoration period now stands condemned, for the twentieth century has in the main conceded that the plays of Wycherley, Vanbrugh, Mrs. Aphra Behn (1640–89) and their lesser fellows are not to be judged as guides to conduct; nor is it now assumed that the amoral standards of the characters were necessarily those of their creators also. However amusing *The Country Wife* may be when skilfully performed—and that it is extremely amusing on the stage few theatregoers would deny—no one is likely to dispute that the spectacle of a libertine feigning impotence as a means to seducing the young wife of an acquaintance is æsthetically repellent, even if its indecency could be condoned.

The career of William Congreve (1670–1729) as a playwright lasted only seven years, during which he wrote four comedies—*The Old Bachelor* (1693), *The Double Dealer* (1694), *Love for Love* (1695), and *The Way of the World* (1700)—and one tragedy, *The Mourning Bride* (1697). He was born at Bardsey in Yorkshire and educated in Ireland, his father being in command of a garrison. After leaving Trinity College, Dublin (where Jonathan Swift was contemporaneously a student), Congreve moved to London and entered the Middle Temple. Instead of following the law, however, he turned to writing and produced a novel of no merit, *Incognita*, in 1691. In his first play, which brought him immediate renown, the famous Thomas Betterton played Heartwell, a surly old bachelor, and the equally famous as well as lovely and virtuous Mrs. Bracegirdle played Araminta. These two also appeared in Congreve's other comedies, Anne Bracegirdle being the first Millamant. *The Mourning Bride* has now only a fragmentary fame as the source of two familiar quotations: 'Music hath charm to soothe the savage breast' and 'Heaven has no rage, like love to hatred turned, Nor hell a fury, like a woman scorned.' *The Way of the World*, since esteemed his finest work, was at first received with disfavour, and that possibly accounts' for Congreve's silence as an author during the remaining twenty-nine years of his life.

Only one writer of tragedies in the Restoration period, Thomas Otway (1652–85), has survived as more than a name. The whole temper of the age was inimical to tragedy on the stage. Although it was a post-war age, it had not the modern habit of recognizing and dramatizing itself as such in a mood of inverted Byronic melancholy and sentimental despair. It wanted to laugh, indecently for preference, and had little liking or aptitude for tragedy. Nathaniel Lee (?1653–92) won some success, more especially with *The Rival Queens* (1677), dealing with the two wives of Alexander the Great, Roxana and Statira; but Otway had genius—and died in poverty at the age of thirty-three after cherishing a vain passion for Mrs. (Elizabeth) Barry who played his tragic heroines. Of his dozen plays, three are outstanding: *Don Carlos* (1676) in rhyme; and *The Orphan* (1680) and *Venice Preserv'd* (1682) in blank verse. The last-named, Otway's masterpiece, is an impressive 'acting piece' but preposterous in theme, hollow in characterization, and morally repulsive. The conspirators against the Venetian senate are political gangsters moved by base personal aims though pretending to high motives. Jaffier's voluntary lodging of his wife with the plotters as hostage for his own loyalty to them is as incredible as it is vile; while Belvidera's end gives point to the line in Sheridan's burlesque, *The Critic (see below,* p. 207), 'O Lord, sir, when a heroine goes mad she always goes into white satin.' Pierre alone is a fully created character— the rebel in grain—and he gives some colour to the view of Otway as an Elizabethan born out of his time. His tragedies have lingering traces of the blood-boltered atmosphere of those of Marlowe and Kyd, though Otway has less spontaneous impetuosity of utterance and more Jonsonian sense of order. Belvidera and Jaffier rage in 'high astounding terms' but their speeches are far more rhetorical than passionate.

Tragedy came to a dead-end in Otway. In Congreve comedy reached a growing-point. Romantic Comedy was carried as far as it could healthily go by Shakespeare; Ben Jonson initiated and exhausted the Comedy of Humours. Congreve left the Comedy of Manners at the juncture where, by shedding the dry husks of intellectual artifice, it could develop in the late eighteenth century into the more warmly genial and human Comedy of Manners of Goldsmith and Sheridan.

Playwriting in the early part of the eighteenth century lay in the shadow of Collier's *A Short View of the Immorality and Profaneness of the English Stage* (1698). Jeremy Collier (1650–1726), a courageous country rector who afterwards became a nonjuring bishop, was as a censor of the drama morally earnest but certainly not critically balanced: he damned without discrimination. He started a controversy which went on for ten years, Congreve being among the playwrights whose words in defence did little but justify the principle that it is sensible for abused authors not to answer back. On the whole, Collier had the best of the argument, and though he did not kill the stage he caused much inconvenience to playwrights and players, several of whom were prosecuted. Even without Collier's intervention, however, the Restoration drama must have faded out in no very different way. Licentiousness amuses for a very little while; it is essentially barren and monotonous, and therefore quickly boring. Lacking both heart and ideas, Restoration drama was self-doomed to early extinction.

John Dryden

To say, as must be said, that Dryden is the most purely rational of the great English poets is in some sense to deny him greatness. Criticism of his poetry has, indeed, seemed as double-faced as Dryden himself; for even his strongest admirers are forced into a defensive posture. One of his later advocates[1] says that Dryden was 'surprisingly wanting in imagination'. This is pointed to as his 'gravest deficiency', and if it covered the facts it would offer a conveniently simple solution of the Dryden problem. But it is not entirely true that he was lacking in imagination. He lacked romantic and emotional imagination, but not intellectual and reflective imagination. His poetry is deficient in colour and human warmth; if it gleams and glitters, it is not with a deep gem-like radiance but with the hard brilliance of faceted and polished steel. Through sheer efficiency he brought verse satire to a high poetic level.

---

[1] Douglas Grant: *Dryden: Poetry, Prose and Plays* (The Reynard Library. Hart-Davis, London, 1952).

He was the master of a precise and perfect functional adaptation of means to ends. His lines cut down with the cleanly merciless sweep of a Toledo blade those they are aimed at; yet while dealing out this perfection of slaughter Dryden's satire developed an interior irony—which was certainly no part of Dryden's purpose—by conferring a kind of martyrdom upon his victims. Men whose very names would have been forgotten by all but literary antiquarians are now permanently and magnificently monumented in Dryden's satires: he slew with equal zest the basely illustrious and the pretentiously obscure and bestowed an inverted immortality where he meant to annihilate.

This is the fatal weakness of satire, that while it is as indispensable to society as death itself, unlike death it does not destroy. The more perfectly contrived the instrument with which satire functions, the more lasting the memorial to the thing assailed. Moreover, it is a double-edged weapon. Posterity rarely probes below the surface of brilliant satire to try anew those whom wit long ago condemned. Was the first Earl of Shaftesbury as Dryden showed him? Whether we know the answer or not, we remember most readily Dryden's portrait of him in *Absalom and Achitophel* and quote with delight such lines as 'A name to all succeeding ages curst' and

> In friendship false, implacable in hate;
> Resolv'd to ruin or to rule the state.

It is salutary to remember always that great satirists are themselves 'implacable in hate'. Only through a cold unrelenting torment of fanatical detestation that consumes any desire for fair dealing and any sense of balance and proportion can a satirist work his purpose, which should be that of a champion of public right but can be that of a moral assassin or, more meanly, of an unscrupulous hired penman. There is indeed in the nature of satire itself a constant danger of debasement to which only writers of high and incorruptible mind are immune. It is hard for a satirist to distinguish between righteous feeling and self-deceiving prejudice, or, even, to avoid the pitfall of 'Much malice mingl'd with a little wit', a line from Dryden's *The Hind and the Panther*. Dryden himself, by facing different ways at several different times, created doubts as to his own integrity, doubts which apologists challenge but can never finally rebut.

The grandson of a baronet, Sir Erasmus Dryden, John Dryden (1631–1700) was born in the vicarage of Aldwinkle All Saints, Northampton, and went as a King's Scholar to Westminster School before entering Trinity College, Cambridge, where he graduated in 1654. He became clerk to his cousin, Sir Gilbert Pickering, Cromwell's chamberlain, and on the death of the Lord Protector in 1658 wrote *Heroic Stanzas Consecrated to the Memory of His Highness* and mainly devoted to Cromwell's military exploits:

> His palms, tho' under Weights they did not stand,
> Still thriv'd; no Winter could his Laurels fade:
> Heaven in his Portrait shew'd a Work-man's Hand
> And drew it perfect, yet without a Shade.

Two years later he published *Astræa Redux. A Poem on the Happy Restoration & Return of His Sacred Majesty Charles the Second*, followed in the next year by *To His Sacred Majesty, a Panegyrick on His Coronation*. These first evidences of Dryden's readiness to turn with the tide were 'not totally forgotten when his reputation raised him enemies', wrote Dr. Johnson who pleaded for him, however, in the *Lives of the Poets* (1779), that 'the reproach of inconstancy was, on this occasion, shared with such numbers, that it produced neither hatred nor disgrace; if he changed, he changed with the nation'. Dryden, the most politic as well as the most political of poets, might himself have excused his impartial conduct with the plea that a cabinet-maker would not have been rebuked for making as good a chair for Charles in 1660 as he made for Cromwell a few years before, or that a physician knows no distinction of creed or dogma in diagnosing his patient's condition. Such analogies are false if poets are to be moral and spiritual directors; but Dryden's estimate of the poet's place in society was more limited. In the preface to *Religio Laici* (1682) he said: 'I pretend not to make myself a Judge of Faith in others, but onely to make a Confession of my own'; and if, five years after this confession of the Anglican faith, he was ardently supporting Roman Catholicism in *The Hind and the Panther*, it is possible to hold, as Johnson did, that 'When opinions are struggling into popularity, the arguments by which they are opposed or defended become more known; and he that changes his profession would perhaps have changed it before, with the like opportunities of instruction.'

In 1663 Dryden married Lady Elizabeth Howard and in the same year wrote *The Wild Gallant*, the first of the score or so of plays in which he was concerned either as sole author, collaborator, or adapter. His adaptations and imitations included *Sir Martin Mar-All* (1667) from Molière's *L'Etourdi*; *The Tempest* (1667), *All for Love* (on Antony and Cleopatra) (1677), *Troilus and Cressida* (1679, also after Shakespeare); *An Evening's Love, or The Mock Astrologer* (1668) from Corneille; *The State of Innocence* (1677), an attempt to turn *Paradise Lost* into a rhyming play. For several years, c. 1667 onward, he was playwright to the King's Company, becoming a shareholder under the terms of an agreement which provided that he should write three or four plays a year. None of his dramatic works has held the stage, and as early as 1671 his 'heroic tragedies' were mocked in *The Rehearsal*, George Villiers, Duke of Buckingham's farcical comedy, which parodies their mannerisms and borrowings and in the character named Bayes satirizes Dryden (and others). Dryden retaliated later by bringing Buckingham into *Absalom and Achitophel* as Zimri:

> A man so various, that he seem'd to be
> Not one, but all Mankind's Epitome.
> Stiff in Opinions, always in the wrong;
> Was Every thing by starts, and Nothing long; . . .

For literary quality as distinct from stageworthiness, *Marriage-à-la-Mode* (1672), *Aureng-Zebe* (1675), *The Spanish Fryar* (1680), and especially *All for Love* are outstanding; but how far short Dryden was of the original he imitated in the last-named can be gauged if the dying speech of his Cleopatra be compared with Shakespeare's. Whereas *Antony and Cleopatra* is all poetry and passion, *All for Love* is cramped by the conventionalism of heroic drama, which shrinks from free emotion and substitutes formal attitudes:

> Already, Death, I feel thee in my Veins;
> I go with such a will to find my Lord,
> That we shall quickly meet.

> A heavy numness creeps through every limb,
> And now 'tis at my head: my eye-lids fall,
> And my dear Love is vanish'd in a mist.
> Where shall I find him, where? O turn me to him,
> And lay me on his breast. Caesar, thy worst;
> Now part us, if thou canst.

It was in the often charming if occasionally improper songs scattered about his plays that Dryden came nearest to natural sentiment and feeling, and nearest also to being a likeable poet.

While the plague raged in London in 1665 Dryden took refuge for a time at Charlton in Wiltshire, writing *Annus Mirabilis: The Year of Wonders, 1666. An Historical Poem* and the most famous of his prose compositions *An Essay of Dramatick Poesie*. In *Annus Mirabilis*, which surveys the 'progress and various successes' of the naval war with Holland and describes the Fire of London, the artificial nature of this kind of poem rather than Dryden's specimen of the kind produces such absurdities as the stanza (16) on the assembly of the British ships, with its associated reference to the comets which appeared at that time:

> To see this Fleet upon the Ocean move
>   Angels drew wide the Curtains of the skies:
> And Heav'n, as if there wanted Lights above,
>   For Tapers made two glareing Comets rise.

and this (271), following the section which purports to give Charles II's prayer during the Great Fire:

> Th' Eternal heard, and from the Heav'nly Quire,
>   Chose out the Cherub with the flaming sword:
> And bad him swiftly drive th' approaching fire
>   From where our Naval Magazins were stor'd.

Yet, notwithstanding artificiality, absurdity, strained imagery, and bathos, *Annus Mirabilis* is a remarkable and technically admirable performance in which the craft of verse runs sometimes near to the art of poetry, with crude imagination lending a hand:

> Thus, to some desart plain, or old wood side,
>   Dire night-hags come from far to dance their round:
> And o'r brode Rivers on their fiends they ride,
>   Or sweep in clowds above the blasted ground.

Dryden was made Poet Laureate in 1668 and Historiographer Royal in 1670, holding the appointments until the Revolution of 1688, when, on the accession of William III and Mary, Thomas Shadwell succeeded to both offices. This was a galling affront to Dryden who, six years before in *Mac Flecknoe*, had nominated Shadwell (?1642–92, minor playwright and poet) as monarch of 'all the Realms of *Non-sense*' in succession to a recently dead and still lesser poet, Richard Flecknoe, who is made by Dryden to say:

> Sh—— alone my perfect image bears,
> Mature in dullness from his tender years:
> Sh—— alone of all my Sons is he
> Who stands confirm'd in full stupidity.
> The rest to some faint meaning make pretence,
> But Sh—— never deviates into sense.

Shadwell had invited this assault by writing *The Medal of John Bayes* in reply to *The Medall: A Satyre against Sedition* (1682) in which Dryden supplemented the attack on Shaftesbury which began in *Absalom and Achitophel* (1681), the first of his great satires. It must always be left for individual opinion and taste to debate whether it was brilliantly clever or only tiresomely ingenuous of Dryden to dress his satirical account of contemporary English politics in scriptural costume which could not at the time have disguised anything from anyone capable of reading the poem, even if its purpose had been to disguise instead of to advertise and defame Shaftesbury (or to 'correct' him, as Dryden would have preferred to say). Something is perhaps gained in wit and audacity by attributing to David, King of Israel, in lines 1–20 the impartial fruitfulness of Charles II:

> Then, *Israel's* Monarch, after Heaven's own heart,
> His vigorous warmth did, variously, impart
> To Wives and Slaves: And, wide as his Command,
> Scatter'd his Maker's Image through the Land. . . .

but little advantage comes from most of the Old Testament machinery which turns France into Egypt, Brussels into Gath, Richard Cromwell into Ishbosheth, the Roman Catholics into Jebusites, the Presbyterians into Levites, Parliament into the Sanhedrin, and so on.

James II's succession in 1685 revived hope among the English Catholics and Dryden joined them in the same year, with the result, as has been seen, that his defence of the Church of England in *Religio Laici* (1682) was counterbalanced by the product of his conversion *The Hind and the Panther* (1687). Whether conviction or prudence was uppermost in Dryden's change of religion is not a literary concern, and it need only be noted that, in these two poems, verse as a medium for argument and apologetics reaches the peak of achievement.

Dryden's main feat as a prosodist was the establishment of heroic verse (heroic couplets, or rhyming couplets—ten-syllable, five feet, or iambic pentameter lines rhyming in pairs) as one of the principal English verse forms. In lesser hands a monotonous measure, the heroic couplet as Dryden used it is adequate for all purposes other than those of romantic poetry: it imposes restraint and regularity to which works of imagination and feeling are not conformable. When, as in his Odes (*To Mrs. Anne Killigrew* and *Alexander's Feast*) and in *A Song for St. Cecilia's Day 1687*, Dryden attempted things beyond the scope of pure intellect he achieved only the Grand Style, aloof alike from feeling and the higher imagination.

In poetry Dryden's last works were his translations of Virgil (1697) and the *Fables, Ancient and Modern* (1700) adapted from Chaucer, Boccaccio, and Ovid. He died in London, and was buried in Westminster Abbey on 13 May 1700.

The restraint and regularity of heroic verse matched that innate bent for directness and economy of statement which makes Dryden's prose so easy and 'modern'. Though verse satire is a socially valuable art it is also a rare one, but prose is always with us and as the great clarifier of English prose Dryden placed the whole nation permanently in his debt. His prose writings contain scarcely a word unfamiliar to present-day readers, and it would be hard to find an involved or an ambiguous sentence. But although Dryden wrote plain prose he did not write pedestrian prose, and the fact that poetry was the subject of his principal essays and prefaces is reflected in the tone of the prose. No one has written better—more sensibly or more eloquently—of Chaucer than Dryden did in the Preface to the *Fables* or of Shakespeare than in the *Essay of Dramatick Poesie*; nor is there a more unassumingly beautiful passage in

English prose than this, from an early page of the *Essay*, describing the scene on the river as the four friends move away from the noise of battle between the English and Dutch navies— to discuss poetic drama:

> Taking then a barge, which a servant of *Lisideius* had provided for them, they made haste to shoot the bridge, and left behind them that great fall of waters, which hindered them from hearing what they desired: after which, having disengaged themselves from many vessels which rode at anchor in the Thames, and almost blocked up the passage towards Greenwich, they ordered the watermen to let fall their oars more gently; and then, every one favouring his own curiosity with a strict silence, it was not long ere they perceived the air to break about them like the noise of distant thunder, or of swallows in a chimney—those little undulations of sound, though almost vanishing before they reached them, yet still seeming to retain somewhat of their first horror which they had betwixt the fleets.

To Dryden, said Johnson,

> we owe . . . the refinement of our language, and much of the correctness of our sentiments. By him we were taught . . . to think naturally and express forcibly. . . . What was said of Rome, adorned by Augustus, may be applied by an easy metaphor to English poetry embellished by Dryden, *lateritiam invenit, marmoream reliquit*, he found it brick, and he left it marble.

From this comes the label 'Augustan Age' applied, often loosely, to the period of Dryden and of those eighteenth-century successors who also aimed at classical correctness. Johnson was himself enough of an Augustan to overlook the foreignness of marble in the English scene and not to observe that the introduction of its equivalent in poetry might be a questionable gain, or even an intrusion out of harmony with the native temperament.

Miscellaneous Writings

Izaak Walton (1593–1683) has obtained a minor though secure immortality from two very different books which nevertheless reflect the same quiet and meditative spirit. He was born an Elizabethan, wrote his masterpiece *The Compleat Angler* (1653) under the Commonwealth, and published the book now generally called *Walton's Lives* (of Donne, Herbert, Hooker, and Wotton) under Charles II in 1670. *The Compleat Angler; or The Contemplative Man's Recreation. Being a Discourse of Rivers, Fish-ponds, Fish, and Fishing* is one of the curiosities of literature, since it must have found the vast majority of its readers among those who know next to nothing and care quite nothing about its subject. Its beauty lies in its unique evocation of an un-blemished personality, Walton's own, and in its preservation of the atmosphere and life of a piece of seventeenth-century rural England. The *Lives*, also, reveal Walton's own spirit and

The Carp

are better remembered on that account than for any direct biographical value. (*See also above*, p. 33.)

It may be no more than individual fancy that suggests a temperamental affinity between Walton and Dorothy Osborne (1627–95), whose love letters to Sir William Temple (1628–99) —whom she married in 1655—are unexcelled among the many fine published collections of English correspondence. Her letters—written mostly at Chicksands in Bedfordshire from 1652 to 1654, but unpublished until 1888—reveal the writer's exquisite personality and give invaluable interior glimpses of an English country house and its occupants during the Com-monwealth. At least one outdoor picture, in an account of Dorothy's doings on a single day, is close in spirit to Walton's pastoral scenes:

> . . . about six or seven a clock, I walke out into a Common that lyes hard by the house where a great many young wenches keep Sheep and Cow's, and sitt in the shade singing of Ballads; I goe to them and compare theire voyces and Beauty's to some Ancient Shepherdesses that I have read of and finde a vaste

difference there, but trust mee I think these are as innocent as
those could bee. I talke to them, and finde they want nothing
to make them the happiest People in the world, but the knoledge
that they are soe. . . .[1]

Sir William Temple (none of whose letters to Dorothy has
survived) was an eminent diplomat and himself a writer of
some distinction (his essays were published in three volumes as
Miscellanea in 1680, 1692, and 1701).[2]

Like Dorothy Osborne's *Letters*, the two most famous
seventeenth-century diaries were not published until the nineteenth century: that of John Evelyn (1620–1706) in 1818 and
that of Samuel Pepys (1633–1703) in 1825. Though these two
were friends for nearly forty years and Evelyn wrote movingly of
him on the day Pepys died, they differed greatly in temperament,
Evelyn being a serious-minded and somewhat solemn person,
while Pepys (in his friend's words) was 'universally belov'd,
hospitable, generous, learned in many things, skill'd in music, a
very great cherisher of learned men' and also—as Evelyn did
not say—an exceedingly great cherisher of unlearned women,
if they were pretty and approachable. Perhaps the two men can
be best and most briefly distinguished by saying that whereas
Pepys loved and savoured Life and everything it offers, Evelyn
was much more selective and had much less fun. Of Pepys's
innumerable interests, the theatre and women were the most
persistent: Mrs. Pepys, his wife though not always his favourite,
has become through his pages as notable a person as her
husband. But while it is Pepys's pleasures and peccadilloes
that have endeared him to several generations of readers, it is
not to be overlooked that he was a great public servant as
Secretary to the Navy Office (now the Admiralty), able and
conscientious, 'none in England exceeding him in knowledge
of the Navy', Evelyn testified. Pepys kept his Diary from
1 January 1660 until 31 May 1669, closing it then because he
feared blindness, a calamity which was so far from actually
befalling him that he lived and did his most important service
for the nation during the thirty years and more that remained

---

[1] Letter 24, 2–4 June 1653. *The Letters of Dorothy Osborne to William
Temple*. Edited by G. C. Moore Smith (Clarendon Press, 1928).
[2] See below, p. 160.

to him. The difference between the tone of Pepys and Evelyn as diarists (Evelyn's journal covered most of his very long life) can readily be judged by comparing the accounts of events, such as the Fire of London, which both describe. Evelyn had neither eye nor care for trifles; but it is often through trifles that Pepys is most revealing, and the pulsing life which makes his Diary the magnificent intimate history of the times that it is depends a great deal upon his noticing and recording things which in themselves and by themselves do not matter a jot. Yet the sum total of the innumerable things in Pepys's Diary that do not matter makes it the most living autobiographical document in English.

If only because they provide a deep well of information about personalities of the age, John Aubrey (1626–97) and Anthony Wood (1632–95) require passing mention. Wood himself drew largely upon the MS. of Aubrey's *Lives of Eminent Persons* (unpublished until 1813) for his own works on the *History and Antiquities of the University of Oxford* [1] and on the lives of Oxford divines and authors, *Athenae Oxonienses* (1691–2).

The seventeenth century was profuse in pamphlets, and (other than Milton's) the most frequently cited are George Fox's *A Paper sent forth into the World from them that are scornfully called Quakers* (1654); Edward Sexby's *Killing no Murder* (1657), a diatribe against Cromwell by one of his former officers who was outraged by his leader's assumption of the rank of Lord Protector; and George Savile, Marquess of Halifax's *Letter to a Dissenter* (1687) and *The Character of a Trimmer* (1688).[2] In addition to the pamphlet mentioned, George Fox's *Journal* (pub. 1694) and William Penn's *Some Fruits of Solitude* (1693) are important in early Quaker literature.

The literary interest of the writings of John Locke (1632–1704)—*An Essay Concerning Human Understanding* (1690), the three *Letters Concerning Toleration* (1689, '90, '92), and the two

---

[1] Wood's English text did not appear until towards the end of the next century, though a Latin translation was edited by Dr. John Fell, Bishop of Oxford, as early as 1674.
[2] See also below, pp. 161–2, on Halifax.

13. Satan raising his legions, from *Paradise Lost*

14. John Milton by E. Pierce

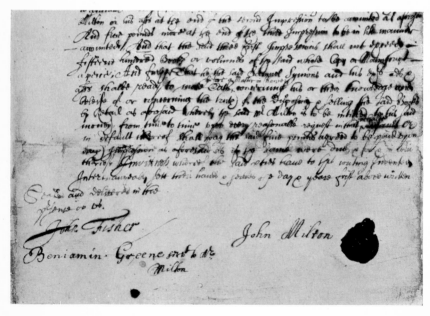

15. Part of the deed for sale of copyright in *Paradise Lost*

16. Frontispiece to the first part
of *The Pilgrim's Progress*

17. John Bunyan by Robert
White

18. Stage scene by Pierre Perrin from the frontispiece to *Ariadne*

19. Thomas Killigrew by William Sheppard

20. Part of one of the bookcases in the Pepysian Library

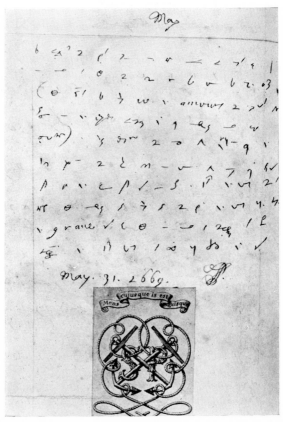

21. The last page from Samuel Pepys' *Diary*

A Choice Collection of Books
being the Library of the late
famous Unborn Doctor, are
to be put to Sale this Day, and
to continue untill all be Sold.
at Mr. I, —g's Auction in the
North West Corner of Middle
Moorfields. Catalogues may
be had at most of the eminent
Booksellers in the four Quarters
of Moorfeilds Gratis, the Books
may be Seen before or at the
time of Sale.

Sutton Nicholls excudit

22. *The Compleat Auctioneer*

23. A London bookseller's advertisement, *c.* 1700

Treatises of Government (1690)—is relatively small in comparison with their value as landmarks in the history of ideas and political philosophy, though that is inseparable from their literary quality. They are written in lucid and arresting prose, as appears from almost any sentences chosen at random:

> He that is nourished by the acorns he picked up under an oak, or the apples he gathered from the trees in the wood, has certainly appropriated them to himself. Nobody can deny but the nourishment is his. I ask, then, when did they begin to be his? when he digested? or when he ate? or when he boiled? or when he brought them home? or when he picked them up?'[1]

Among the lesser poets writing in the second half of the century, the most popular were Matthew Prior, whose published work belongs mainly to the eighteenth century, and Samuel Butler, author of *Hudibras*.[2] John Wilmot, Earl of Rochester (1647–80), the most notoriously obscene poet of the age, was yet a poet with superabundant creative energy which he dissipated in satiric disgust of Charles II and his mistresses, and in satyric rage against the whole race of women which led him to begin a pastoral poem 'Fair *Cloris* in a Pig-Sty lay' and a song

> Love a Woman! you're an Ass,
> 'Tis a most insipid Passion;
> To chuse out for your Happiness,
> The silliest Part of God's Creation.

The most impressive lyrical poet of the half century, Thomas Traherne (?1634–1704), published *Christian Ethicks* in his lifetime (1675) but his finest works both in verse and in prose remained unprinted until *Poems* appeared in 1903 and *Centuries of Meditations* in 1908. He is among the best of the metaphysical religious poets; and he is also a poet without qualification. His medieval delight in colour takes us back to such a poem as *Pearl*,[3] and he combined spiritual fervour and mystical rapture with deep tenderness. Traherne is perhaps more evidently his own particular self in prose than in verse. What might be called

---

[1] *Second Treatise on Civil Government*: ch. V 'Of Property'.
[2] Prior and Butler are discussed below, p. 152 ff.
[3] Ward: I, p. 10 ff.

his mannerisms if that were not a misleading word are assimilated into his poetry; in his prose, characteristic phrases and
passages can be more easily isolated: 'An empty book is like an
infant's soul, in which anything may be written. It is capable
of all things, but containeth nothing.' '. . . I alone am the end
of the World: . . .' 'You never enjoy the world aright, till
the Sea itself floweth in your veins, till you are clothed with
the heavens, and crowned with the stars.' And, a passage
widely known:

> The corn was orient and immortal wheat, which never should
> be reaped, nor was ever sown. I thought it had stood from ever-
> lasting to everlasting. The dust and stones of the street were as
> precious as gold: the gates were at first the end of the world.
> The green trees when I saw them first through one of the gates
> transported and ravished me, their sweetness and unusual beauty
> made my heart to leap, and almost mad with ecstasy, they were
> such strange and wonderful things.

Traherne's prose style is akin to that of Sir Thomas Browne,
the ornamental style condemned to extinction by the practical
workaday style of Dryden and his successors. In the closing
years of Dryden's life appeared the earliest works of Daniel
Defoe, the man above all others destined to further the purposes of plain prose. When *Robinson Crusoe* came out in 1719
Defoe was approaching sixty, but from 1697 onward he had
been an indefatigable pamphleteer and journalist and with
him begins the age of journalism and journeymen of letters.

CHAPTER V

BOOK SELLING AND NEWS DISTRIBUTION

WHILE it would be an overstatement to say that literature in modern times—roughly since the invention of printing—has depended for its existence upon economic factors, it is nevertheless indisputable that the progress towards worldwide literacy, which in the long run must determine the nature as well as the prosperity of literature, has been made possible by the enterprise and business acumen of publishers and booksellers during five centuries. Caxton was much more than a machine-minded tradesman. He printed and sold books, but he was also a man of taste with scholarly instincts and abilities, and his services to English literature were manifold. Besides introducing the printed book into England, he made English poetry into a going concern by printing Chaucer and Gower, while he contributed invaluably to English prose with his edition of Malory. But, as noted earlier (Ward: I, 83–4 note), Caxton found it necessary to attend to what would now be called commercial considerations by seeking noble patronage as a means of ensuring the sale of enough copies of his books to keep the printing business afloat.

The coming of the printing press to displace the monastic scribe had the revolutionary effect of causing supply to outstrip demand for the first time in the history of book production. The chained book—slowly and laboriously hand-written on precious vellum or parchment, and therefore, as a rare possession, to be safeguarded from thieves and from absent-minded or predatory borrowers—was soon to become an antiquarian relic, though early printed books were also often chained. Since Caxton printed religious service books as well as secular verse and prose he could count upon the Church as a market for part of the output of his press. He therefore enjoyed ecclesiastical as well as lay patronage, and such personal and institutional patronage was to continue as a governing—though gradually diminishing—factor in literature until, first, a reading public large enough to support the book trade appeared, and, second, religious and political censorship ceased and left the trade free to develop without fear of persecution. The first of these conditions was not met until the eighteenth century; the second not wholly until the Victorian age brought a more liberal-minded conception of government.

The Commerce of Literature [1]

The eighteenth century, the great age of British commercial expansion and therefore, necessarily, of increasingly effective organization in all branches of trade and industry, was the century in which English books became established throughout as articles of commerce. Books had been 'coming out' for many generations, sometimes smuggled into readers' hands by independent pirate printers and sellers, but mostly issued under monopoly or some restrictive privilege.[2] Of publishing, genuinely so-called, there had been little in the sixteenth and most part of the seventeenth century. Publishing was at last to become in the eighteenth century a systematic and efficient trade directed by men with a genuine vocation and a natural aptitude for fostering the talents yet restraining the vanities of a multiplying band of professional authors.

The relationship of printers, publishers, and booksellers is too complex to be treated in detail here. Their three functions were for long combined, or only partially separated. Indeed, all were originally designated *stationers*,[3] a comprehensive description perpetuated in the title of the Stationers' Company, which played an important part in the affairs of the book trade

---

[1] For the facts in this section I have drawn mainly upon F. A. Mumby's *Publishing and Bookselling: A History from the Earliest Times to the Present Day* (Cape, London, new edn. 1954).

[2] The only instance of such privilege remaining in the twentieth century is that still held by the Universities of Oxford and Cambridge and the Queen's (or King's) Printers in the printing of the Bible (Authorized Version) and the Book of Common Prayer. This privilege also carries, however, the onerous responsibility of absolute accuracy and the highest standards of production.

[3] The word *stationer* first came into use to distinguish the stationary shopkeeping seller of books and writing materials from the peripatetic chapman and the stallkeeper. It is only in comparatively recent usage that the word has become limited to a seller of writing materials (and more or less associated fancy articles). Though he is sometimes reluctantly a stationer also, the present-day bookseller usually regards stationery as an inferior though profitable business line.

from the middle of the sixteenth century until the early years of the twentieth, when the Copyright Act of 1911 rendered unnecessary the traditional procedure of entering the titles of books on the Register at Stationers' Hall as a means of establishing title to ownership. Until such notable characters as Jacob Tonson (?1656–1736), William Taylor (c. 1688–1724) and his successor the first Thomas Longman (1699–1766), Bernard Lintot (1675–1736), Robert Dodsley (1703–64), and John Newbery (1713–67) brought into the business their forceful personalities, bookprinting and bookselling had been largely a struggle between the monopolists and those who, holding no privilege, courageously defied monopoly, or surreptitiously and piratically printed or reprinted books in which they held no rights, or acquired and published material despised by the prosperous monopolists. In one or both of the last two categories came Shakespeare's and other sixteenth-century plays which are among the treasures of literature. It is possible that but for the chaotic state of the book trade which forced smaller tradesmen to scavenge and pillage, some important Elizabethan and other writings would not have been preserved. On the other hand, had the trade been freer, fewer or none would have taken to piracy, for they could have obtained, legitimately, better texts than the garbled ones they acquired by dubious means.

Though the Stationers' Company long ago became an honoured as well as a veteran body, in the course of the centuries during which its function was not only to protect the interests of its members but also to control the affairs of the whole trade, its influence was sometimes oppressive and tyrannical. In the early sixteenth century foreign printers and binders, freely admitted into England under a statute of 1484, were strictly limited in number after a calamitous riot led by native apprentices. The few remaining foreign workers were then placed under the surveillance of the Stationers' Company, which received, belatedly, a charter of incorporation in 1557, in the reign of Mary. From that time all books were to be entered, before publication, in the Register of the Company, and while this served as a measure of protection to the owners it also provided means of censorship for the prevention of heresy and sedition in print. The officers of the Company were empowered, moreover, to search premises suspected of harbouring proscribed matter.

With those measures the organization of the book trade may be said to have begun; but from earlier times a few names of printers and publishers are well remembered. Caxton's assistant and successor, Wynkyn de Worde (*d.* ?1534), lacked his master's interest in good literature for its own sake and set himself to provide small cheap books with a popular appeal. Yet, if only unawares, he produced some notable works, among them the first extracts (issued anonymously) from *The Book of Margery Kempe*.[1] By Wynkyn de Worde's day St. Paul's Churchyard, where he took a shop in 1509, was already the booksellers' centre, and the neighbourhood retained a close connection with publishing business until Paternoster Row, adjacent to the Churchyard, was obliterated in a single night during the Second World War.

Few readers of general literature hear the name of any English publisher earlier than Richard Tottel (*d.* 1594) who ventured outside the field of his monopoly in law books and issued Lydgate's *Falls of Princes* (1554), the Earl of Surrey's translation of Virgil's *Æneid* (1557) and, in 1559, the famous *Tottel's Miscellany*,[2] which he helped to compile. But John Day (1522–84), as the first to print in Anglo-Saxon characters and one of the earliest of English music-printers, was no less important than Tottel; he also brought out in 1570, long after its original performance, the first authentic edition of *Gorboduc* and Roger Ascham's *The Scholemaster* (1570). Day, too, was a monopolist, in alphabet books (ABCs) and catechisms..

The disrepute in which public authorship was held by gentlemen in the Elizabethan age and later, and their reluctance to put their writings into print, was at least in part due to the fact that literature, at the instigation of enterprising printer-publishers, was becoming a regular trade, and though a gentleman did not need to shrink from buccaneering on the high seas and singeing the Spaniard's beard, he could hardly risk the suspicion that he was on the pay-roll of some measly bookseller. (So in the Victorian age eminent wholesale merchants did not dare to flirt with retail trade.) Edmund Spenser, lower in the social scale than his revered friend Sir Philip

[1] See Ward: I, 72 ff.   [2] See Ward: I, 107 ff.

II. Jacob Tonson by Sir Godfrey Kneller

Sidney, published his poems unashamedly, and chiefly with William Ponsonby (?1546–1604) who at length, after the author's death, managed to get permission from Sidney's relatives to print and issue *Arcadia* in 1590.

Men of letters who were also men of fashion long continued to hold themselves aloof from commercial dealings with publishers.[1] Scribblers could now be hired for a miserable pittance to turn out anything, from one of those noble translations which were a feature of the Elizabethan book trade, to controversial pamphlets and street ballads. These last came from the press in quantities so vast that one publisher who specialized in ballad sheets—Richard Jones (*fl.* 1564–1602)[2]—entered in the Stationers' Register in 1586 no fewer than 123 on a single occasion.

But although scrupulous printers with presses and businesses to keep running were being compelled to go in search of authors and to commission books to be written, thus originating an important side of modern publishing, no commanding figure had yet appeared among them. Little is known of Richard Field (*fl.* 1579–1624) apart from his Stratford birth and his printing of *Venus and Adonis* (1593) and *Lucrece* (1594), the only pieces that Shakespeare appears to have cared about in book form, for (also in 1594) another printer, John Danter, pirated *Titus Andronicus*. It could be supposed that Shakespeare had so poor an opinion of *Titus* that anyone might print it without hindrance, but the same pirate also brought out a poor text of *Romeo and Juliet* in 1597; and Danter was in most ways a shady character. The most renowned of the Shakespeare pirates, Thomas Thorpe (?1570–?1635), set the literary world an everlasting puzzle with his dedication of the first edition of the *Sonnets* (1609) to 'the onlie begetter'. That Mr. W. H. may have been only Thorpe's rummaging 'book-scout'—in this instance a supremely lucky one—and not Southampton or any other friend of Shakespeare is a fascinatingly deflating possibility put forward by Sir Sidney Lee.[3]

---

[1] Thomas Gray, as late as 1751, would take nothing from Dodsley for *An Elegy in a Country Churchyard*, holding that it was unbecoming in an author to receive money from a bookseller. In after years Gray changed his opinion.

[2] He also published Marlowe's *Tamburlaine* and other notable works.

[3] See Ward: I, 216.

Two years before her death Elizabeth abrogated all monopolies, but on James I's accession in 1603 the Stationers' Company acquired the first of a sequence of grants of exclusive right which influential members used to secure control of a large part of the trade. A proportion of the Society's annual trading profits was to be set aside for charity, a provision which the independent printers alleged was not carried out. It must be allowed to the credit of the Stationers' Company, however, that they financed the printing and publishing of the Authorized Version of the Bible (1611) and contributed funds to the revisers. The Company's monopolies were not swept away until 1779, but in the meantime the personal influence of Tonson, Dodsley, and others had transformed the book trade and its relations with authors.

While registration at Stationers' Hall had nominally, yet not effectually, given protection to the printer or other registree, authors' rights were unprotected until the passing of the Copyright Act of 1709, which granted copyright for twenty-one years for books already in print, and a maximum of twenty-eight years for new books. Registration at Stationers' Hall was still required. This statute was far from satisfactory to the owners of literary property, who regarded enforceable legal protection for a comparatively short term of years as a poor exchange for what had commonly been assumed to be a perpetual right, even though the right might be infringed by the unscrupulous. Yet the 1709 measure brought the beginnings of order into a trade which had largely fallen into chaos, partly through the cumulative effect of a long series of restrictive ordinances, capriciously administered even when not spitefully and stupidly drafted, which maintained the old spirit of persecution that had hanged a publisher (John Twyn) for an alleged seditious pamphlet in the reign of Charles II and put Defoe thrice into the pillory on account of his pamphlet *The Shortest Way with the Dissenters*. Moreover, until the 1709 Act restored its validity by giving it legal force, the system of registration at Stationers' Hall had broken down.

Yet no Act of Parliament could have brought about a radically improved state of affairs if the trade had not itself been on the high road to self-reformation. Indeed, if it is true that the first draft for the 1709 Act was devised by Swift, the impulse for legal regularization came from within what was to become the highly respected literary profession.

The new era may conveniently be dated from 1683, when Jacob Tonson bought a half share in the publication rights of Milton's *Paradise Lost*. Samuel Simmons, the original publisher, had paid £18 in all to Milton and Milton's widow between 1667 and 1680, when he acquired the entire rights. Simmons' own profits could hardly have been more than modest, and it could not have been foreseen in 1683 that Tonson would go on to make more profit from *Paradise Lost* than from any of the poems by Dryden and other renowned contemporaries who were to be among his authors. Soon Tonson was paying Dryden 250 guineas (equivalent to some 1,500 guineas in present-day currency) for the first edition of *Fables*, and in 1709 he originated the Shakespeare industry by publishing a seven-volume edition of the works, which he had commissioned Nicholas Rowe to edit 'for the general reader'.[1] Tonson afterwards took his nephew Jacob into the business. They became Pope's first publishers before he went to Bernard Lintot. He came back to them to edit another edition of Shakespeare, published in 1725 with only limited success. Later, Tonson became Addison's publisher and, in 1712, joint publisher of *The Spectator*. Not less important for the professional standing of the book trade and for the raising of its general status, Tonson made his way into high society as a foundation member and secretary of the Kit-Cat Club (*see below*, p. 131 n.).

Perhaps the most widely known of booksellers and printers, Thomas Guy (?1645–1724), owes his enduring repute to other activities. Though Guy began business as a trafficker in smuggled Dutch-printed Bibles, thus injuring the monopoly rights then owned by the Stationers' Company, he afterwards acquired for several years from the University the sole right of printing in Oxford. The wealth which enabled him to leave a great fortune for the endowment of Guy's Hospital in London was, however, the product of his well-calculated financial dabbling in such concerns as the South Sea Company, from which he freed himself before its ruinous collapse. He was in Parliament as member for Tamworth, Staffs., from 1695 to 1707.

[1] See below, pp. 227–8, on eighteenth-century editions of Shakespeare.

34

Mr Tonson

you were no sooner gone, but I felt in
my pocket, & found my Lady Chudleighs
verses: which this Afternoon I gave Mr
Walsh to read in the Coffee house. His opinion
& the same with mine, that they are much
than any which are printed before the Book: so
thinks also Mr Wycherley. I have them by me: but
do not send them, till I heare from My Lord
Clifford, whether My Lady will put her name to
them or not. Therefore I differ; they may be
printed last of all the Copys. I have also written
this day to Mr Chetwood, & let him know, that the
Book is immediatly going to the press again My
Opinion is, that the printer should begin with
the first Pastoral, & print on to the end of the
Georgiques, or farther if occasion be; till Dr
Chetwood corrects his priface which he writes
me word is printed very false. You cannot take
too great care of the printing this Edition, ex
actly after my Amendments: for a fault of that
nature will disoblige me Eternally. I am
glad to heare from all Hands, that my Ode is
esteemd the best of all my Poetry, by all
the Town: I thought so my selfe when I writ
                                                    it

Part of a letter to Jacob Tonson from John Dryden

According to Samuel Johnson's estimate, Pope received above £5,000 as his total proceeds from the translation of Homer's *Iliad*, while the *Odyssey* is said to have brought him well over £4,000. His publisher Bernard Lintot did not profit in proportion, the surreptitious importation of a cheap pirated edition from Holland forcing Lintot to produce a still cheaper edition which left him an infinitesimal margin. It is as Pope's publisher that he remains well known in book-trade annals, though he also issued works by John Gay and other prominent writers, including George Farquhar. Like Jacob Tonson and Thomas Guy, Lintot became well known outside the book trade, serving as High Sheriff of the County of Sussex after his retirement.

The third, with Tonson and Lintot, of the great eighteenth-century publisher-booksellers, Robert Dodsley, began as a footman-poet: his *Servitude* appeared in 1729 and three years later *A Muse in Livery; or, The Footman's Miscellany*. These brought him to the notice of prominent men of letters, including Pope, who was instrumental in getting Rich to produce at Drury Lane in 1735 Dodsley's *The Toy Shop*. Its success persuaded him to leave domestic service, and on 17 May in the same year he opened his bookshop in Pall Mall. This became both a flourishing business and a famed literary rendezvous.

Dodsley developed into the most enterprising and successful publisher of the period during which Johnson, Gray, Swift, Burke, and Goldsmith were active: he paid Johnson 10 guineas for the poem *London*; 15 guineas for *The Vanity of Human Wishes*; £100 for the play *Irene*. It was probably from Dodsley that the suggestion came for Johnson's *Dictionary*, the compiler's fee being agreed at £1,575 (though that sum was exceeded), shared between Dodsley and his four associates, who included Thomas Longman, founder of the firm of Longmans, Green and Company, publishers of the present book. Johnson wrote to Longman, on receiving the contract, inviting him 'and the rest of the Gentlemen [to] breakfast with me that we may sign'.[1]

[1] The reputable publishers named above had a scoundrelly competitor in Edmund Curle (1675–1747), who was frequently in trouble with Parliament, and was tossed in a blanket by Westminster School boys for issuing a garbled version (with 'false Latin in it') of an oration by the captain of the school. But though 'he had no scruples either in business or private life, . . . he published and sold many good books' (*D.N.B.*), including an edition of Pope's letters which may or may not have been authorized.

The system of sharing the costs and profits of particular books was a familiar and convenient eighteenth-century trade practice. It made possible the production of works too expensive or too risky for any single publisher, and it marked a further step away from personal patronage. The subscription system (still used occasionally for complimentary, institutional, or luxury publications), whereby the author or the bookseller touted in advance for orders (and payment) for copies of the proposed work, was also in vogue. Though this procedure might be financially prudent, it was rarely commendable, being for the most part a begging process, with attendant humiliations; and it was open to the twofold objection that appeared in the case of Johnson's edition of Shakespeare, which was not ready until some eight years after it was promised and long after Johnson had lost the subscribers' names and spent the money.

By the end of the eighteenth century the pattern of English publishing was settled for the next century and a half: the figures in the pattern were the author, the publisher-bookseller (a double function later to be divided between publisher and bookseller), and the public. Though the infinitely fragmented patronage of the public requires its own forms of importunity— through publishers' travellers' canvassing of booksellers and libraries, and through press and other advertisements directed to the individual bookbuyer; and though it also imposes upon professional authors its own forms of subservience, through the striving to give the public what the public wants, it is nevertheless certain that the public frequently buys better books than it supposed it wanted, buys them often with a minimum of persuasion, and buys them sometimes (it might appear) through an inexplicable temporary gift of second sight.

Journalism and the Coffee Houses

English printed journalism, as a medium for the dissemination of current news, goes back primitively to the sixteenth-century street ballads which provided, in crude verse, crude accounts of crime and catastrophe. In the 1620s, imported from the Netherlands but soon to be printed in England, came the first of the serious news-journals, largely concerned with happenings

abroad. These brought in their train censorship on the one
hand and tendentious propaganda on the other, for Parlia-
mentarians and Royalists alike used the scurrilous pens of
party journalists. The beginnings of journalism as a reputable
profession date from 1659, when Henry Muddiman turned
from schoolteaching to the compiling of newsbooks. He had
started two such publications before launching, in 1665, *The
Oxford Gazette* while the Court was taking refuge in the university town from the plague in London. This publication, the
first English newspaper in the modern sense of a periodical
containing general news, subsequently became *The London
Gazette* and, nearly three centuries later, continues to appear
with that title, though its contents have long been confined to
official (government and Court) news and notices. The price
of the earliest newsbooks (of about sixteen pages) was one
penny; Muddiman's were sent post free to subscribers for
£5 a year.

Although Samuel Pepys considered him 'an arch rogue'
because he admitted writing for the Parliamentary cause 'only
to get money' (*Pepys's Diary*, 9 January 1660), Muddiman is a
worthy person to stand as the father of English journalism if
only because, with *The London Gazette*, he temporarily drove
out his chief rival, the infamous Sir Roger L'Estrange, who had
published (1663–6) *The Intelligencer* and *The News*. L'Estrange
returned to journalism in 1681 with *The Observator*, continuing
it until 1678 as an organ of government opinion, presented in
a series of arguments in dialogue between an always triumphant
Tory and a discomfited Whig.

Before the end of the seventeenth century an insatiable
craving for news had been fostered by the papers, and by
discussion in the multiplying coffee houses where verbal news
and opinions supplemented the printed sheets. The combined
effects of periodical publications and coffee-house gatherings
were to be so important in the directing and developing of
eighteenth-century literature, that both must be considered as
having a vital part in the creation of the atmosphere and circumstances congenial to Defoe and his contemporaries and
successors. The *State Trials*[1] report a judge as saying in 1680:

[1] Vol. VII, p. 1120; quoted in H. R. Fox Bourne, *English Newspapers*
(1887), I, 49.

'So fond are men in these days, that when they will deny their children a penny for bread, they will lay it out for a pamphlet; and the temptations are so great that no man can keep twopence in his pocket because of the news.' L'Estrange wrote in *The Observator* (21 March 1684): 'I have observed very ill effects many times from the ordinary written papers of parliament news by making the coffee-houses and all the popular clubs judges of those counsels and deliberations which they have nothing to do withal.' The authorities' conviction that the free discussion of public affairs either in print or in speech was an encroachment on matters with which the people had nothing to do, led to that long series of restrictions—by censorship and indictment or, indirectly, by taxation—against which the newspapers, and the printing press generally, struggled during the eighteenth century and after.

Though some effort was made to suppress them on the plea that they became hotbeds of political discontent, the coffee houses were not only less vulnerable to the stifling of opinion than was the press, but also, by fostering social intercourse— its humanity and its urbanity—they helped to create the audience for that new type of periodical, of which *The Tatler* and *The Spectator* in the hands of Steele and Addison were to become the most distinguished and to pass lastingly into English literature.

Coffee houses had spread from Egypt and Turkey to most European countries during the seventeenth century, the first in England being opened at Oxford in 1650. Two years later one was opened close by Cornhill in the centre of London. By the end of the century they were numerous enough to have become specialized: a particular coffee house would attract a clientele drawn together by a special interest, commercial, intellectual, or social: thus Will's Coffee House, near Covent Garden and named after its proprietor, William Unwin, was a resort of poets; White's Chocolate House (opened in 1697 by Francis White) is mentioned in the first number of *The Tatler* as the source from which its news of gallantry, pleasure, and entertainment would come, while foreign and domestic news would come from St. James's Coffee House, and all learned articles from the Grecian. White's has survived as one of the most exclusive of the present-day London clubs, and Lloyd's

Coffee House (founded by Edward Lloyd in Lombard Street in the early eighteenth century) after being the meeting place of men whose interest lay in some branch of the shipping industry, developed into the great Lloyd's corporation which gathers and publishes shipping intelligence from all the oceans and is the world centre of marine insurance.

CHAPTER VI

DEFOE AND SWIFT

Daniel Defoe

In so far as it is possible to be a writer of genius while giving no overt sign of inspiration, Daniel Defoe (1660–1731) achieved that miracle in a career which produced half a dozen masterpieces, as well as some three hundred pieces of journey-work on a range of topics—from politics to apparitions—which left few aspects of the contemporary scene unnoticed. It was not that Defoe himself experienced a commonplace life: he travelled much, though probably less extensively than might be inferred from his writings; he was concerned in Monmouth's rebellion (1685); before he was thirty-five he had twice failed in business after spells of prosperity, and in the last year of his life he was in retreat from pursuing creditors; he outraged political and ecclesiastical authorities, stood in the pillory, and went to gaol; at other times he was the devious propagandist and emissary of statesmen, his flexible pen gliding from one policy to its opposite.

In addition to all this, Defoe was endowed with a remarkable inventive faculty which guided his imagination into channels peculiar to himself. While he imagined, his mentality kept him so painstakingly on ground level that the gaudiest fiction took on a semblance of drab and homespun fact. His massed works include a *History of the Union of England and Scotland* (1709), a *History of the Wars of Charles XII of Sweden* (1715), possibly a *General History of the Robberies and Murders of the Most Notorious Pyrates* (1724), and certainly a *Political History of the Devil* (1726), all four treated with studied sobriety and, it might be said, with a deliberate avoidance of tone and colour. Defoe's practice of blurring, even at times of obliterating, the boundary line between fiction and fact has caused him to be rated as the greatest liar in English literature, a title which belongs of better right to a nineteenth-century writer who, if not Defoe's disciple, was at least his admirer. George Borrow's *Lavengro* and

The Romany Rye are a baffling amalgam of autobiography and fiction, of fact and invention, but whereas Borrow lied in wantonness and egoism—for the perverse satisfaction of lying and of striking a self-flattering attitude as a more than lifesize figure—Defoe was moved by an innate passion for verisimilitude. Fact allured him more than fiction; fiction was powerless to engage his interest unless it could pass for fact. Yet the stuff of fact and the attractions of fact are limited. Fact may itself lie by default if it permits only fragments of a story to appear; while, as the works of many 'objective' historians attest unawares, unswerving loyalty to fact is often a short cut to tedium.

Defoe.was a child of five when plague raged in London in 1665. Some faint memories of that foul visitation may have stirred in him when, in his early sixties, he produced *A Journal of the Plague Year* (published 1722), which claimed to be 'written by a Citizen who continued all the while in London'. It is the most characteristic of Defoe's writings, its material being so 'realistic' that efforts have been made to establish an earlier date than 1660 for Defoe's birth, in order to build up a case for the *Journal* as the outcome of personal recollection. Defoe the literary craftsman would no doubt have been gratified by the knowledge that his invented history would so impose itself upon the consciousness of posterity as to take on something of the authority of a source document; no doubt, also, this would greatly have surprised him. If he wrote *A Journal of the Plague Year* as make-believe history, he also wrote it as a warning, for plague seemed again likely to spread from the Continent to England, and Defoe had earlier in that year 1722 brought out a tract on *Due Preparations for the Plague, as well for Soul as Body*.

The clarity of Defoe's prose is perhaps the natural corollary of the direct utterance of a born Dissenter; its plain efficiency is as workmanlike as the bricks and tiles made at the Tilbury works which Defoe ran successfully for several years; its air of immediate reality, even when the story it tells is as remote as that in *Robinson Crusoe*, comes from Defoe's instinctive skill in the arts and devices of journalism. It was, indeed, the timely arrival of the Age of Journalism that made Defoe possible.

Defoe's periodical, *The Review*, launched on 19 February

1704,[1] after a few weekly numbers at a penny settled into a thrice-weekly publication, modifying its sub-title and the nature of its contents from time to time. Defoe's main original purpose in *The Review* was to concentrate public attention on the news from France, then at war with England; later the paper was more particularly concerned with 'the state of the English nation' and, after the Union of England and Scotland, with the state of the British nation. But the political news which was then the backbone of *The Review* appears, in retrospect, less important than a trifling feature which, after occupying a single page in each issue with the affairs of an imaginary 'Scandalous Club', presented as 'a Weekly History of Nonsense, Impertinence, Vice, and Debauchery', shortly hived off as a separate twice-weekly journal called *The Little Review*. In that form it lasted only from May to August 1705. Though the doings of the Scandalous Club as recorded by Defoe now hold little interest or amusement, they gave Richard Steele a notion which was to mould the character of *The Tatler* when he started it in 1709. Defoe should therefore receive credit for planting seed which bore literary fruit of two kinds: the Periodical Essay, perfected by Steele and Addison; and its gargantuan offspring, the Novel, brought to maturity by Fielding and others who developed a continuous fictional narrative from the brief character-sketches and episodes in essay form which *The Tatler* and *The Spectator* popularized.

Daniel Defoe's place and date of birth are not precisely recorded, but the date was almost certainly September 1660 and the place the parish of St. Giles, Cripplegate, London. His father, James Foe, formerly a tallow chandler, was then a butcher by trade, and by religious conviction a Dissenter, his forebears having been Protestant emigrés from Flanders. With an ear for euphony and a touch of snobbery Daniel afterwards called himself Defoe and took steps to secure a coat of arms. He went to school at the Dissenting Academy at Newington Green, on the northern outskirts of London, kept by Charles

---

[1] *The Review* was one of the longest-lived of the very numerous early eighteenth-century periodicals. Defoe kept it going until 11 June 1713, i.e. for nine years, whereas Steele and Addison ran *The Tatler* and *The Spectator* for less than two years in each instance.

Morton (who subsequently went to America and became Harvard's first vice-president). Years later, Defoe made particular reference to the school as a place where the pupils were 'made masters of the English tongue'. He went into the hosiery business, probably as a wholesaler rather than as a shopkeeper, and at the beginning of 1684 married Mary Tuffley, daughter of a merchant who was also a practising Dissenter. She brought a dowry of several thousand pounds, but Defoe nevertheless went bankrupt a few years later, becoming much involved in litigation and dabbling in odd enterprises, one of which—a civet cat farm at Newington—provided his enemies with a favourite gibe.

He was a devoted and active supporter of the new regime from the time of William III's landing to supplant James II in 1688. By what means Defoe obtained his introduction to government circles and regained solvency is unknown, but by 1694 he had Court connections and was soon successfully re-established in business as proprietor of the Tilbury brick and tile factory, though that also failed in 1703. In 1697 appeared his first important work, *An Essay upon Projects*, with a Preface to 'Thomas Dalby, Esq., One of the Commissioners for Managing His Majesty's Duties on Glass, etc., . . . as the most proper Judge of the Subjects Treated of', viz. projectors (what might now be called company promoters, good and bad), banks, highways, assurances, friendly societies, a pension-office, wagering, fools, bankrupts, academies, merchants, seamen. The final sentence of *An Essay upon Projects* is of special interest as an early manifesto of Defoe's ideals as a writer of prose:

> As to Language, I have been rather careful to make it speak *English* suitable to the Manner of the Story, than to dress it up with Exactness of Stile; chusing rather to have it Free and Familiar, . . . than to strain at a Perfection of Language, which I rather wish for, than pretend to be Master of.

In the remaining three or four years of William III's life, Defoe wrote, in support of the regime, numerous political pamphlets and, in rhyming couplets, *The True-Born Englishman* (1701). The occasion of this work was the currency given to the phrase 'true-born Englishman' by those who derided William III as a foreign intruder on the English throne.

Defoe's verse diatribe (it lacks the subtlety that would entitle it to the rank of satire claimed for it by the author) labours the point that the English are in fact a mongrel people and that they were incapable of gratitude, even to the royal champion who had succoured them in their extremity. Notwithstanding its popularity with the public, largely through pirated editions, the poem brought much abuse upon Defoe from the increasingly vocal anti-William party. At the king's death in the next year a round of troubles began for Defoe. In December 1702, incensed by the disabilities imposed upon nonconformists by the Occasional Conformity measure, he published anonymously *The Shortest Way with the Dissenters*, which was taken at first as a serious proposal for eliminating dissenters ruthlessly by death or banishment. It soon dawned upon the Church party, however, that Defoe's real intention was to reduce their policy to absurdity and by ironical overstatement to demolish it.

> 'Tis vain to trifle in this matter [Defoe wrote], the light foolish handling of them by Mulcts, Fines, etc. 'tis their Glory and their Advantage; if the Gallows instead of the Counter, and the Gallies instead of the Fines, were the reward of going to a Conventicle, to preach or to hear, there wou'd not be so many sufferers, the Spirit of Martyrdom is over; they that will go to Church to be chosen Sheriffs and Mayors, would go to forty Churches rather than be Hang'd. . . .

> . . . I am not supposing that all the Dissenters in *England* shou'd be Hang'd or Banish'd, but as in cases of Rebellions and Insurrections, if a few of the Ring-leaders suffer, the Multitude are dismist, so a few obstinate People being made Examples there's no doubt but the Severity of the Law would find a stop in the Compliance of the Multitude.

As soon as the true purpose of the *Shortest Way* was recognized and the authorship discovered, a reward of £50 was offered for Defoe's arrest. The notice circulated described him as 'A middle-sized spare man about forty years old, of a brown complexion and dark brown-coloured hair, but wears a wig; a hooked nose, a sharp chin, grey eyes, and a large mole near his mouth.' He was indicted on a charge of libel against the Church, and, after hiding on the premises of a Spitalfields weaver, was taken in May 1703, tried in July, fined 200 marks,

pilloried thrice, and jailed at Newgate. He became a popular
hero, but that did not compensate the failure of his Tilbury
business, and he again became bankrupt in 1703. His indefinite
sentence of imprisonment ended in November of the same year
at the instance of Robert Harley (afterwards 1st Earl of Oxford)
the statesman in whose service Defoe's pen was often employed.
In the following sixteen years—from the age of forty-three to
the age of all but sixty—Defoe was continuously at work,
writing prolifically and travelling much as a mouthpiece and
listening ear for Harley's policies. His publications were mostly
political, and little but *The Review* and the curious *A True
Relation of the Apparition of Mrs. Veal the Next Day after her Death
to Mrs. Bargrave at Canterbury, the Eighth of September 1705* (1706)
are now noticed. It is said that Defoe went down to Canterbury
to hear the story as it had been related by Mrs. Bargrave to a
neighbour. This device of an intermediate narrator enables
Defoe to put the account into the mouth of a speaker and thus
to create a sense of greater immediacy than if it were presented
plainly as the work of a reporting journalist: the neighbour is
made to say of Mrs. Bargrave 'she is my intimate friend, and
I can avouch for her reputation for these last fifteen or sixteen
years, on my own knowledge'. This short piece is probably
the most matter-of-fact of all ghost stories, though it has some
odd inconsistencies. Mrs. Veal, appearing *post mortem* to Mrs.
Bargrave, appears to be aware of her own incorporeality, for
at the last second she eludes a proffered kiss and subsequently
evades an offer of tea; yet she remarks upon the material of her
dress and Mrs. Bargrave touches it, afterwards citing the fact
as evidence of the reality of the visitation. The story no doubt
appealed to Defoe through his interest in the supernatural,
but it may very well have been also (or even primarily) an
advertisement written to order for a bookseller, since it makes
pointed commendatory references to 'Drelincourt on Death',
i.e. *Drelincourt's Book of Consolations against the Fears of Death*,
a work of popular piety then in circulation.

Despite its brevity and the slightness of its treatment, *Mrs.
Veal* is singularly interesting among Defoe's writings as a tentative step in the direction which was to lead to his mature works
in the five amazingly abundant years beginning at 1719 when,
on 25 April, *The Life and Adventures of Robinson Crusoe* came out

anonymously, to be followed by *Memoirs of a Cavalier* (1720), *Captain Singleton* (1720), *Moll Flanders* (1722), *A Journal of the Plague Year* (1722), *Colonel Jack* (1722), and *Roxana, the Fortunate Mistress* (1724), besides his regular outpouring of fugitive pieces, mainly on current affairs. In 1724 began also his valuable account of *A Tour Thro' the Whole Island of Great Britain*; the second volume of this was issued in 1725, the third and final volume in 1726.

If Defoe had died at the age of fifty-eight he would appear in literature as a rather shabby hack-writer who, in a sudden burst of dissenting indignation, wrote a single small master-piece of bland yet blasting irony. His place among English writers would be minor and inconspicuous. He lived to be seventy, and in the first half of that final decade elevated him-self, unawares, to a permanent unique position with *Robinson Crusoe*—no other book of its kind has been written—and to a considerable place in the general history of the English novel with this and his other works of fiction. Furthermore, *A Journal of the Plague Year* is unique as being pseudo-history which historians respect; while the *Tour* is an important first-hand contribution to eighteenth-century social history.

That *Robinson Crusoe* owes the germ of its existence to the four and a half years' solitary exile of a Scottish sailor, Alexander Selkirk, on Juan Fernandez island from 1704 to 1709 is one of the popular clichés of literary history. Selkirk's story was published in 1712 by the Captain Rogers who brought him away from the island and it achieved an almost legendary popularity. Beyond question Selkirk's experience was to the fore in Defoe's mind when he started *Robinson Crusoe* several years afterwards, but the sources of the book are many, and it is significant that at the beginning of 1720 Defoe published an account of Ralegh's voyages, particularly of the Guiana venture, for Crusoe's island is imagined in that region, off the mouth of the Orinoco, whereas Selkirk's was on the other side of the world, in the South Pacific. No doubt numerous hints from actual happenings were drawn upon freely for the Crusoe story, but the book as it stands is all Defoe's. It is con-trived with such cunning that no one can say whether or not the few clumsinesses are due to the author's oversight, or whether they are there to strengthen the sense of actuality in a narrative related in the first person by a man of action, a cast-away in direful straits, who would be a stranger to the niceties ·of literary composition. So, also, it is impossible to know whether Defoe intended Crusoe to be something of a prig and a bore, or whether the tedium of certain meditative and religiose passages is due to artificial spinning-out of the material and to a wish to give the tale an aura of piety. Some of the shrewdest observations of character come, almost casually it might seem, in passages which, superficially assessed, are tedious. Thus, in the opening pages, the hero's father in a Polonius-like address attempts to dissuade him from going to sea, and young Robinson 'sincerely affected with this Discourse . . . resolv'd not to think of going Abroad any more. . . .' Then, like a dash of icy water in the face of filial deference, comes immediately, 'But alas! a few Days wore it all off. . . .'

The main features of Defoe's style have already been remarked, but it may be added in relation to *Robinson Crusoe* (and to his works generally) that the avoidance of a high temperature in his prose, even when it is dealing with episodes in themselves fraught with excitement or apprehension, is not due to a habit of mannered understatement. Defoe's prose is 'natural' in the way that nature or the universe is natural. In life, for the most part, *things happen* without our being warned that they are about to happen; and while they are happening the universe appears profoundly indifferent. Defoe's prose, as a medium of expression, gives no preliminary warning that startling things are about to happen; and while they are happening it betrays no agitation, it has no *tremolo*. One of the most exciting moments in any book is the moment when Crusoe, after years on his uninhabited island, first sees a human footprint there. But no flicker of excitement gets into the sentence which describes the episode. With no preliminary working-up of tension, the words are slipped-in on a page previously concerned with Crusoe's goats and grapes:

> It happen'd one Day about Noon going towards my Boat, I was exceedingly surpriz'd with the Print of a Man's naked Foot on the Shore, which was very plain to be seen in the Sand.

The words are commonplace enough, but it is unfortunate that we cannot know if Defoe here subordinated probability to effect. Why only a single footprint if, as afterwards appears, cannibals occasionally came to the shore to feast? Did Defoe appreciate that the improbably isolated footprint was far more sinister than a score could have been?

It is in the recording of events (and in satire) that Defoe's prose keeps its balance most securely. It tends to wobble only in those patches of pious reflection which appear to be cobbled on to *Robinson Crusoe*, not genuinely a part of the whole fabric. The fact is, of course, that Defoe would have been a much finer writer than he was if he had not had so patched a mind. He wrote too much on too many subjects: he was, to his injury, a politicians' tout as well as a literary man-of-all-work. Yet if he had known more about fewer matters might he also have produced fewer masterpieces, as well as less ephemera?

The theme of *Memoirs of a Cavalier*, published on 21 May 1720, is advertised in its subtitle: 'a *Military Journal* of the *Wars* in Germany, and the *Wars* in England, from the Year 1632, to the Year 1648. Written Threescore Years ago by an *English* Gentleman, who first served in the Army of *Gustavus Adolphus*, the glorious King of *Sweden*, till his Death; and after that, in the Royal Army of King *Charles* the First, from the Beginning of the Rebellion, to the End of that War.' This, like *A Journal of the Plague Year*, is now generally accepted as an example of Defoe's liking for mystification. It was at one time supposed that the *Memoirs* were derived from a manuscript relating to an actual Andrew Newport, but this is no longer credited and the book is treated as Defoe's own work, based on his reading of history aided by his creative imagination.

Defoe's skill as a narrator appears instantly in the opening lines of his books. Each has its different and appropriate accent; each glides insinuatingly to capture the reader's interest. The feature is important enough to warrant illustration from Defoe's principal works.

I was born in the Year 1632, in the City of *York*, of a good Family, tho' not of that Country, my Father being a Foreigner of *Bremen*, who settled first at Hull. (*Robinson Crusoe*.)

It may suffice the Reader, without being very inquisitive after my Name, that I was born in the County of *Salop*, in the year 1608; under the Government of what Star I was never Astrologer enough to examine; but the Consequences of my Life may allow me to suppose some extraordinary Influence affected my Birth. (*Memoirs of a Cavalier.*)

. . . If I may believe the Woman, whom I was taught to call Mother, I was a little Boy, of about two Years old, very well dress'd, had a Nursery Maid to tend me, who took me out on a fine Summer's Evening into the Fields towards *Islington* . . . (*Captain Singleton*: part of second sentence.)

My True Name is so well known in the Records, or Registers at *Newgate*, and in the Old-Baily, and there are some things of such Consequence still depending there, relating to my particular Conduct, that it is not to be expected I should set my Name or the Account of my Family to this Work; perhaps, after my Death it may be better known. . . . (*Moll Flanders.*)

It was about the Beginning of *September* 1664, that I, among the Rest of my Neighbours, heard in ordinary Discourse, that the Plague was return'd again to *Holland*; . . . (*A Journal of the Plague Year.*)

York . . . Salop . . . Islington . . . Newgate and the Old Bailey . . . Holland. It is unlikely that this repeated geographical precision is only a matter of coincidence, and much more likely that the immediate introduction of a place-name was a device—capable, as can be seen, of flexible variation—adopted by Defoe to establish the sense of actuality at which he constantly aimed and which was sensibly aided by his preference for the first-person method of narration.

Defoe missed becoming the first major English novelist only by his lack of a single requirement—though a requirement of the first importance—the ability to create characters with the essential quality of livingness. In all great novels the characters have an interior personal life, they do not exist in their actions alone nor merely as creatures of their environment; we have the conviction that they could be moved alive into other circumstances. We may be illuded into thinking of Crusoe as a real person, but he has no existence apart from the happenings that befall him. Moll Flanders, too, is embedded in her own narrative, and though the narrative is as absorbing as any of its kind and probably, as a piece of prose, the soberest life-story of a prostitute ever written, Moll is more a mouthpiece than a woman of flesh and blood. The nearest Defoe came to creating a character in the round was with 'one very merry fellow', William Walters, the Quaker ship's-surgeon in *Captain Singleton*: even when shot flew thick about his ears 'there was *William*, as composed, and in as perfect Tranquillity as to Danger, as if he had been over a Bowl of Punch. . . .' William lives, independently of his background.

While much of *A Journal of the Plague Year* is documentary in kind—orders issued by the Lord Mayor, vital statistics, etc.—its fascination, however horrid, comes not only from its anecdotes (such as that of the piper who found himself in the dead-cart) and its reporting of gossip and superstitions, but even more from the sensation it conveys so powerfully of things happening here and now. Defoe was a born journalist, a journalist of genius; and in this book journalism is raised to a level that few men of letters and few historians can hope to outreach. True, it is feigned history and pseudo-reporting; nevertheless its method is that of ideal journalism.

A Tour thro' the Whole Island of Great Britain is read today 'above all for the light it throws on the economic and social condition of England half a century or so before the coming of the Industrial Revolution'.[1] Defoe gathered the material during his journeyings on Harley's business, though his travels were probably not confined to political excursions. Except by students of the history of the period the *Tour* is a book to browse in rather than to read through; its topics are too multifarious for rapid assimilation. Besides masses of factual information, however, there is much that is lighter and entertaining. Reaching Bath, Defoe observes:

> In the Morning you (supposing you to be a young Lady) are fetch'd in a close Chair, dress'd in your Bathing Cloths, that is, stript to the Smock, to the Cross-Bath. There the Musick plays you into the Bath, and the Women that tend you, present you with a little floating Wooden Dish, like a Bason; in which the Lady puts a Handkerchief, and a Nosegay, of late the Snuff-Box is added, and some Patches; Tho' the Bath occasioning a little Perspiration, the Patches do not stick so kindly as they should.

[1] G. D. H. Cole: Introduction to Everyman's Library edition of the *Tour* (2 vols. Dent, London, 1928).

The concluding volume of the *Tour* came out in the last year of George I's reign, when Defoe was sixty-six. He continued to write prolifically through the last five years of his life—on conduct in married life, on commerce, on police measures. He finished *The Compleat English Tradesman* in 1727 (the first volume had appeared in 1725) and at his death left *The Compleat English Gentleman* unpublished: this was, perhaps, symbolic of Defoe's career, for he was himself the complete tradesman in literature and always something less than the complete gentleman he wished to be; he had the solid qualities of the class in which he was born, never the fine manners of the class he aspired to.

For more than his last twenty years he lived at Stoke Newington, the district in which his schooldays were spent, and there doubtless he would have died but for importunate creditors, from whom he went into hiding, dying in lodgings in Moorfields next to his native parish of St. Giles. His grave is in the Dissenters' nearby burial ground at Bunhill Fields.

Jonathan Swift

The lives of Defoe and Swift (1667–1745) overlapped by more than sixty years. When Swift was born Defoe was seven; when Defoe died in 1731, at the age of seventy-one, though Swift had fourteen more of his seventy-eight years to run he had finished all but a few fragments of his life's work and was soon to pass into the mental twilight that long preluded his death. As writers, then, Defoe and Swift were full contemporaries; each wrote didactically and satirically on political and theological subjects; each was on terms with leading statesmen and other notables; each was to have his adult masterpiece taken over as a children's classic; each was a master of English prose style.

That Defoe was a stalwart Dissenter and Swift a stalwart Churchman is a difference reflected in their differing prose styles, for even while clarity and lucidity are the hallmarks of both, the clear water of Defoe is at once more refreshing and less stimulating than the sparkling wine of Swift. If there are places in the one where the water appears stagnant, with the other there are occasions in plenty when the wine turns sour. The hazards of bankruptcy, prison, and pillory left Defoe imperturbable; Swift, though relatively well used by society, was all perturbation. Defoe's *Shortest Way with the Dissenters* is no less a triumph of effective satire than Swift's *Modest Proposal*, though the former is as smooth as butter while the other is as bitter as gall and as corrosive as acid.

Any reader's response to these two writers may well be more temperamental than intellectual. Defoe may seem flat, insensitive, and dull to some; to others Swift's angry championship of the oppressed in his Irish pamphlets, and his contempt for lackeydom in *Directions to Servants*, his loathing of human brutishness (as he thought it) in the last part of *Gulliver's Travels*, may appear as symptoms of a gnawing inward grievance personal in origin. But while Swift is known to have had disappointments and to have borne them ill-humouredly, the disgust which on occasion tended to weaken his satire was in some measure pathological. Satire is so powerful a weapon of correction that it is the more unfortunate that it can fall too readily into the grasp of the maladjusted and the physically afflicted, with whom it becomes an instrument of personal vengeance upon mankind. Swift, Pope, Byron—brilliant and just though their satirical attacks may be—are nevertheless vulnerable in that respect. The satirist should be above suspicion of personal motive, for only when surveyed in a universal aspect is mankind to be sanely judged; the more the judge is involved with the defendant, the more he may be held to belittle himself and to nullify the sentence he passes. Defoe's satire was more confined than Swift's. His target was not mankind, but only a section of the English community; his particular indignation does not pass over into a general fury and he thus escapes the satirist's besetting temptation to view his local microcosm with a magnifying eye. Swift was a more spectacular, a more romantic, writer than Defoe: Defoe had no Stella; no Vanessa; no dire malady to stir compassion.

Jonathan Swift, who became in the latter part of his life a hero to the people of Ireland, was not the only English subject who has passionately championed the cause of the Irish in their own country. Though he was born (a posthumous child) in Dublin, on 30 November 1667, his father's family was of Yorkshire descent, his mother came from Leicester, and John Dryden was his cousin. At Kilkenny Grammar School Swift had William Congreve among his fellow pupils. He proceeded to Trinity College, Dublin, where he neglected much of the set curriculum, preferring to concentrate on history and poetry. These were insufficient to qualify him for a degree in the normal course, and the B.A. to which he was later admitted by 'special grace' was a concession without distinction. About 1692 he entered the household of Sir William Temple and his wife (née Dorothy Osborne[1]) at Moor Park, Surrey, as Secretary, his duties including a mission to William III.[2] His expectation that Temple would obtain for him a position of consequence being unfulfilled, Swift went back to Ireland, where he was ordained in 1694, but he returned to Moor Park in 1696, editing Temple's letters and miscellaneous papers (published 1700–1, Temple having died in 1699). Some verses published in 1692 brought from Dryden the comment 'Cousin Swift, you will never be a poet', a judgement never quite falsified, though Swift was to write a great deal of verse in subsequent years. His début as a prose writer was more auspicious.

During his second term with the Temples, Swift wrote (in 1697) *The Battle of the Books* and about the same time or possibly a little earlier *A Tale of a Tub. Written for the Universal Improvement of Mankind*. These were published (like almost all his work, anonymously) in a single volume in 1704.

Hardly enough attention has been given to the fact that *A Tale of a Tub* is a parody as well as a satire. Swift imitates the practice of contemporary authors who congested their publications with tiresome collections of prefaces and other introductory matter which oppose an almost impenetrable barrier to the reader. But parody and satire are not of a single kind. Parody should be transmutation as well as an imitation. However tedious the original, the parody must in itself avoid tedium whilst throwing a highlight upon the special characteristics of the original. This double achievement was beyond Swift's talent and, in form and effect at least, the preliminary paraphernalia of *A Tale of a Tub* follow too closely in the tracks of

[1] See above, pp. 78–9.
[2] Too much emphasis seems to have been laid upon the supposed menial nature of Swift's duties while with Temple, and upon the belief that he was embittered thereby. Swift, always ambitious, was also always disappointed: hoping for an English bishopric he was fobbed off in the end with an Irish deanery.

the masters of tedium. The chief intention of the piece was to be in some sort a defence of the government and the Church against such ideas as those formulated by Hobbes (in *Leviathan*) and other advocates or apologists for absolutism. Swift's title alludes to the sailors' custom of throwing a tub into the sea as a distraction to any threatening whale. The narrative treats of a father whose legacy to his sons—Peter (signifying the Church of Rome), Martin (the Reformed, i.e. Anglican, Church), and Jack (the Calvinists, and Dissenters generally)—is a coat to each, with the set injunction that none of these garments is to be altered. By differing degrees of casuistry this injunction is set aside, and the coats, symbolizing pure Christianity, are either ornamented (signifying ritual) or, by Jack, torn to rags (fanatical asceticism). Martin, standing for Swift's own Anglican communion, after being led astray by Peter, endeavours by moderation to restore his coat to its original state; but, as always with Swift, his own party does not escape assault. Nor does the *Tale* keep rigidly to its main theme; the numerous digressions are among its liveliest features.

At the time *A Tale of a Tub* was written, though *Gulliver's Travels* was some thirty years in the future, the mood that dominates the account of Gulliver's final adventure among the Houyhnhnms and Yahoos was already stirring in Swift; and—as in the *Modest Proposal*, three years after *Gulliver*—there is in the early work an inclination, perhaps as much sadistic as satirical, to harp upon horror.

> . . . in most Corporeal Beings, which have fallen under my Cognizance, the *Outside* hath been infinitely preferable to the *In*: Whereof I have been farther convinced from some late Experiments. Last Week I saw a Woman *flay'd*, and you will hardly believe, how much it altered her Person for the worse. Yesterday I ordered the Carcass of a *Beau* to be stript in my Presence; when we were all amazed to find so many unsuspected Faults under one Suit of Cloaths: Then I laid open his *Brain*, his *Heart*, and his *Spleen*; But I plainly perceived at every Operation, that the farther we proceeded, we found the Defects encrease upon us in Number and Bulk: from all which, I justly formed this Conclusion to my self; That whatever Philosopher or Projector can find out an Art to sodder and patch up the Flaws and Imperfections of Nature, will deserve much better of Mankind, and teach us a more useful Science, than that so much in present

Esteem, of widening and exposing them (like him who held *Anatomy* to be the ultimate End of physick).

Swift was led to write *The Battle of the Books (An Account of a Battel between the Antient and Modern Books in St.* James's *Library)* by a controversy between Temple on the one hand and, on the other, the classical scholars William Wotton and Richard Bentley. An imagined assembly of modern writers demands that the ancients shall yield to them the higher peak of Parnassus, and conflict begins after Æsop has described the moderns as spinning like the spider from their own entrails whereas the ancients, like the bee, go straight to nature. The *Battle* is more lighthearted and more varied in tone than *A Tale of a Tub*: Dryden is introduced in a helmet 'nine times too large for the head'; in a passage which ends with one of the few 'beautiful' sentences to be found in Swift's writings, Pindar

> . . . with a mighty Stroak, cleft the wretched *Modern* [Cowley] in twain, the Sword pursuing the Blow; and one half lay panting on the Ground, to be trod in pieces by the Horses Feet, the other half was born by the frighted Steed thro' the Field. This *Venus* took, wash'd it seven times in *Ambrosia*, then struck it twice with a Sprig of *Amarant*; upon which, the Leather grew round and soft, and the Leaves turned into Feathers, and being gilded before, continued gilded still; so it became a *Dove*, and She harness'd it to her Chariot.

There has been little change in 250 years in authors' opinions of critics. Swift described Criticism as 'a malignant deity' and goes on to picture her in terms which also express the views of many present-day poets, novelists, and others, who have, however, no current language of invective such as that which enabled Swift to cleanse his bosom:

> . . . *Criticism* . . . extended in her Den, upon the Spoils of numberless Volumes half devoured. At her right Hand sat *Ignorance*, her Father and Husband, blind with Age; at her left, *Pride* her Mother, dressing her up in the Scraps of Paper herself had torn. There, was *Opinion* her Sister, light of Foot, hoodwinkt, and headstrong, yet giddy and perpetually turning. About her play'd her Children, *Noise* and *Impudence*, *Dullness* and *Vanity*, *Positiveness*, *Pedantry*, and *Ill-Manners*. The Goddess herself had Claws like a Cat: Her Head, and Ears, and Voice, resembled

those of an Ass; Her Teeth fallen out before; Her Eyes turned
inward, as if she lookt only upon herself: Her Diet was the
overflowing of her own *Gall*: . . .

The great enigma of Swift's life, his relationship with Esther
Johnson (1681–1728), had its beginnings at Moor Park where

A letter from Swift to Vanessa

she was living in the Temple's household. Swift claimed to
have known her since she was six,[1] though he did not go to
Moor Park until *c.* 1692, when she would have been eleven
and he about twenty-five. Starting as his pupil, she was to
become for the remainder of her life his ardent admirer and
dearest friend, conceivably his undeclared wife, though there
exists no proof of their marriage. The letters which make up

[1] So he said in his paper *On the Death of Mrs. Johnson (see next page)*; but
in another place he says she was sixteen.

24. A coffee-house at the end of the seventeenth century

25. Robinson Crusoe from the frontispiece to the
first edition

26. A satirical print against the Whigs showing Daniel Defoe with the Pope and the Devil

27. Joseph Addison by Michael Dahl

28. Jonathan Swift by Charles Jervas

THE
DUNCIAD,
VARIORVM.
WITH THE
PROLEGOMENA of SCRIBLERUS.

DEFEROR IN VICVM

VENDENTEM THVS ET ODORES

LONDON.

Printed for A. DOB . 1729.

29. Title-page of the *Dunciad* by Alexander Pope

30. Scene from *The Rape of the Lock* by Alexander Pope

31. A view in the garden of Pope's villa at Twickenham

the *Journal to Stella*, published rather more than twenty years after his death (part in 1766; the rest in 1768), have become, next to *Gulliver's Travels*, his most famous composition. Since they give, for the period covered, a close account of Swift's doings in London and of his dealings with statesmen and others, they are an invaluable biographical and historical record. As a personal and psychological document they are unique; they are also disturbing and to some minds may be more repellent than engaging. Purporting to be addressed both to Esther and to her companion Rebecca Dingley (who were then living in Ireland), they are nevertheless love letters to Stella herself, making use of an intimate pet language of a kind embarrassing in public view or hearing, and particularly so in this case since we know too little and may guess too much concerning Stella's feelings and, maybe, sufferings. Of Swift, also, in this connection we know too little and can only ask questions to which there is no answer. Why did not he and Stella marry? Or if they did, why was it kept secret? And why, in view of his known devotion to Stella, did he conduct from 1708 an abortive affair with Esther Vanhomrigh (twenty-three years younger than he), whose frustrated love for him and the breaking of their relationship were contributory to her death in 1723? It is impossible to suppose that he was a heartless philanderer; much easier to believe that he had earlier forebodings of the madness in which his life ended. Yet while any such forebodings would be an obstacle to marriage, they would surely preclude also an emotional relationship short only of marriage. The enigma remains. When Stella died on 28 January 1728 Swift wrote of her at length in a private memorandum *On the Death of Mrs. Johnson*, unpublished until 1765, twenty years after his own death. Of her qualities of heart, of her modesty and her charity, there could be no question, but Swift witnesses also to her remarkable mental qualities:

> Never was any of her Sex born with better Gifts of the Mind, or more improved them by Reading and Conversation. . . . I cannot call to Mind that I ever once heard her make a wrong Judgement of Persons, Books, or Affairs. Her Advice was always the best, and with the greatest Freedom, mixed with the greatest Decency. She had a Gracefulness somewhat more than Human in every Motion, Word, and Action.

I

He added later, not without pedantic formality:

> . . . She understood the Nature of Government, and could point out all the Errours of Hobbes, both in that and Religion.

When Temple died Swift went again to Ireland, receiving the living of Laracor and a prebend in the cathedral of St. Patrick, Dublin. He made many visits to London, however, and there established friendships with most of the leading writers— Addison and Steele, his old school-fellow Congreve, Pope, Gay, and others—as well as with politicians, first the Whigs, until their pro-Dissent policy caused him to embrace the Tory and pro-Church party, whose penman and pamphleteer he became.

In 1713 Swift was made Dean of St. Patrick's, and while continuing to pamphleteer on behalf of the English ministers he did not in any of those occasional pieces repeat the success of his 1711 peace pamphlet *The Conduct of the Allies*. With Pope, Gay, Congreve, Arbuthnot, and others, he joined in the formation (1713) of the Scriblerus Club (*see below*, p. 164), which undertook to compose the *Memoirs of Martinus Scriblerus*. After Queen Anne died in 1714 and the Tory ministry went out of office, Swift retired to Ireland (1715), disappointed at having secured no higher ecclesiastical office. From that time he was the powerful defender of Irish causes, less from love of Ireland and its people than from comprehensive detestation of the English Whig government, whose treatment of Irish matters no doubt outraged Swift's sense of justice as well as hardening his political antipathies. He wrote in 1720 a *Proposal for the Universal use of Irish Manufactures*, and in 1724 began the series of pamphlets called *The Drapier's Letters*, which were so sharp a thorn in the Whigs' side that the concession for the manufacture of 'Wood's Halfpence',[1] made notorious under that nickname in the *Letters*, was withdrawn before the coinage entered Ireland.

The identity of 'the Draper' (though well enough known in Ireland to make him revered) was not publicly declared

---

[1] The government had granted a patent to supply copper coins for circulation in Ireland to an English merchant and tradesman, William Wood, whose profit would have been about £25,000. Swift protested that the purchasing power of the coins would be much below their face value and that the plan was a fraud on the Irish people, whom he urged not to handle the debased money.

until Swift received the freedom of the City of Dublin at the time he issued, in 1729, the most famous of his pamphlets, *A Modest Proposal for Preventing the Children of the Poor from Being a Burthen to their Parents or Country, and for making them Beneficial to the Publick*, which in matter-of-fact terms veined with blistering irony propounded that a hundred thousand one-year-old children should be sold annually for food at ten shillings each. The righteousness of the cause and the intensity of passion it stirred in Swift may be held to justify the horror which it is the whole point of the satire to arouse. Nevertheless, in some of its details the pamphlet goes beyond the bounds of satire and spills over into a region of morbidity where the dark angel in Swift's make-up was prone to seek ghoulish delight. The last word on the central matter of *A Modest Proposal*, however, should properly be left to the author:

. . . I desire those Politicians, who dislike my Overture, and may perhaps be so bold to attempt an Answer, that they will first ask the Parents of these Mortals, Whether they would not at this Day think it a great Happiness to have been sold for Food at a Year Old, in the manner I prescribe, and thereby have avoided such a perpetual Scene of Misfortunes, as they have since gone through, by the *Oppression of Land-lords*, the Impossibility of paying Rent without Money or Trade, the Want of common Sustenance, with neither House nor Cloaths to cover them from these Inclemencies of Weather, and the most inevitable Prospect of intailing the like, or greater Miseries, upon their Breed for ever.

Travels into Several Remote Nations of the World, by Lemuel Gulliver, first a Surgeon, and then a Captain of Several Ships was introduced to its publisher, Benjamin Motte, in a letter signed Richard Sympson, who stated that he was acting on behalf of his cousin Mr. Lemuel Gulliver. This was a piece of mystification by Swift, for the letter was his, written in a feigned hand. Motte undertook to pay the author £200, and the book, published anonymously late in 1726, was an immediate success. To what extent Swift's *Gulliver's Travels* has become a worldwide best-seller during its two centuries cannot be estimated, since the millions of copies read by children are abridged and bowdlerized to the point at which the book ceases to be Swift's satire and remains only an adventure story, an unsurpassed adventure story certainly, but as that alone it would scarcely have interested its author. Yet this emasculated *Gulliver's Travels* holds the field, for relatively few except students turn in adult life to Swift's own book.

Gulliver's Travels appears to have started as one of the proposed contributions to the Scriblerus Club *Memoirs*, in which Martinus is represented as going to the same lands as Gulliver was to visit. The voyage to the island of the Lilliputians satirizes contemporary English political and religious dissensions and the European war by diminishing the scale of the contestants until their rivalries and battles appear no more important than ridiculous squabbles among pygmies. To the giants of Brobdingnag on his second voyage Gulliver gives an account of the condition of Europe and thus reveals to the king there a state of affairs as revoltingly absurd to his mind as the people of Lilliput were to Gulliver's. The king concludes, with Swiftian misanthropy, that the history related to him is only

> an Heap of Conspiracies, Rebellions, Murders, Massacres, Revolutions, Banishments . . . Avarice, Faction, Hypocrisy, Perfidiousness, Cruelty, Rage, Madness, Hatred, Envy, Lust, Malice, or Ambition . . . I cannot but conclude the Bulk of your Natives to be the most pernicious Race of little odious Vermin that Nature ever suffered to crawl upon the Surface of the Earth.

The third voyage, to the flying island of Laputa and elsewhere, gives opportunity for satire addressed to intellectuals (philosophers and scientists) and financial speculators, with a horrifying end-passage on the Struldbrugs, beings endowed with earthly immortality. The Yahoos in the 'unknown land' of the final voyage symbolize the extreme of Swift's disgust with humanity: physically repulsive to sight and smell, formed nearly enough in human shape to stand as a parody of the vilest in men and women, they are 'the most unteachable of all Brutes': 'I confess I never saw any sensitive Being so detestable on all accounts; and the more I came near them, the more hateful they grew.' The four-footed Houyhnhnms, on the contrary, are of 'a very mild Aspect, never offering the least Violence . . . orderly and rational . . . acute and judicious'.

The more I see of men, Swift would not have hesitated to say, the more I love horses.

As a prose satire *Gulliver's Travels* is the greatest in the language; it is also among the greatest works of imagination even when in children's editions Swift's major purpose is drained away. No moment in a child's reading life can surpass that in which he first comes to the page describing Gulliver's waking in Lilliput to find himself pegged to the ground by a network of slender cords, his body swarmed over by forty or more 'human' creatures not six inches high.

Any doubt of the identity of Swift's own views with those expressed vicariously in *Gulliver's Travels* and elsewhere is removed by the personal statement in one of his letters to Pope (29 September 1725):

> . . . I have ever hated all Nations, Professions, and Communities; and all my Love is towards Individuals: . . . principally I hate and detest that Animal called Man, although I heartily love *John*, *Peter*, *Thomas*, and so forth. . . . Upon this great Foundation of Misanthropy (though not in *Timon's* manner) the whole Building of my Travels is erected; and I never will have peace of Mind, until all honest Men are of my Opinion: . . .

In their ease of manner Swift's letters are the most pleasing of all his writings and hardly any correspondence in English excels his, though Steele's is more heartwarming.

The poetry of Swift is less summarily dismissed now than formerly, yet its bulk is more remarkable than its merit, and its interest is more autobiographical than poetic. *Cadenus and Vanessa* (1726) tells obliquely of the relationship with Esther Vanhomrigh; several poems are written to Stella; while in some five hundred anticipatory lines *On the Death of Dr. Swift* he attempted a self-portrait in which not all the features are identical with those posterity has drawn, though in the main the portrait is just and at moments precise:

> As with a moral View design'd
> To cure the Vices of Mankind,
> His Vein, ironically grave,
> Exposed the Fool and lash'd the Knave.

A brain tumour afflicted Swift in the last phase of his life, affecting sight and hearing and causing insanity in the final three years. Ten years before his death he was writing to Pope (7 February 1735/6):

> I have no body now left but you: Pray be so kind to outlive me, and then die as soon as you please, but without Pain, and let us meet in a better Place. . . . My State of Health is not to boast of; my Giddiness is more or less constant; I have not an Ounce of Flesh between Skin and Bone; I sleep ill, and have a poor Appetite.

He outlived Pope by a year. On his grave, beside Stella's in St. Patrick's Cathedral, was cut his self-epitaph: *Ubi saeva indignatio ulterius cor lacerare nequit*—'Where fierce indignation can no longer tear the heart'.

CHAPTER VII

THE PURSUIT OF URBANITY: STEELE TO POPE

WHETHER confined to the twelve years of Queen Anne's reign (1702–14) or extended to the hundred years and more that took in Dryden's writings at the beginning and Johnson's at the end, the term 'Augustan Age' (*see above*, p. 77) is far from being the neat and precise label that its familiarity suggests. In so far as 'Augustan' implies classical order and discipline, form and balance, and some degree of cool and chaste grandeur, much that is typical in eighteenth-century life and letters belies the label. Nor is 'Age of Reason' more appropriate, since the eighteenth century had among its writers and thinkers, its aristocracy and its middle classes, many eccentrics[1] who were the very embodiment of unreason. It was an age in which the sense of propriety and restraint of a few was offset by widespread self-indulgence and excess: an age of material greed, of spiritual lassitude (which it took a Wesley to combat), of wild speculation in the stock markets, of ruinous gambling in clubs and private houses, of crime and debauchery, of brutality and squalor such as Fielding fought against both as magistrate and as writer and Hogarth exposed in paintings and engravings of rakes and harlots and gin-sodden poor. Furthermore, the caricatures of Gillray and Rowlandson, scarifying as satirical exposures of human follies and enormities, are nevertheless infected by something base in the atmosphere of the time and are the product of a brutalized visual sense ameliorated by brilliant technical accomplishment.

Illusory as the largely romantic twentieth-century view of the eighteenth century may often be, however, few persistent illusions lack initial substance. For a happy—or at least a comfortable—small minority the eighteenth century was an age of gracious living. This may have been little more than a

---

[1] Edith Sitwell's *The English Eccentrics* (London, Faber, 1933), finds a generous quantity of odd human material in the eighteenth century.

veneer, but the veneer has lasted—in gracious houses and furnishings, gracious formal gardens and landscaping, gracious paintings, gracious and stately music. Yet the æsthetic good manners thus evidenced have too often been imagined a condition of the eighteenth century as a whole.

Eighteenth-century literature, too, was often stately; but it was seldom gracious. While it was frequently good-mannered it was also frequently boorish and spiteful, occasionally (though usually with a good reformatory intent) disgusting. In perspective it may appear more integrated than the literature of other centuries, though it is in truth diverse and in many respects confusingly self-contradictory.

'Eighteenth-century literature', if that innocuous phrase be taken to indicate a particular style of writing, is not, however, coextensive with the period 1701–1800. Though a new mode developed in the early part of the century, a revolutionary change of outlook and temper displaced it long before Wordsworth and Coleridge's *Lyrical Ballads* of 1798, from which the beginning of the Romantic Revival is commonly dated. If for the moment, without qualification, *sense* be considered the predominant factor of eighteenth-century literature and *sensibility* that of the succeeding period, sensibility to nature and human sentiment will nevertheless be found in Goldsmith's writings of the 1760s and, in the same decade, sensibility to the supernatural (even if only through a spurious medievalism) in Horace Walpole's tales. Yet, while these and other signs of an impending breach with the mode were perceptible in the sixties, Gibbon's *Decline and Fall of the Roman Empire*—one of the greatest and most characteristic eighteenth-century works—started publication only in 1776 and was not completed until 1788, five years after William Blake's first poems: thus the work of a true visionary overlapped in date that of a complete rationalist.

Since no single formula embraces the output of the whole century, it will suffice for the present need to isolate a few unique qualities of the peculiarly eighteenth-century writers. Of these Steele and Addison were among the first; and they were of the age, whereas individual genius had to a large extent set both Defoe and Swift apart from the age and above it.

Richard Steele

Dublin was the birthplace of Richard Steele (1672–1729) as it had been five years earlier of Jonathan Swift. His father—an attorney in the Irish capital, though possibly of English birth—died when the boy was five, if the account in No. 181 of *The Tatler* is authentic; his mother seems to have lived until 1713, a letter to his wife in the spring of that year saying 'since the Death of my Poor Mother I find a growing Melancholy encrease upon me'. He was sent to school at the Charterhouse in London, where Addison also was, and from there went to Oxford, first at Christ Church and then at Merton College, becoming next a cadet in the Life Guards and at length a captain and secretary to the colonel of the Coldstream Guards, Lord Cutts (Coutts). To him Steele dedicated in 1701 his tract *The Christian Hero: An Argument Proving that No Principles but Those of Religion are Sufficient to Make a Great Man*, the intrinsic importance of which is much less than its interest as a conspectus of attitudes and opinions that he was to develop in other writings.

Steele was then about twenty-nine, on paper a pious and earnest young man with a pompous style which, happily, he shed later for an easy and informal manner contrasting attractively with the smoothly academic and orotund style of Addison. The dedication speaks of *The Christian Hero* as the product of meditation during guard duty 'when the Mind was perfectly Disengag'd and at Leisure in the Silent Watch of the Night'. In later years Steele wrote that the tract was designed 'principally to fix upon his own Mind a strong Impression of Virtue and Religion, in opposition to a stronger Propensity toward unWarrantable Pleasures'. Thackeray jeered at it in *English Humorists of the Eighteenth Century* as the product of 'a theologian in liquor'. Steele's weakness in this respect and his chronic indebtedness were largely responsible for the affectionately condoling term of address, 'poor Dick Steele', and letters to his second wife contain such expressions as: 'If you do not hear of me before three to-morrow afternoon believe I am too fuddled to take care to observe your Orders', and on the following day (26 October 1708) 'I am very sick with too much Wine last night'.[1] The propensity to unwar-

[1] *The Correspondence of Richard Steele*, edited by Rae Blanchard (Oxford University Press, 1941), p. 242.

rantable pleasures which Steele confessed was no baseless self-condemnation. In 1699 or 1700 he became the father of an illegitimate child, and according to Mrs. Manley (1663–1724), an early friend of Steele and a scurrilous writer, 'He affected to be extreme Religious, at the same Time when he had two different Creatures lying-in of base Children by him.'[1]

Steele interpreted Christianity as a reasonable and prudential faith, and though neither he individually, nor eighteenth-century man collectively, was reasonable or prudential in action, Reason and Prudence as intellectual concepts and theoretical principles of conduct are familiar in eighteenth-century literature, even when, as in Richardson's *Pamela* (*see below*, pp. 180–1), prudence as a protective apron for virginity becomes ridiculously if not despicably confused with innocence. Steele reprobates in *The Christian Hero* 'the Love-Histories we daily hear young Fellows relate of the Favours and Fondness of Debauch'd Women to 'em'. He was already, in contrast with the attitude of the older generation, an early champion of woman: rational, humane, and impatient of the modish artificiality as well as of the witless bawdry which so tediously ushered out a large part of seventeenth-century literature:

> . . . it is, among other Reasons, from want of Wit and Invention in our Modern Gallants, that the beautiful Sex is absurdly and vitiously entertain'd by 'em: For there is in their tender Frame, native Simplicity, groundless Fear, and little unaccountable Contradictions, upon which there might be built Expostulations to divert a good and Intelligent young Woman, as well as the fulsome Raptures, guilty Impressions, senseless Deifications, and pretended Deaths that are every day offer'd her.

After writing with little profit three plays—*The Funeral* (1701), *The Lying Lover* (1703), and *The Tender Husband* (1705) —Steele became in 1706 Gentleman-Waiter (i.e. usher) to Queen Anne's consort, Prince George of Denmark, at a salary of £100 a year tax free; and in May of the following year, as he

---

[1] *The New Atlantis* by Mrs. Mary De La Rivière Manley (1709) led to the authoress's arrest for slandering eminent persons, but she was discharged and in 1711 became editor of *The Examiner* in succession to Swift. Her assertions on any matter cannot be credited unless there is reliable independent confirmation.

informed his prospective second mother-in-law, he was 'appointed by the Secretaries of State to write the Gazette,[1] with a salary of three hundred pounds a Year paying tax of forty-five pounds'. Steele lost both these offices: the first on the death of the Prince in 1708, the other in 1710 when a Tory administration came in. Though he retained under the new government the office of Commissioner of Stamps, which he had held since January 1710, Steele was heavily in debt, as he had been before and was to be off and on until in 1724 he fled from his London creditors and spent his last five years in Carmarthenshire, Wales, his wife's family home, dying in the town of Carmarthen on 1 September 1729.

Between 1709 and 1724 Steele edited not only *The Tatler* and (with Addison) *The Spectator*,[2] but also *The Guardian* (1713), *The Englishman* (1713-14; 2nd series, 1715), *The Lover* (1714), *The Reader* (1714), *The Plebeian* (1719), and *The Theatre* (1720), all short-lived. He also wrote prologues, epilogues, dedications, numerous political pamphlets, as well as his best-known play, *The Conscious Lovers*, first acted at Drury Lane on 7 November 1722 and having what was then accounted a successful run of eighteen performances, with Colley Cibber and Mrs. Oldfield among the players.

In 1713 he became member of Parliament for Stockbridge, in Hampshire, but was expelled from the Commons in the next year, Defoe (then a government agent) having been set on to find in Steele's writings matter to justify a charge of sedition. His pamphlet, *The Crisis* (January 1714), in support of the Hanoverian succession, sold 40,000 copies, but was held to reflect upon the Queen and to be derogatory of her ministers. Steele regained favour under a new government, however, when George I followed Anne on the throne at the end of July 1714. He was knighted on 9 April 1715, became Governor of Drury Lane Theatre at £700 a year, Surveyor of the Royal Stables at Hampton Court, and received grants from the King's Bounty and the Secret Service Committee. Yet his political troubles were still not at an end. Again falling foul of the ministry over the Peerage Bill in 1718, he lost his Drury Lane appointment and quarrelled finally with Addison.

[1] Officially titled 'Gazetteer', his task was to edit *The London Gazette*.
[2] These two journals are considered below, p. 133 ff.

Steele's letters are an indispensable adjunct to his biography [1] and those he wrote to his second wife illuminate many facets of his personality. He married first (early in 1705) Margaret Stretch, a widow who had inherited her brother's estates in Barbados, but of whom nothing further is known than that she died in December 1706. In August 1707 began his letters of courtship to Mary Scurlock (heiress of a Carmarthen lawyer), whom he first met at his wife's funeral. The second marriage took place on 9 September 1707 and ended with the death of Mary (by that time Lady Steele) on 26 December 1718 at the age of forty.

Some 400 of Steele's letters to Mary have been printed, and although many are very brief, even those that run to no more than a single line add some touch to a portrait of a husband almost as intimate and as rare as that of Samuel Pepys in his Diary. After a few months of marriage Steele addressed his wife consistently as Dear Prue, sometimes writing to her more than once a day, though they might both be in town and the message might be no more than 'Dear Prue, I enclose two Guinneas and will come home exactly at seven. Yrs Tenderly, Richd Steele', or 'Dear Prue, Don't be displeased that I do not come home till eleven o'clock. Yours ever, Richd Steele', or 'Dear Prue, Sober or not, I am Ever Yours, Richard Steele.' His affection endured throughout the marriage, his last extant letter to her being subscribed, 'Yr Most Affectionate Most Obedient Husband & Servant'. Yet they had not only money difficulties. Though in the month following their wedding she is 'the most agreeable Creature living' and has his heart 'by all the Tyes of Beauty, Virtue, Good-nature, and Freindship', eight months later (June 1708) he writes: 'I wish I knew how to Court you into Good-Humour, for Two or Three Quarrels more will dispatch Me quite'; in August 1708: 'I shall make it the business of my life to make you easy and happy: Consult yr cool thoughts & You'le know that 'tis the Glory of a Woman to be her husband's Freind and Companion and not his Sovereign Director. I am with Truth, Sincerity and Tendernesse Ever yr Faithfull Husband, R. Steele.'

[1] The notes by Rae Blanchard in his edition of the *Correspondence* (*cited above*, p. 121 n.), provide much valuable information on Steele's life and times.

The dictatorial Prue appears to have become (though not immediately, and then somewhat intermittently) conformable to her husband's notions of a fit wifely bearing; but, unlike Mrs. Pepys, she was careless about dress: 'Pray be well dressed', Steele enjoins her in June 1708 when she is to call at his office; in December of that year: 'I desire you to dresse your self decently before you appear before me for I will [not] be so easily pleased as I have been being now in a fair Way of being a Great man.' In the early part of 1716 when she is in Wales and asks him for a little flattery, he tells her: '. . . though you have every perfection you have one extravagant fault which almost frustrates the good in You to Me, and that is that you do not Love to dress, to appear, to shine out even at my request, and to make me proud of You. . . .'

His affection is expressed in many ways: by endearments, by little presents—of 'a Quarter of a pound of Bohee, and as much of Green Tea'; or he sends 'Dear Prue . . . seven-pen'orth of Wall nutts at five a penny Which is the greatest proof I can give you at present of my being with my whole Heart, Yrs Richd. Steele'; and though he can remind her parsimoniously (December 1716) 'Your man Sam owes me Three pence which must be deducted in the account between you and me', only a few weeks later when she writes from Carmarthen that she has a pain in her head he replies: 'When I lay in yr place and on yr Pillow I assure [you] I fell into Tears last night to think that my Charming little insolent might be then awake and in pain, and tooke it to be a Sin to go to Sleep.'

The young Steele in 1701 had commended Christianity as a 'reasonable' religion, and the tears the Drury Lane audience is reputed to have shed when *The Conscious Lovers* was performed twenty-one years later flowed, so the author contended in his preface to the play, 'from Reason and good Sense'. To say that Steele paid no more than prolonged lip-service to Reason would be to misrepresent him and to charge him with insincerity foreign to his character. Nevertheless it is true that while, in theory and with a bow to the intellectual spirit of the age, Steele advocated the life of reason, he was himself that bugbear of the eighteenth-century intellectuals, a man of sentiment. The tussle between reason and sentiment in Steele could easily be interpreted, in twentieth-century terminology,

as schizophrenia, a case of split personality. But Steele was no
'case'; he was very definitely a personality, endearingly innocent of strict logic but as unsplit as personalities invariably
were before modern psychology invented schizophrenia and
made it a fashionably contagious mental disease. If Steele was
conscious of not measuring up either to his own aspirations or
to the pedantic tendencies of the age, he took himself as he was
without heroics or histrionics and without whimpering. If he
was sometimes fuddled, as his letters acknowledge—well, he
was fuddled. He did not dissipate energy in morbid self-
inspection or futile repining; he did, however, set about to
correct abuses and to civilize the age, himself included. As a
young man in the army he had taken a low view of women; he
had fought a duel and nearly killed his opponent. Thereafter
he used his pen to raise the status of women and to bring
duelling into disrepute.

The Christian Hero, his first-fruit of repentance, made him
something of a butt in the regiment. Finding that 'from being
reckoned no undelightful companion he was soon reckoned a
disagreeable fellow', he endeavoured to rehabilitate himself by
writing a comedy—a comedy, however, in which virtue and
vice were to appear in their true aspect, though 'full of incidents that move laughter'. The play that resulted does still
move to laughter in reading, notwithstanding its gloomy title,
The Funeral: or, Grief à-la-mode (1701), and notwithstanding,
also, that neither here nor in his other plays did Steele show
himself capable of handling a plot with any inventive ability
or organizing skill. He borrowed clumsily and half-heartedly
from Corneille in *The Lying Lover*, from Molière in *The Tender
Husband*, from Terence in *The Conscious Lovers*, here paraphras-
ing a passage, there translating almost literally, elsewhere
getting a hint for the story. As narratives his plays are extremely
tedious, yet they have incidental merits that might conceivably
justify occasional stage performances at the present time. The
characters have a way of being interesting in themselves (no
doubt in such degree as they are projections of that interesting
person their creator), though the parts they play are often
either empty or silly; the dialogue, more often than not,
engages attention by good sense, by humour, by liveliness, by
wit; while occasionally Steele's characters are delivered of neat

sayings that later epigrammatists would not have disdained: 'when the Husband begins, the Heroe ends' (*The Tender Husband*, IV, ii); 'he is a Man, and therefore a Hypocrite' (*The Conscious Lovers*, II, ii); 'The Art of Love, Sir, is the Art of Giving' (*The Lying Lover*, I, i); of a lady's maid, 'as much a second-hand thing as her Clothes' (*The Funeral*, I, i); 'All Human Life's a mere Vertigo' (*ibid.*, I, i); 'Fits are a mighty help in the Government of a Good-natur'd Man', an observation by a (supposed) widow, who adds, 'but in an Ill-natur'd Fellow have a care of 'em—he'll hate you for Natural Infirmities; will remember your Face in its Distortion, and not value your Return of Beauty' (*ibid.*, I, i).

As a satirist Steele was perhaps too genial and tender: he provokes a comprehending smile but scarcely plants a barb in such passages as that in which Sable the undertaker drills his mutes in the business of looking dismal (*The Funeral*, I, i), or (later in the same scene) that in which the lawyer, Puzzle, discourses on legal gibberish and tautology, a topic resumed many years later in *The Conscious Lovers* (III, i); those in which Mr. Sealand speaks of the growth of the merchant class while other characters sneer at his trade (*ibid.*, IV, ii; V, i); that in which Cimberton (a nastier forerunner of Jane Austen's Mr. Collins) expresses his lubricious and mercenary views on women, a scene (*ibid.*, III, i) in which Steele is more savage than was his custom.

Within a limited compass Steele could originate, but he lacked the skill to coordinate and sustain. This kept him from becoming a playwright of the first rank, just as it kept him from developing *The Tatler* and *The Spectator* type of essay into the novel: he planted seed which others cultivated and brought to maturity. It has been pointed out[1] that a single play by Steele, *The Tender Husband*, gave Fielding Sir Harry Gubbin as a model for Squire Weston (*Tom Jones*), Goldsmith Humphry Gubbin for Tony Lumpkin (*She Stoops to Conquer*), and Sheridan Biddy Tipkin for Lydia Languish (*The Rivals*).

Jeremy Collier has received little but abuse for his strident outburst in *A Short View of the Profaneness and Immorality of the*

---

[1] By Steele's biographer, G. A. Aitkin: see his introduction to *The Complete Plays of Richard Steele* (The Mermaid Series. London, Fisher Unwin, 1926), p. xxvi.

English Stage (*see above*, p. 70), yet that work was taken to heart by Steele and was to some extent responsible for his determination to reform the theatre. The dedication of *The Lying Lover* to the Duke of Ormond (in whose regiment Steele had first enlisted) proclaims that the play is designed 'to banish out of Conversation all Entertainment which does not proceed from Simplicity of Mind, Good-nature, Friendship, and Honour'; the Preface speaks of the author's 'honest Ambition to attempt a Comedy which might be no improper Entertainment in a Christian Common-wealth'; while the Prologue declares that

> our Author treads the Stage
> With just regard to a reforming Age. . . .

When after nineteen years Steele next brought out a play, he referred to 'the *Goths* and *Vandals* that frequent the Theatres' (Preface to *The Conscious Lovers*). It was to those as well as to the gentler sort who had wept at the scene (IV, ii) in which Bevil, Junior brings Myrtle, his challenger, to see that there is 'nothing manly' in duelling,[1] that Steele addressed the Prologue, with its summing-up of his intentions:

> By new and desp'rate Rules resolv'd to Write;
> Fain would he give more just Applauses Rise,
> And please by Wit that scorns the Aids of Vice;
> The Praise he seeks, from worthier Motives springs,
> Such Praise, as Praise to those that give, it brings . . .
> No more let Ribaldry, with Licence writ,
> Usurp the Name of Eloquence or Wit;
> No more let lawless Farce uncensur'd go,
> The lewd dull Gleanings of a *Smithfield* Show.
> 'Tis yours, with Breeding to refine the Age,
> To Chasten Wit, and Moralize the Stage . . .

Whether the amoral Restoration drama perished of internal decay or was hastened to its end by changes of taste which sought 'with breeding to refine the age', it is a fact that not only Restoration drama but drama itself was moribund before

---

[1] In *The Lying Lover* (V, ii) the case against duelling as an affair of honour is more emphatically urged by Young Bookwit: 'Honour! The horrid application of that sacred word to a revenge against friendship, law, and reason is a damned last shift of the damned envious foe of the human race. . . .'

Steele died. Colley Cibber, the actor-manager, continued to manufacture acting pieces; Fielding wrote numerous farces, comedies, and tragedies in the quarter century or so between 1728 and his death, but they count for little beside his novels; and the leading playwrights of the intermediate generation— George Farquhar, Susannah Centlivre, and Nicholas Rowe [1]— were all dead by 1723. Not until Goldsmith and Sheridan took to playwriting in the sixties and seventies did a semblance of life reappear on the stage, only to flicker out again until it was revived by T. W. Robertson and his successors a whole century later.

Joseph Addison

One of Steele's characters, Penelope, in *The Lying Lover*, expresses her preference for 'a man that has agreeable faults rather than offensive virtues'. To her friend Victoria's incredulous 'Offensive virtues, madam?' she answers: 'Yes, I don't know how—there's a sort of virtue, or prudence, or what you'll call it, that we can but just approve. That does not win us. . . .'
It is not likely that Steele was giving a quizzical side-glance at his friend Addison when he wrote thus, and it may well be that Addison's virtues were free of offence; yet posterity's majority verdict is almost certainly that the worthy and admirable Mr. Addison's leading qualities are such 'as we can but just approve'. This was not the opinion of his friends and contemporaries, however:

> Every witness who has spoken of Addison from intimate knowledge has told us of the almost magical attraction which he exercised in private and personal relationships. A brilliant mind, extensive scholarship, fortitude of character, and an elusive gift of humour, made him an admirable companion. [2]

Like Steele, Addison cuts no great figure in literature apart from his contributions to periodicals; and without those his

---

[1] See the general chapter on Eighteenth-Century Drama: below, p. 190 ff.

[2] Peter Smithers: *The Life of Joseph Addison* (Clarendon Press, 1953), p. 34. This biography lays stress on Addison's political and administrative career, and the author, after fourteen years' intensive work, records a feeling 'of deep admiration for a man who set himself a noble pattern of life in youth, and who, in spite of defects of character which he mastered, lived and died consistently therein ' (p. viii).

place would be below that of Steele, who did no little to reform the drama, even if he helped to reform it out of existence. Addison was thirty-seven when he began to write for *The Tatler*. After the three years (1709–12) of *The Tatler* and *The Spectator* he produced *Cato: A Tragedy*, now a fossil relic, and *The Drummer*, a comedy amusing to none then or since. He is not to be valued by his literary output alone, however; nor is it to be overlooked that he might seem more likeable to us if more were known about his personality.

> Addison abhorred irrelevant self-revelation by authors and was meticulous in his own avoidance thereof. . . . The reticence and self-criticism which was such a remarkable feature of his character has apparently served to conceal from posterity all but the barest details of his daily life, . . . The circle of wits in the coffee-house, their writings, their friendships and their quarrels, which made up so large a part of the lives of many of them, are of secondary significance in Addison's career. He was and envisaged himself as an important figure in the administrative and political life of England, and he held posts for which the aristocratic and wealthy competed fiercely. So fully rounded was his view of life that literary output became a by-product, though a very important one, of a life well lived.[1]

Joseph Addison (1672–1719), the second child and eldest son of the Rev. Lancelot Addison, was born in his father's cottage-rectory at Milston, a Wiltshire village. The boy, already reticent and extremely sensitive, was educated at Amesbury and Salisbury until, his father having become in 1683 Dean of Lichfield, he went to the Grammar School there and laid the foundations of his later excellence as a classical scholar. When fourteen he left Lichfield for the Charterhouse in London and there met young Richard Steele. Though both went to Oxford (Addison to Magdalen) there is no evidence that they associated there, and Steele left without a degree nearly a year after Addison took his B.A. in 1691. As a writer of Latin verse Addison sought and secured the favour of John Dryden, whose publisher, Jacob Tonson, soon became Addison's also. Elected a Fellow of Magdalen, his reputation as a classical scholar brought him wider notice, and in 1699 a Treasury grant and leave of absence from Oxford enabled

[1] Smithers, *op. cit.*, pp. v, vi.

him to travel. He spent from the autumn of that year to the
spring of 1704 in France, Italy, and the Netherlands.

On returning to London he became a member of the famous
Kit-Cat Club,[1] though lodging modestly and for a while
penuriously in a garret near the Haymarket. In 1704 he was
commissioned by Tory ministers to compose a poem celebrating
Marlborough's victory at Blenheim, with a £200-a-year post as
Commissioner of Excise Appeals as reward. Tonson published
this in December as *The Campaign, a poem to His Grace the Duke
of Marlborough by Mr. Addison*, its nearly five hundred lines in
rhyming couplets being formally heroic, lifelessly martial,
loudly verbose, and, to twentieth-century war-sick ears,
faintly ridiculous and faintly repulsive—though the final line
of the following has become a familiar quotation:

> So when an Angel by Divine Command
> With rising Tempests shakes a guilty Land,
> Such as of late o'er pale *Britannia* past,
> Calm and Serene he drives the furious Blast;
> And, pleas'd th' Almighty's Orders to perform,
> Rides in the Whirl-wind, and directs the Storm.

The Campaign was enthusiastically and profitably received,
with few dissenting voices, one being Defoe's, who commented
acidly in verse that whereas he himself wrote poems for nothing
Addison required £200 a year—'fix'd his pension first, or he
had never sung'; Pope quoted him ironically in *The Dunciad*;
and Swift applauded Addison's wisdom in refraining from more
poetry, as he did for years. But *The Campaign* served the author
well. In 1705 Addison became an Under-Secretary of State
and a Commissioner of the Peace; in 1706 he was chosen to
accompany Lord Halifax on a mission from Queen Anne,
ostensibly to present the Order of the Garter to the Electoral

---

[1] A Whig confraternity established at that time and including (besides
Steele and Addison) Congreve, Vanbrugh, and some thirty or forty
statesmen and noblemen, with Jacob Tonson as secretary. The original
meeting-place was at a pastry cook's near Temple Bar kept by Christopher
Cat, whose mutton pies were called Kit-cats. The portraits of the members
(now in the National Portrait Gallery), commissioned by Tonson and
painted by Sir Godfrey Kneller, were half-lengths (36 in. × 28 in.) to fit
the restricted wall-space in the club's new dining-room built by Tonson
in his house at Barn Elms. These paintings (and half-length portraits
generally) are referred to as Kit-Cats.

Prince of Hanover (afterwards George I) but more especially to discuss the Act of Settlement.

A major disappointment befell Addison in 1707 when his opera *Rosamond,* with music by Thomas Clayton, failed at Drury Lane; but his progress as a man of affairs continued. He entered Parliament in 1708 as member for Lostwithiel in Cornwall; he courted at Holland House the widowed Countess of Warwick; at the end of 1709 he became Secretary to the government in Ireland, and 'as the pressure of government business became heavy his literary activities ceased almost entirely'.[1] Two years later the Whig ministry fell and Addison lost office. Then ensued the partnership with Steele[2] in *The Tatler* and *The Spectator.* Early in 1713 he bought for £8,000 the Manor of Bilton, near Rugby, although he had been writing gloomily not long before about his financial prospects.

While at Oxford Addison first drafted *Cato,* and worked on it sporadically in after years. He completed it for performance at Drury Lane on 14 April 1713, with Booth as Cato, Anne Oldfield as his daughter Marcia, and Cibber and Wilks in other parts. The play ran for a month with resounding success, and would have continued but for Mrs. Oldfield's advanced pregnancy. The play was also successful in print, reaching the eighth edition in as many months. The political ambiguity of the tragedy contributed to its popularity. Johnson wrote in his essay on Addison in *Lives of the Poets*: 'the time . . . was now come, when those who affected to think liberty in danger, affected likewise to think that a stage-play might preserve it. . . . The Whigs applauded every line [of *Cato*] in which Liberty was mentioned, as a satire on the Tories; and the Tories echoed every clap, to shew that the satire was unfelt.' No doubt the imposing rhetoric of Addison's lines delivered in the grand manner of the eighteenth-century theatre accounted for the near-frenzy of its original hearers. Cold on the page, *Cato* is now a dry carcass. Nevertheless it remains—however withered and bloodless—to witness to the eighteenth-century ideal of classical drama; it fails, not because the theme lacks tragic potentiality (within the circumscribed emotional range allowed by classical principles Corneille and Racine wrote

[1] Smithers, *op. cit.,* p. 142.   [2] See below, p. 133 ff.

world masterpieces on such themes), but because of Addison's inadequacy as a poet.[1]

In the remaining six years of Addison's life there was nothing of literary importance. He returned to office with the Whigs at the accession of George I in 1714, becoming again Secretary to the Irish government, subsequently a Commissioner of Trade and Plantations, and in 1717 Secretary of State for the Southern Department. He married the dowager Countess of Warwick in 1716, and a daughter was born to them in January 1719. Addison lived only five months longer. He was buried in Henry VII's Chapel, Westminster Abbey.

The Tatler and *The Spectator*

The works of man are as subject to ceaseless erosion as the works of nature: looking back we see only what has survived the weathering of time and circumstance. In literature we are aware of little but what is best from the past, whereas we see the writings of our own day in mass, before time has washed away the detritus. Within the first two decades of the eighteenth century over three hundred periodicals were started; of these, only two have a front place in literature.

The conditions which caused these periodicals to abound were also the conditions which caused the bulk of them to perish soon. Some (*The Spectator* certainly) did aim to interest a wider-than-London public; but the majority lived or died by the favour of coffee-house and boudoir, purveying gossip and scandal, and truckling to partisan prejudice. The survival of *The Tatler* and *The Spectator* is due to the faith and enterprise of Steele and Addison, who ventured to offer readers in town and country a range of subjects and a style of writing which few would themselves have desiderated. Few things in literature are more surprising, indeed, than that Addison found a welcoming audience for his serial critical essays in *The Spectator* on Milton, on Wit, and on Imagination.

It has been noted above (*see* p. 98) that Defoe's 'Scandalous Club' feature in *The Review* led Steele to see the possibility of developing some such idea in a periodical giving as much

---

[1] Amid much tediously protracted carping, John Dennis made just and lively critical observations in his *Remarks upon Cato, a Tragedy*, written in 1713 while the play was the talk of the town. See below, pp. 145, 163.

The TATLER.

By Isaac Bickerstaff Esq;

———————— *Garrit aniles*
Ex re Fabellas———— Hor.

From *Tuesday December* 6. to *Thursday December* 8. 1709.

From my own Apartment, December 7.

MY Brother *Tranquillus* being gone out of Town for some Days, my Sister *Jenny* sent me Word she would come and dine with me, and therefore desired to have no other Company. I took Care accordingly, and was not a little pleased to see her enter the Room with a decent and Matron-like Behaviour, which I thought very much became her. I saw she had a great deal to say to me, and easily discovered in her Eyes, and the Air of her Countenance, that she had abundance of Satisfaction in her Heart, which she longed to communicate. However, I was resolved to let her break into her Discourse her own Way, and reduced her to a Thousand little Devices and Intimations to bring me to the Mention of her Husband. But Finding I was resolved not to name him, she began of her own Accord; My Husband (said she) gives his humble Service to you: To which I only answered, I hope he is well; and without waiting for a Reply, fell into other Subjects. She at last was out of all Patience, and said, (with a Smile and Manner that I thought had more Beauty and Spirit than I had ever observed before in her) I did not think, Brother, you had been so ill-natured. You have seen ever since I came in, that I had a Mind to talk of my Husband, and you won't be so kind as to give me an Occasion. I did not know (said I) but it might be a disagreeable Subject to you. You do not take me for so old-fashioned a Fellow as to think of entertaining a young Lady with the Discourse of her Husband. I know, nothing is more acceptable than to speak of one who is to be so; but to speak of one who is so! Indeed, *Jenny*, I am a better bred Man than you think me. She showed a little Dislike at my Raillery; and by her bridling up, I perceived she expected to be treated hereafter not as *Jenny Distaff*, but Mrs. *Tranquillus*. I was very well pleased with this Change in her Humour; and upon talking with her on several Subjects, I could not but fancy, that I saw a great deal of her Husband's Way and Manner in her Remarks, the Phrases, the Tone of her Voice, and the very Air of her Countenance. This gave me an unspeakable Satisfaction, not so much because I had found her an Husband, from whom she could learn many Things that were laudable, but also because I looked upon her Imitation of him as an infallible Sign that she intirely loved him. This is an Observation that I never knew fail, though I do not remember that any other has made it. The natural Shieness of her Sex hindered her from telling me the greatness of her own Passion; but I easily collected it, from the Representation she gave me of his. I have every Thing, says she, in *Tranquillus* that I can wish for; and enjoy in him (what indeed you have told me were to be met with in a good Husband) the Fondness of a Lover, the Tenderness of a Parent, and the Intimacy of a

Friend. It transported me to see her Eyes swimming in Tears of Affection when she spoke: And is there not, Dear Sister, said I, more Pleasure in the Possession of such a Man, than in all the little Impertinencies of Balls, Assemblies, and Equipage, which it cost me so much Pains to make you contemn? She answered, smiling, *Tranquillus* has made me a sincere Convert in a few Weeks, tho' I am afraid you could not have done it in your whole Life. To tell you truly, I have only one Fear hanging upon me, which is apt to give me Trouble in the Midst of all my Satisfactions: I am afraid, you must know, that I shall not always make the same amiable Appearance in his Eye that I do at present. You know, Brother *Bickerstaff*, that you have the Reputation of a Conjurer; and if you have any one Secret in your Art to make your Sister always beautiful, I should be happier than if I were Mistress of all the Worlds you have shown me in a Starry Night--- *Jenny* (said I) without having Recourse to Magick, I shall give you one plain Rule, that will not fail of making you always amiable to a Man who has so great a Passion for you, and is of so equal and reasonable a Temper as *Tranquillus*. Endeavour to please, and you must please; be always in the same Disposition as you are when you ask for this Secret, and, you may take my Word, you will never want it. An inviolable Fidelity, good Humour, and Complacency of Temper, out-live all the Charms of a fine Face, and make the Decays of it invisible.

We discoursed very long upon this Head, which was equally agreeable to us both; for I must confess, (as I tenderly love her) I take as much Pleasure in giving her Instructions for her Welfare, as she her self does in receiving them. I proceeded therefore to inculcate these Sentiments, by relating a very particular Passage that happened within my own Knowledge.

There were several of us making merry at a Friend's House in a Country Village, when the Sexton of the Parish-Church entered the Room in a Sort of Surprize, and told us, That as he was digging a Grave in the Chancel, a little Blow of his Pickax opened a decayed Coffin, in which there were several written Papers. Our Curiosity was immediately raised, so that we went to the Place where the Sexton had been at work, and found a great Concourse of People about the Grave. Among the rest, there was an old Woman, who told us, the Person buried there was a Lady, whom I do not think fit to mention, tho' there is nothing in the Story but what tends very much to her Honour. This Lady lived several Years an Exemplary Pattern of Conjugal Love, and dying soon after her Husband, who every Way answered her Character in Virtue and Affection, made it her Death-Bed Request, That all the Letters which she had received from him, both before and after her Marriage, should be buried in the Coffin with her. These I found upon Examination were the Papers before us. Several of them had prominence to social affairs, to entertainment, and to culture, as to politics. The first number of *The Tatler* (12 April 1709) took the position that readers of the political journals, 'who neglect their own Affairs to look into Transactions of State', were for the most part 'Persons of strong zeal and weak Intellects' who needed to be instructed 'after their Reading, what to think'. From a heavier pen than Steele's this would have been pompous, pretentious, pedagogic, and a little insolent. It is neither satire nor irony; yet a little of both, with wit and humour and that touch of impudent fun and gay abandon which constitutes Steele's individual style. Charming and enlivening though his style is, however, it lacks weight and intellectual depth, qualities which could be and were amply provided by Addison. Without Addison *The Tatler* and *The Spectator* would have been like small boats without ballast, to be capsized by any light breeze; with Addison and no Steele, the ballast alone might have sunk them incontinently.

For all his lightness, however, Steele was a great civilizer, and would still have been so if he had done no more than champion the cause of women. It would hardly have occurred to Addison (who had no very enlightened opinion of the other sex) to cater for women readers; but it was so much in Steele's mind that *The Tatler* might otherwise have been differently named. He said in the first number: 'I resolve also to have Something which may be of Entertainment to the Fair Sex, in honour of whom I have invented the Title of this Paper.' Steele never wrote better than when women were his theme. He then kept a sure, however seemingly precarious, balance between honest admiration and formal gallantry, between playfulness and sincerity, between sentimentality and genuine feeling. In No. 4 of *The Tatler* he introduces two ladies of fashion, naming them Clarissa and Chloe, beauties both, who affect their lovers in opposite ways:

. . . The Admirers of *Chloe* are eternally Gay and well-pleas'd: Those of *Clarissa* Melancholy and Thoughtful. . . . There were of each Kind just now here. Here is One that Whistles, Laughs, Sings, and Cuts Capers, for Love of *Chloe*. Another has just now writ Three Lines to *Clarissa*, then taken a Turn in the Garden, then came back again, then tore his Fragment, then call'd for some Chocolate, then went away without it.

Female  Tatler.

By Mrs. Craekenthorpe, *a Lady that knows every thing.*

From **Monday** September 26, to **Wednesday** September 28, 1709.

R. ——— is a Gentleman I would willingly excuse for his great Abilities, as well as the Habit he wears; but as his *Eminence* and *Figure* may be of prevalence to the World to make it follow his Example, so I find my self oblig'd, after all the Admonitions of his Friends have been of no Force with him, to declare, that he's a mixture of for expofing their want of it, I shall for this one time, (and they may affure themfelves it shall be the laft) admit 'em into my Cognizance. Their *Graces* (who has no *Horfes* to rub down, for if they had been poffefs'd of thofe of the *Sun*, they would have been *pawn'd* to the *Stationer* long fince) is introduc'd talking with my Man *Francis*, who is made to be as *ragged*, and *famifh'd*, as a certain worthy Perfon that was diftinguifh'd at *Oxford* only

---

Numb. 12.

THE
OBSERVATOR.

On a Highflying Clergyman's aukward way of vifiting a dying Parifhioner, and refufing to bury him, becaufe he would not leave his Game at Cards. The Canons in fuch Cafes. On a pleafant Converfation betwixt Sir William Read, her Majefty's Oculift, and Roger, about Sir William's calling Dr. Sacheverel Brother-Oculift. Reflections on the Skill of the Doctor and his Party in Opthalmicks, and their blinding inftead of opening the Eyes of the People. The Compliment of a Whig to a Knot of Sacheverellites. On S——'s Anfwer to Mr. Biffet.

From **Wednefday**, February 7. to **Saturday**, February 10. 1711.

Countrym. HERE's a Letter, Mafter, from a Gentleman, to whom we have been formerly oblig'd for Information of things material, with a heavy Complaint of one, who is Reader of ' had a Warrant ferv'd upon them, and carry'd ' them before a certain Juftice of Peace, who by ' his Chriftian Name fhould be fomething of a ' Jew, and by his Sirname a Highflier, 'tis fo near-' ly related to the Top of the Houfe. This bright

---

The GROULER:
OR,
Diogenes *Robb'd of his Tub.*

From *Saturday,* January 27. to *Thurfday* February 1. 1711.

DIOGENE be fick, very well; he no naturaliz'd, me be de more fick; me be naturaliz'd; me be de provok'd; me be in de Paffion; me will write de Paper for him; me will groul like de very Dog; for vat do me get by being de *Engel*ifh-man? Vat ha me for me Shilling? Vat do de Parliament make a de Vark about? Me no Be- de Poulet, de Pidgeon, de any Ting for de Soup, de Ragou, de Frichafie; fo de *French* be de Fool to de *Irifh*; he be de Pack-horfe to work for dem, for a littel Money, a littel Vittels, a littel Cloaths, dat be all dey do get for de Study of de Brain, and de great Travel.

In *England* me be de Companion for de Quality; dey do fay very oft, *Monfieur, do me de Honour to*

There is in the last sentence a touching quality as well as a playful one; however artificial the theme may be, something real has got into it. In the union (as here) of sophistication and innocence of feeling lay Steele's unique contribution to the urbanity of *The Tatler* and *The Spectator*. Before that urbanity could be attained, however, a stabilizing element was needed, and Addison provided it through his scholarship, analytical ability, and gravity, and the solid sense of humour which was the complement of Steele's gaiety. It is unfortunate that Johnson did not write at length of Steele, as he did of Addison in *Lives of the Poets*, where he concludes:

> It seems to have been his principal endeavour to avoid all harshness and severity of diction; he is therefore sometimes verbose in his transitions and connections, and sometimes descends too much to the language of conversation; yet if his language had been less idiomatical, it might have lost somewhat of its genuine Anglicism.

And Johnson sums up that Addison's English style was 'familiar but not coarse, . . . elegant but not ostentatious'. While in the periodical essays of Steele and Addison there may be no obvious disparity of style, there is also no great difficulty in distinguishing between them: Addison's writing is thicker in texture, and its humour, though not essentially less amusing, lacks the sly side-glances and occasional dancing steps that enliven Steele's. In the most famous of *The Spectator* papers, the Sir Roger de Coverley group, Steele introduces the characters with the differentiating skill of a playwright, and when he writes of them subsequently he drops easily into conversation, whereas Addison prefers indirect reporting or set description, or even to take up a subject or a story which has little if any organic link with Sir Roger or the others. In so far as the Novel can be said to have grown in due course from the seed planted by these essays, it was more from Steele than from Addison that the creative fictional element came.

The Tatler was by turns a newspaper—it reported events in Marlborough's campaign on the Continent—a gossip sheet, a magazine, and a general miscellany of social criticism. It lasted until 4 January 1710/11, ceasing with No. 272. Addison wrote forty numbers, and other writers contributed occasionally,

Whereas there is already printed Four Volumes of the Spectators which
Include from Number one to Number Three hundred Twenty one
And Whereas there is two Volumes more now printing which will take
in from Number Three hundred Twenty one to to Number four hundred
& Eighty or thereabouts which will make Six Volumes And Whereas
it is intended by the Authors whose Names are hereinafter mentioned
to Continue writing the said Spectator to the end of this present
Month of November which will make a Seventh Volume.

Now Know all Men by these presents that Joseph Addison of St James
W.Aminster Esqr and Richard Steele of St Giles in the fields Esqr for
and in consideration of the Summe of Five hundred Seventy and
five pounds to them or one of them in hand paid by Samuel
Buckley of London printer & Bookseller the Receipt whereof
They the said Joseph Addison & Richard Steele doe hereby respectively
Acknowledge they the said Joseph Addison and Richard Steele have
and each and either of them Hath Granted Bargained Sold
Assigned Transferred and Set over And by these presents They
the said Joseph Addison and Richard Steele Doe and each and
either of them doth Grant Bargain Sell assign Transfer and Set
over Unto the said Samuel Buckley his Executors Administrators
and Assigns all that their full and Sole right and Title of in and to
one Moiety or full half Share of the Copys of all and every the
above mentioned Seven Volumes of Spectators which said
Moiety or full half share to remain unto the said Samuel
Buckley his heires and Assigns for Ever In Witness whereof
the said Joseph Addison and Richard Steele have hereun to
Set their hands & Seals this Fourth day of November Annoqz
Domi 1712.

Witness:d Richard Thwaites;   Joseph Addison
               David Verdon
        at the Fountain Tavern in the Strand.

                                                 Richard Steele :

but the great majority were by Steele himself. The real reason for killing *The Tatler* can only be guessed, but it is likely to have been a step dictated by political expediency. Yet *The Tatler* was no sooner dead than Addison and Steele were preparing to bring *The Spectator* to birth, as they did on 1 March 1711. Writing the first number in the form of a biographical sketch of the fictional chronicler, Mr. Spectator, Addison said:

> . . . I live in the World, rather as a Spectator of Mankind, than as one of the Species: by which means I have made my self a Speculative Statesman, Soldier, Merchant, and Artizan, without ever medling with any Practical Part in Life. I am very well versed in the Theory of an Husband, or a Father, and can discern the Errors in the Oeconomy, Business and Diversion of others, better than those who are engaged in them; as Standers-by discover Blots, which are apt to escape those who are in the Game. I never espoused any Party with Violence, and am resolved to observe an exact Neutrality between the Whigs and Tories, unless I shall be forced to declare my self by the Hostilities of either Side. In short, I have acted in all the Parts of my Life as a Looker-on, which is the Character I intend to preserve in this Paper.

The device of the Spectator Club was mooted in No. 1 by Addison, and Steele developed it with particulars of the fictional members in the second number; Sir Roger de Coverley of Worcestershire, a bachelor of fifty-five living in Soho Square when in town; an unnamed Member of the Inner Temple; Sir Andrew Freeport, a City Merchant; Captain Sentry; Will Honeycomb, 'of that Sort of Man who is usually called a well-bred fine Gentleman. To conclude his Character, where Women are not concern'd, he is an honest worthy Man.' There was also, though he attended but seldom, a philosophical, learned, saintly, well-bred clergyman of probity and integrity with 'a very weak constitution'.

The declared purpose of *The Spectator* was 'to enter into the Passions of Mankind, and to correct those depraved Sentiments that give Birth to all those little Extravagances which appear in their outward Dress and Behaviour'. The paper appeared daily until 6 December 1712, when Steele brought it to a close in No. 555 with a valedictory address over his own signature.

It is impossible to glance at *The Spectator* without having one's

attention caught and held to some one of the hundreds of subjects that were discussed. Who would not (for example) read
on to find what follows after the opening sentence of No. 56?—
'The *Americans* believe that all Creatures have Souls, not only
Men and Women, but Brutes, Vegetables, nay even the most
inanimate things, as Stocks and Stones.' Each number of the
paper was a single essay, though when Addison embarked on
the discussion of the nature of Wit he continued it in instalments throughout a week; his ambitious critical essays on
Milton's *Paradise Lost* ran on eighteen successive Saturdays; the
series on Imagination took eleven daily instalments. These
were not displays of intellectual self-indulgence by Addison.
The paper depended upon the maintenance of its circulation
and could not afford to aim above the heads of its readers. In
the last of the Milton series Addison concluded (No. 369):

> . . . Had I thought, at my first engaging in this Design, that it
> would have led me to so great a Length, I believe I should never
> have entred upon it; but the kind Reception which it has met
> with among those whose Judgments I have a Value for, as well
> as the uncommon Demands which my Bookseller tells me has
> been made for these particular Discourses, give me no Reason to
> repent of the pains I have been at in composing them.

In No. 10 Addison said that the publisher was distributing
3,000 copies daily; in the last number Steele said that 9,000
copies of each bound volume had been sold. 'The circulation
of the most popular numbers has been estimated at from fourteen to twenty thousand and the average at ten thousand daily.
These figures are almost certainly too high, but circulation
approaching them would be much in excess of anything previously attained by a literary publication.'[1]

Whatever its sales may have been, *The Spectator* remains one
of the most remarkable enterprises in English literary journalism. The modern reader is daunted by its total bulk, and the
varieties of pleasure that its contents can give have been largely
obscured by stereotyped selections which lean too heavily
upon the de Coverley papers. *The Spectator* is a library-in-little
to be browsed in, though a castaway might be happy to read on
from No. 1 to No. 555.

[1] Smithers, *op. cit.*, p. 244.

Alexander Pope

No one has written on Pope more justly than Samuel Johnson, whose biographical and critical study in *Lives of the Poets* needs little further adjustment after more than a century and a half than is necessitated by Johnson's intermittent tendency to become obtrusively moralistic and excessively literal. Of Pope's *Elegy to the Memory of an Unfortunate Lady* he wrote, 'Poetry has not often been worse employed than in dignifying the amorous fury of a raving girl'—an observation that might equally condemn Shakespeare for *Romeo and Juliet*; and on line 365 in *An Essay on Criticism*—'The sound must seem an echo to the sense'—Johnson commented: 'the desire of discovering frequent adaptations of the sound to the sense, have produced, in my opinion, many wild conceits and imaginary beauties'. Since Pope's poetry introduces the barest minimum of amorous fury and wild conceits Johnson was able to view it with a minimum of temperamental bias, free alike from the antipathy which was to sway the nineteenth-century Romantics and from the bellicose partiality of the twentieth-century anti-Romantics. He saw Pope's greatness and also his littleness: as the finest lapidary artist in English poetry and as the creature who spoke of himself as a spider and behaved like a scorpion.

Whatever ground there may have been for his wish to relate his family to the nobility, Alexander Pope (1688–1744) was in fact the son of a London linen draper. A weakly boy, his health was permanently affected when he was twelve by an illness which crippled him for the rest of his life. In middle age (Johnson wrote):

> . . . His stature was so low, that, to bring him to a level with common tables, it was necessary to raise his seat. But his face was not displeasing, and his eyes were animated and vivid. By natural deformity, or accidental distortion, his vital functions were so much disordered, that his life was a *long disease*. . . . He was . . . extremely sensible of cold, so that he wore a kind of fur doublet, under a shirt of a very coarse warm linen with fine sleeves. When he rose, he was invested in boddice made of stiff canvas, being scarce able to hold himself erect till they were laced, and he then put on a flannel waistcoat. One side was contracted. His legs were so slender, that he enlarged their bulk with three pair of stockings, which were drawn on and off by the

maid; for he was not able to dress or undress himself, and neither went to bed nor rose without help. His weakness made it very difficult for him to be clean. His hair had fallen almost all away; and he used to dine sometimes with Lord Oxford, privately, in a velvet cap. His dress of ceremony was black, with a tye-wig, and a little sword.

Whereas in childhood Pope was said to have been gentle and of a sweet disposition, with so attractive a voice that he was called 'the little nightingale', he grew waspish and capable of malice towards his friends, while he was malevolent to his enemies. This distortion of his nature, to be traced originally to his physical condition, was no doubt aggravated by the fact that, as a Roman Catholic, he was debarred from a university education. When the London shop was given up and the family moved to the village of Binfield in Windsor Forest (with a fortune of some £20,000 which the father kept in a chest and drew upon heavily), he was sent to a Twyford academy and later to a school at Hyde Park Corner, London. A Roman Catholic priest had previously taught him the elements of Greek and Latin and he became an insatiable reader, with a particular devotion to Homer and Ovid.

Beginning to write verses while a schoolboy, he took poetry as his almost exclusive interest from the time his schooldays ended with his return to Binfield at the age of twelve. His elderly father encouraged the young poet, who modelled himself upon Dryden and was taken to see him presiding at Will's coffee-house in Covent Garden, shortly before Dryden died.

The *Ode on Solitude* is said to have been written when Pope was twelve; he next undertook the *Imitations of English Poets* (Chaucer, Spenser, Waller, Cowley, Rochester, Dorset, and Swift); and composed his *Pastorals* in 1704, when he was sixteen. These last (published five years later in the sixth of Tonson's *Poetical Miscellanies*), though they contribute nothing important to English poetry, are of interest as showing Pope partly trusting his own eyes, in such lines as 'Here the bright crocus and blue violet grow', but more especially using, with easy competence, a conventional poetic diction—as in the lines to which Handel afterwards gave lasting currency as an aria in his opera *Semele*:

> Where'er you walk, cool gales shall fan the glade,
> Trees, where you sit, shall croud into a shade:
> Where'er you tread, the blushing flow'rs shall rise,
> And all things flourish where you turn your eyes.

The verses written in succession to the *Pastorals* (*Windsor Forest*; *Messiah*; *The Temple of Fame*; *Ode on St. Cecilia's Day*; *The Dying Christian to his Soul*; *Elegy to the Memory of an Unfortunate Lady*) are again scarcely more than imitations and exercises, though carried out with uncommon skill and assurance.[1] During those years, 1704–9, he made the first of his literary friendships, with Wycherley; two years later he was established. An advertisement in No. 66 of *The Spectator* (16 May 1711) announced: 'This Day is publish'd *An Essay on Criticism* . . . Price 1s.' It had been composed in 1709 when Pope was twenty-one, and was issued anonymously. Seven months after its publication Addison wrote in *The Spectator* (No. 253, 20 December 1711) that it was a masterpiece in its kind, and devoted to it most of that number of the paper. Of the major parts of the *Essay on Criticism* Addison remarked that 'The Observations . . . are placed in so beautiful a Light, and illustrated with such apt Allusions, that they have in them all the Graces of Novelty, and . . . Truth and Solidity.' The closer a reader's familiarity with Pope's first masterpiece, the more just appears Addison's judgement that its graces are those of novelty, beauty, truth, and solidity. The beauty consists not in ornamentation nor in employment of the picturesque, but in precision and economy of statement: it is the beauty of a perfectly adjusted instrument, not the beauty of a flower, for as Pope's own couplet declares,

> True Wit is Nature to advantage dress'd,
> What oft was thought, but ne'er so well express'd.

He is not of those who

> With gold and jewels cover ev'ry part,
> And hide with ornaments their want of art.

[1] Steele thought well enough of *Messiah* to print it in *The Spectator* (No. 378, 14 May 1712), with some changes suggested by himself, and this introductory note: 'I will make no Apology for entertaining the Reader with the following Poem, which is written by a great Genius, a Friend of mine, in the Country, who is not asham'd to employ his Wit in the Praise of his Maker.' By the time this early poem was published Pope had become a celebrity with *An Essay on Criticism*.

The novelty of which Addison speaks distinguishes the whole poem, the like of which had not before (and has not since) been done in English. The truth and solidity lie in the sustained argument, but also in the many lines which, beginning as epigrams, long since took on the familiarity of proverbs and became part of the national store of distilled wisdom: e.g. 'A little learning is a dang'rous thing'; 'Be not the first by whom the new are tried, Nor yet the last to lay the old aside'; 'True ease in writing comes from art, not chance, As those move easiest who have learned to dance'; 'To err is human, to forgive, divine'; 'fools rush in where angels fear to tread'; 'pleased to teach, and yet not proud to know'; 'The bookful blockhead, ignorantly read, With loads of learned lumber in his head.'

An Essay on Criticism may be a novelty in English literature but it had both a classical and a neo-classical ancestry, by descent from the *Ars Poetica* of Horace through the *Art Poétique* (1674) of Boileau, who wrote in the age of Racine when France was already as self-consciously classical as England would become within the next half-century. The fundamental tenet of these writers was that poetry must be considered first and foremost as an art, in which the thing to be said must submit to the mould of form: manner must take charge, not emotion. This doctrine would seem less tyrannical if poetry were analogous to architecture, where the laws of construction rule. But there is no such analogy. Poetry is not a visual art but an intellectual, emotional, and spiritual activity. The taste, ingenuity, and dexterity with which Pope assembles words and burnishes phrases, so that his art appears as fine as a jeweller's or a mosaicist's—all this can be admired and delighted in to the utmost. Yet it leaves life out of reckoning, and can do little with life when it is taken into account.

The strangling limitations of a formalized art of poetry such as Pope advocated are demonstrated in the one poem in which he came to grips with a subject which could not be intellectualized. In *Eloisa to Abelard*, presented as a monologue by the woman after the tragedy, emotion is all the while battering its wings against the confining bars of the heroic couplet, a verse unit perfect for concentrated thought and epigram but an imprisoning cell when deep feeling calls for expression. The admiration which most of Pope's mature work commands, and the peculiarly satisfying pleasure it gives within its limits, does not permit the conclusion to be burked that his theory of poetry is fallacious and heretical. It attempts to dwarf the human spirit to fit a neat and charming little æsthetic casket, and is blind to the truth that poetry must be capable of enlargement to the full scale of the human spirit's limitless variety of need for communication.

At least one protest was heard amid the general chorus in praise of *An Essay on Criticism*, though the protest was not against the theory. In the lines

> Appius reddens at each word you speak,
> And stares, tremendous, with a threat'ning eye,
> Like some fierce Tyrant in old tapestry

Pope baited John Dennis, whose *Appius and Virginia* and other tragedies are of less account than the critical writings in which he poured upon his contemporaries unmeasured personal abuse. Although Dennis was in some respects a contemptible person he was not, as has been said above (p. 133, n.), entirely negligible as a critic, and when he turned on Pope he scored some immediate hits. After Dennis had attacked *Cato*, Addison was embarrassed by an intemperate anonymous pamphlet, written by Pope and designed to avenge his friend. It brought not gratitude to Pope but repudiation and explanation from Addison to Dennis, and thus the train was laid for the explosive animosity which culminated in the bitter lines on Addison ultimately embedded in Pope's *Epistle to Dr. Arbuthnot* (see below, p. 149).

Pope was now famous, but he was not rich; and since his religion made him ineligible for official employment, he was compelled to seek other means of supplementing the allowance from his father. Having retained a strong liking for the classics, Homer in particular, he projected an annotated translation of the *Iliad* for subscribers, in six large volumes at six guineas the set. The hazards and profits of this venture have been referred to above (p. 91). The translation occupied him from 1712 to 1718, the first volume coming from the press in 1715, the year in which he moved with his parents from Windsor Forest to the villa by the river Thames at Twickenham, in Middlesex, which has since borne his name, Pope's Villa.

Provided that Pope's translations of the *Iliad* and the *Odyssey* (1725–6) are read as eighteenth-century English poems on Homeric themes, they can be praised without reserve; viewed as translations of Homer they are inappropriate, for of all the world's poets Homer is least conformable to the narrow discipline of Pope's art of poetry, to which Virgil, on the other hand, would have been reducible if Pope had chosen the *Æneid* for translation. His aim, however, was to add fortune to fame and in this he succeeded.

Meanwhile, in the year (1712) in which he began on the *Iliad*, the first version of *The Rape of the Lock* appeared in Bernard Lintot's *Miscellanies*. The original two cantos were

> Received of *the Hon: Mrs Granville* Two Guineas, being the first Payment to the Subscription, for the Translation of HOMER'S ILIADS ; to be delivered, in Quires, to the Bearer hereof, in the manner specify'd in the Proposals.
>
> *A. Pope.*

afterwards increased to five and the full edition came out in 1714. In comparison with, say, *Paradise Lost*, *The Rape of the Lock* is no more than a literary trinket; yet it is perfect, and perfection has no governing scale of magnitude. This is the one achievement which gives Pope an indisputable place among the English poets: here he had no theory to whip up, no grudges to pay off, no philosophy to propound. It is a creation fit for the century which produced Mozart's music, exquisite figures in porcelain, and the paintings and drawings of Watteau. A consummate piece of artificiality, it originated in the reality of a family quarrel, a Lord Petre having taken by force a snippet from a certain Arabella Fermor's head. Arabella approved the poem in its original version—it was, indeed, written to appease the Fermors—but when Pope enlarged it, introducing the delicious sylphs and other aery creatures, Arabella was less agreeable. However playful *The Rape of the Lock* may be, it is serious in its poetic kind, being strictly of the mock-heroic genre and again 'after' Boileau, of whose *Le Lutin* it is perhaps more an emanation than an imitation. Pope 'presents Belinda at her toilet, a game of ombre, the snipping of the lock while Belinda sips her coffee, the wrath of Belinda and her demand that the lock be restored, the final wafting of the lock, as a new star, to adorn the skies'. With wonderful dexterity the whole poem is kept absolutely in key and absolutely to its miniature scale, the catalogue of omens being a delicately ludicrous series of diminishing anticlimaxes:

> Some dire disaster, or by force, or slight ;
> But what, or where, the fates have wrapt in night.
> Whether the nymph shall break Diana's law,
> Or some frail China jar receive a flaw;
> Or stain her honour, or her new brocade;
> Forget her pray'rs, or miss a masquerade;
> Or lose her heart, or necklace, at a ball; . . .

The third of Pope's four major works, *The Dunciad*, first published, anonymously, in 1728, was occasioned by Lewis Theobald's pamphlet detailing the errors in Pope's edition of Shakespeare (1725). Theobald was made the hero of this satire on Dullness in the first edition, but Pope replaced him by Colley Cibber in the 1744 version. It would be useless to assume that present-day readers will inevitably find great pleasure or continuous interest in *The Dunciad*. Exciting though it was to contemporaries, who took the common human delight in seeing one another lambasted, it now has too many obscurities which can only be made clear by too many footnotes, a high proportion of which suggest that Pope expended excessive talent on next-to-nobodies. In passages which leave the particular for the general or the universal, Pope lifts himself from the toils of the goddess Dullness who in this poem enmeshed him hardly less than the individual dunces he went out against. The better Pope appears off and on, and is in full possession in the final lines:

> She comes! she comes! the sable Throne behold
> Of *Night* Primæval, and of *Chaos* old! . . .
> . . . at her felt approach, and secret might,
> *Art* after *Art* goes out, and all is *Night*.
> See skulking *Truth* to her old cavern fled,
> Mountains of Casuistry heap'd o'er her head! . . .

> *Religion* blushing veils her sacred fires,
> And unawares *Morality* expires.
> Nor *public* Flame, nor *private*, dares to shine;
> Nor *human* Spark is left, nor Glimpse *divine*!
> Lo! thy dread Empire, CHAOS! is restor'd;
> Light dies before thy uncreating word:
> Thy hand, great Anarch! lets the curtain fall;
> And Universal Darkness buries All.

The powerful close of *The Dunciad* shames the triviality and spleen of much in its earlier parts. Pope had become arrogant and over-confident of his own intellectual reach. In the *Essay on Man* (1732–4) he attempted a universal philosophy in four Epistles: I. 'Of the Nature and State of Man with respect to the Universe'; II. 'Of the Nature and State of Man with respect to himself as an Individual'; III. 'Of the Nature and State of Man with respect to Society'; IV. 'Of the Nature and State of Man with respect to Happiness'. It has not been left to the present century to conclude that Pope, in presuming that a total of 1,300 lines was adequate to the undertaking, made himself vulnerable to such satire as he himself would have leapt to write if the *Essay on Man* had been by another hand. Johnson, who had spoken of the *Iliad* translation as 'that poetical wonder . . . a performance which no age or nation can pretend to equal', said that Pope in the *Essay on Man* was 'in haste to teach what he had not learned':

> Having exalted himself into the chair of wisdom, he tells us much that every man knows, and much that he does not know himself: . . . This Essay affords an egregious instance of the predominance of genius, the dazzling splendour of imagery, and the seductive powers of eloquence. Never were penury of knowledge and vulgarity of sentiment so happily disguised.

Even in splendour of imagery and seductive eloquence Pope's touch is less certain here than in earlier works: he precedes the lovely line 'Die of a rose in aromatic pain'[1] with 'quick effluvia darting thro' the brain' (I, 199–200); and while he is capable of such unforgettable if not especially profound lines as

> Hope springs eternal in the human breast;
> Man never Is, but always To be blessed. (I, 95–6)

[1] See below, p. 155 and n.

he does not disdain the calculated bathos of

> Why has not Man a microscopic eye?
> For this plain reason, Man is not a Fly (I, 193–4).[1]

Harsh things have been said and written of Pope: Johnson speaks of his 'incessant and unappeasable malignity' towards Colley Cibber, but records also Bolingbroke's tribute, 'I never in my life knew a man that had so tender a heart for his particular friends, or a more general friendship for mankind.' Mankind has been more inclined to think of Pope as spiteful and embittered than as tender and friendly. A satirist inevitably appears curmudgeonly; it is his purpose to castigate mankind for mankind's good, not for mankind's comfort. Pope's character has sometimes been deduced from one notorious passage, that on Addison:

> Shou'd such a man, too fond to rule alone,
> Bear, like the Turk, no brother near the throne,
> View him with scornful, yet with jealous eyes,
> And hate for arts that caus'd himself to rise;
> Damn with faint praise, assent with civil leer,
> And without sneering, teach the rest to sneer;
> Willing to wound and yet afraid to strike. . . .[2]

Finding in this picture no resemblance to the Addison other men drew, nor to the Addison known through his writings, posterity has excusably suspected that the passage presents a subconscious mirror-image of Alexander Pope himself.

---

[1] Cf. *Peri Bathous: or, Martin Scriblerus his Treatise of the Art of Sinking in Poetry* (1727), a demi-satire—probably by Pope himself—on the use of bathos. (Reissued in a critical edition by Edna Leake Steeves: King's Crown Press, New York, 1952.)

[2] *Epistle to Dr. Arbuthnot*, ll. 197–203.

CHAPTER VIII

LESSER VERSE AND PROSE 1701-25

By their commanding stature amid the ruck of contemporaries, Defoe, Swift, Steele, Addison, Pope inevitably attract immediate attention in any approach to the eighteenth century, but the processes of change from seventeenth-century to eighteenth-century ideals and achievements may more easily be traced through the lesser writers.

We are prone, at our distance in time, to overstress the differences between the two centuries and to underestimate the extent to which the earlier 1700s continued in the shadow of the political and religious turbulence of the preceding half-century. Obvious differences there were. If the earlier period is regarded as a metaphysical age and the later as materialistic, the distinction is not seriously misleading, though at what point and by what means the metaphysical was displaced by the materialistic is hard to discern. Pope's *Essay on Man*, like *Paradise Lost*, proposed to justify God's ways to Man— a metaphysical ambition; and Samuel Johnson's religious consciousness was little less acutely sensitive than that of any seventeenth-century Covenanter.

The eighteenth century was caught in a dilemma which man is still far from resolving. The seventeenth century was the last of the ages of faith, the eighteenth century the first of the would-be ages of reason. No age, however, has yet been an age of reason; attempts at such an age have broken down because, it seems, the life of reason starves the soul and plunges man into a profound discontent. Man is still too immature, or by his nature unfitted, to adjust himself to the life of reason, which allows no recourse to supernatural aids or consolations. The reasonable man must stand upright on his own feet and alone.

The main sources of the eighteenth-century dilemma were strangely unrelated: *philosophy* and *trade*. Only in recent times has *natural philosophy* come to be distinguished separately from the general body of philosophy as *science*. Philosophy in the eighteenth century embraced science, and served as a two-pronged devil's fork. The one prong, *philosophy* as such, encouraged the persuasion that by taking thought—i.e. by the operations of reason—man would solve the riddle of the universe; the other prong, *science* (*natural philosophy*), by means of observation and deduction was to guide reason to that end. The great enemy of the life of reason, in eighteenth-century eyes, was *enthusiasm*,[1] which, to the rational man, connoted a state of emotional or spiritual over-balance or excess, and it was anathema to orthodox Christians, since Enthusiasts (of whatever sectarian affiliation) claimed a direct personal relationship with God and denied the authority of priesthood. The easygoing mid-eighteenth-century clergy viewed the Evangelical Revival generated by George Whitefield and John Wesley as a deplorable outburst of Enthusiasm, but it survived antagonism and outlived contemporary rationalism and latitudinarianism to become a world force.

The growth of prosperity through trade, then more and more netting the globe, was the other powerful eighteenth-century incentive to rationalism. There were, of course, those who believed that goodness was the key to commercial success, a belief strengthened by the experience of the many members of the Religious Society of Friends (Quakers) who became prosperous as bankers, merchants, and manufacturers. In general, however, there appeared to be little if any connection between righteousness and the acquisition of wealth, particularly when so dubious an enterprise as the slave trade was seen to produce magnificent dividends. With philosophy and prosperity a man could obviously have lifelong content; while, for gentlemen, religion was surely a superfluity.

Much of the lesser eighteenth-century literature needs to be considered against some such background of ideas in ferment. The major writers, though not divorced from it, were not dominated by the background and their works are more nearly independent productions, in the sense that, e.g., *The Dunciad* was an achievement peculiar to Pope, although its

[1] An exhaustive analysis of its nature and a history of its manifestations are given from the Roman Catholic angle, though temperately and with scholarly thoroughness, in *Enthusiasm* by Ronald Knox (Clarendon Press, 1950).

material was drawn from the background or picked from the
literary undergrowth of the time. In the Argument to Book III
of *The Dunciad* he tilts at 'the visions of wild enthusiasts, projectors, politicians, inamoratas, castle-builders, chemists, and
poets'; and (IV, 472–82) at the 'gloomy clerk, Sworn foe to
mystery' voicing the creed of those who

> . . . reason downward, till we doubt of God;
> Make Nature still encroach upon His plan;
> And shove Him off as far as e'er we can:
> Thrust some mechanic cause into His place;
> Or bind in matter, or diffuse in space.
> Or, at one bound o'erleaping all His laws,
> Make God man's image, man the final cause,
> Find virtue local, all relation scorn,
> See all in self, and but for self be born:
> Of nought so certain as our reason still,
> Of nought so doubtful as of soul and will.

Verse Writers

If the satirical mode of which Pope was to be the supreme and
final master can be said to have had an originator in England,
no one is better entitled to be so named than Samuel Butler
(1612–80), to whose mock-heroic *Hudibras* (in three parts:
1663, '64, '78) we may here look back as a bridge linking *The
Faerie Queene* (Hudibras is a character named in Book II, ii, 17
of Spenser's poem) and *Don Quixote* with the eighteenth-
century verse-satirists. Though Dryden intervenes and was
Pope's great master in poetry, it was more by technique than
by temper that the two were linked. Dryden's largeness of
vision safeguarded him from the spleen which gives a sour and
bitter taste to a good deal of Butler and some of Pope. The
octosyllabic couplets of *Hudibras* fall into a plodding monotony
which never endangers the agile ten-syllable couplets of Pope's
masterpieces; and also, by harping on too many strings—from
Spenser, Cervantes, Rabelais, and Scarron—and at the same
time lampooning Presbyterians and Independents, Butler
missed the directness and clarity imperative for excellence in
satire. Whereas Pope's satires are as well organized as a first-
class stage performance, *Hudibras* has the irresponsible bustle
of a country fair.

Too little is known of Samuel Butler's life to allow *Hudibras* to be fitted enlighteningly into his personal history. He was the son of a Worcestershire farmer, and went to the free school at Worcester, afterwards becoming page to the Duchess of Kent. He was for a while in France and the Netherlands, and in England held several offices as clerk and secretary, and as steward of Ludlow Castle. He failed in later life to get preferment at Court and is said to have died in poverty. The originals for his presbyterian knight Sir Hudibras were probably the two puritan justices of the peace to whom he had been clerk, Sir Samuel Luke of Bedfordshire and Sir Henry Rosewell of Devon. Hudibras, like Quixote, is a figure of wry humour abroad on a starveling horse, followed by a squire who acts as interlocutor in the many arguments on sectarian matters. Sir Hudibras spoke

> A *Babylonish* dialect,
> Which learned Pedants much affect. . . .
> For he could coyn or counterfeit
> New words with little or no wit:
> Words so debas'd and hard, no stone
> Was hard enough to touch them on. . . .
> He could raise Scruples dark and nice,
> And after solve 'em in a trice:
> As if Divinity had catch'd
> The Itch, of purpose to be scratch'd; . .
> He knew the Seat of Paradise,
> Could tell in what degree it lies:
> And, as he was dispos'd, could prove it,
> Below the Moon, or else above it: . . .
> Whether the Serpent at the Fall
> Had cloven Feet, or none at all. . . .

A closer though slighter link between the two centuries exists in the poetry of Matthew Prior (1664–1721), who collaborated with Charles Montagu, 1st Earl of Halifax, in *The Hind and the Panther Transvers'd to the Story of the Country and City Mouse* (1687), a satire on Dryden's *The Hind and the Panther*, and used the *Hudibras* metre in one of his few long poems, *Alma; or, the Progress of the Mind*. Prior was at his best in amorous and playful verse. He wrote attractively to small children, as in 'A

Letter to the Honourable Lady Margaret Cavendish Holles-Harley', beginning

> My noble, lovely, little PEGGY,
> Let this, my FIRST-EPISTLE, beg ye,
> At dawn of morn, and close of even,
> To lift your heart and hands to heaven:

and in 'To a Child of Quality Five Years Old', ending

> For as our different Ages move,
> 'Tis so ordain'd, wou'd Fate but mend it,
> That I shall be past making Love,
> When she begins to comprehend it.

He extended a light satirical tone even to grim topics, as in this from 'An Epitaph':

> Interr'd beneath this Marble Stone,
> Lie Saunt'ring JACK, and Idle JOAN. . . .
> Slothful Disorder fill'd His Stable;
> And sluttish Plenty deck'd Her Table.
> Their Beer was strong; Their Wine was *Port*;
> Their Meal was large; Their Grace was short.
> They gave the Poor the Remnant-meat,
> Just when it grew not fit to eat.

and in this from 'Jinny the Just':

> Less smooth than her Skin and less white than her breast
> Was this pollisht stone beneath which she lyes prest:
> Stop, Reader, and Sigh while thou thinkst on the rest.
>
> With a just trim of Virtue her Soul was endu'd,
> Not affectedly Pious nor secretly lewd
> She cut even between the Cocquet and the Prude.

At moments Prior is something of a latter-day Herrick, but Herrick had more sincerity of feeling than artifice; in Prior the balance is reversed. There may be small art in his poetry, but art there is: the art of elegance in the mechanics of verse, and the polish which was so much a part of eighteenth-century urbanity.

> Thy melting Numbers, and polite Address,
> In ev'ry Fair raise passion to excess.
> In either sex You never fail, we find,
> To cultivate the heart, or charm the mind.

These gushing lines 'To Mr. Prior from a Lady Unknown'
were written by Anne Finch, Countess of Winchilsea (1661–
1720), in whose verse Wordsworth found some merit, while
Pope and Shelley discovered in her 'Pindarik Poem' *The
Spleen* two lines that haunted them:

> Now the Jonquille o'ercomes the feeble Brain;
> We faint beneath the Aromatic Pain, . . .[1]

Her work displays the mannered artifice of eighteenth-century
poetry at its most characteristic, and its profuse visual imagery
has an elusive attraction which struggles, for the most part in
vain, against an embarrassing fundamental silliness. When
occasionally, as in 'A Nocturnal Reverie', she encourages the
reader's hopes with such lines as

> When fresh'ned grass now bears itself upright,
> And makes cool banks to pleasing rest invite,
> Whence spring the woodbine and the bramble-rose,
> And where the sleepy cowslip shelter'd grows; . . .

the hopes are dashed by her forcing the poem beyond bounds
until it sinks into chatter.

Ambrose Philips (1675–1749) and John Philips (1676–1709)
were unrelated, but both were prominent in their generation
and Ambrose's *Pastorals* (1709) received serious critical attention from the Addison circle. This aroused the unremitting
animosity of Pope, who made game of Philips, and in the
Epistle to Dr. Arbuthnot he refers (lines 179 ff.) to his rival
pastoralist as

> The Bard whom pilfer'd Pastorals renown,
> Who turns a *Persian Tale* for Half-a-crown,
> Just writes to make his Barrenness appear,
> And strains from hard-bound Brains, eight Lines a-Year; . . .

'Philips had taken Spenser, and Pope took Virgil for his
pattern. Philips endeavoured to be natural, Pope laboured to

---

[1] Cf. Pope's *Essay on Man* (I, 199–200): '. . . quick effluvia darting
through the brain, Die of a rose in aromatic pain'; and Shelley's *Epi-
psychidion* (ll. 450–2): '. . . from the moss violets and jonquils peep, And dart
their arrowy odour through the brain Till you might faint with that
delicious pain.'

be elegant.'[1] Philips is now remembered by hardly more than one of the poems which earned him the nickname Namby Pamby—the lines 'To Miss Charlotte Pulteney in her Mother's Arms', beginning

> Timely blossom, infant fair,
> Fondling of a happy pair,
> Every morn, and every night,
> Their solicitous delight. . . .

While in Johnson's opinion Philips 'added nothing to English poetry', he yet made the pointed remark of the 'namby-pamby' pieces that 'if they had been written by Addison they would have had admirers'.

Of Ambrose Philips's early life nothing is known but that he went to St. John's College, Cambridge; John Philips, the son of an archdeacon of Shrewsbury, was born at Bampton in Oxfordshire, and educated at Winchester and Christ Church, Oxford. He intended to become a physician, but his burlesque poem *The Splendid Shilling* (1705) brought him literary repute and he was commissioned by the Tory ministers to produce *Blenheim* (1705), a poem to offset the Whigs' engagement of Addison to write *The Campaign* (*see above*, p. 131). In 1708 Philips had a further popular success with *Cyder*, a blank verse poem 'on the cultivation of cider apples, and the manufacture and virtues of cider'; this 'was received with fond praises, and continued long to be read, as an imitation of Virgil's *Georgick*, which needed not shun the presence of the original'. *The Splendid Shilling* applies pseudo-Miltonic blank verse to a comic theme which shows Philips's preoccupation with gormandize; and it contrasts with the happy lot of him whose 'splendid shilling' buys oysters and ale and other delights, the state of the needy poet whose

> parched Throat
> Finds no Relief, nor heavy Eyes Repose:
> But if a Slumber haply does invade
> My weary Limbs, my Fancy's still awake,
> Thoughtful of Drink, and eager, in a Dream
> Tipples imaginary Pots of Ale: . . .

---

[1] Johnson: *Lives of the Poets.*

Thus do I live from Pleasure quite debarr'd,
Nor taste the Fruits that the Sun's genial Rays
Mature, *John-Apple*, nor the downy *Peach*,
Nor *Walnut* in rough-furrow'd Coat secure,
Nor Medlar, Fruit delicious in Decay.

The Fable of the Bees; or Private Vices, Public Benefits (1714) by
Bernard de Mandeville (1670–1733), a Dutch physician living
in London, was an enlarged edition with a prose commentary
of his earlier *The Grumbling Hive, or Knaves Turn'd Honest* (1705),
a verse satire. Neither version has independent literary merit,
but as a philosophizing diatribe against the human race and
society it provoked replies from such eminent philosophers as
William Law and George Berkeley (*see below*, pp. 165–6).

Whatever may be the poetic rank of Isaac Watts (1674–
1748), he is immortalized by his hymns, which include 'Jesus
shall reign where'er the Sun Doth his successive Journeys run',
'When I survey the wond'rous Cross On which the Prince of
Glory dy'd', and 'There is a Land of pure Delight Where
Saints Immortal reign', published in *Hymns and Spiritual Songs*
(1707), and 'Our God, our Help in Ages Past', from *The
Psalms of David Imitated* (1719). His *Divine Songs, for the Use of
Children* (1720) contain not only perennial nursery moral
jingles, e.g.

> Let dogs delight to bark and bite,
> For God hath made them so; . . .

> But, children, you should never let
> Such angry passions rise;
> You little hands were never made
> To tear each other's eyes.

and

> How doth the little busy bee
> Improve each shining hour. . . .

and

> 'Tis the voice of the sluggard; I heard him complain,
> 'You have wak'd me too soon, I must slumber again.'

but also the lovely 'Cradle Hymn' beginning

> Hush! my dear, lie still and slumber,
> Holy angels guard thy bed! . . .

Thomas Parnell (1679–1718), of Dublin birth and education, became one of the Pope and Swift circle in London from 1706, and through the latter's interest was made vicar of Finglas in the Dublin diocese. His posthumous *Poems on Several Occasions* (published by Pope in 1722) are neither first-rate nor merely mediocre. The *Night-Piece on Death* and *The Hermit* express that eighteenth-century mood which found pleasure in melancholy[1] and solitude, but Parnell also chose themes remarkable for oddity—'Health: an Eclogue', 'The Flies: an Eclogue', 'On a Lady with Foul Breath', 'On the Number Three'. He wrote a few attractive lyrics in doggerel metre, but his only immortalized line ends this passage from 'An Elegy, to an Old Beauty':

> 'Tis now thy daughter's daughter's time to shine,
> With more address, or such as pleases more,
> She runs her female exercises o'er,
> Unfurls or closes, raps or turns the fan,
> And smiles, or blushes, at the creature man,
> With quicker life, as gilded coaches pass,
> In sidelong courtesy she drops the glass.
> With better strength, on visit-days she bears
> To mount her fifty flights of ample stairs.
> Her mien, her shape, her temper, eyes, and tongue,
> Are sure to conquer—for the rogue is young;
> And all that's madly wild, or oddly gay,
> We call it only pretty Fanny's way.

After the death of Sir David Lyndsay[2] in 1555 Scots vernacular poetry went into a long decline, until collections of old songs made by Allan Ramsay (1686–1758) and others, and Ramsay's own works, revived the genius of northern poetry. Ramsay was in business as a wig-maker in Edinburgh before he turned to bookselling, and in 1718 he produced *Christ's Kirk on the Green*, enlarging an old poem on a village fair. In *The Tea-Table Miscellany* (1724 and later volumes) and *The*

---

[1] See below, p. 212 ff.   [2] See Ward: I, 102 ff.

Ever Green (1724) he gathered old and new songs by various hands, but his chief contribution to the revival was a pastoral play, *The Gentle Shepherd* (1725), containing such delightful songs as that beginning

> My *Peggy* is a Young Thing
> Just enter'd in her Teens
> Fair as the Day, and sweet as *May*,
> Fair as the Day, and always gay,
> My *Peggy* is a Young Thing,
> And I'm not very auld,
> Yet well I like to meet her at
> The wawking of the Fauld.[1]

He was the most notable near forerunner of Burns, who was born the year after Ramsay died.

Henry Carey (died 1743), poet, playwright, and composer, who published volumes of poems in 1713 and 1729, is remembered by little except 'The Ballad of Sally in our Alley' and by the irresistibly absurd title of his burlesque, *Chrononhotonthologos* (1734), 'the Most Tragical Tragedy that ever was Tragediz'd by any Company of Tragedians', which has characters bearing names no less lengthily absurd. His talent for ridicule is neatly and amusingly exercised in 'Namby Pamby: or, a Panegyric on the new versification addressed to A—— P——, Esq.', lampooning Ambrose Philips's poems on the Pulteney children:[2]

> Namby Pamby ne'er will die
> While the Nurse sings Lullaby.
> Namby Pamby's doubly mild,
> Once a Man, and twice a Child;
> To his hanging Sleeves restor'd,
> Now he foots it like a Lord;
> Now he pumps his little Wits,
> All by little tiny Bits.

Prose Writers

The first years of the eighteenth century saw the publication of notable works by three writers who died before the century

---

[1] wawking of the Fauld] a festival custom ('watching the fold') when the lambs were weaned.

[2] See above, p. 156.

began. The *Letters* and *Miscellanea* of Sir William Temple (1628–99) edited by Swift in volumes which appeared in 1700 and 1701 supplemented two earlier collections of *Miscellanea* (1680, '92). Temple, an eminent diplomat and man of affairs, is now best known in literature as the person to whom Dorothy Osborne's letters [1] were addressed before their marriage. His style wanted the ease and charm of hers, and while his essays are formally graceful and refined they are at moments heavily prosy. A cross-breed, as it were, between Bacon and Addison, he lacked the power of compression of the one and the easy sophistication of the other. Temple wrote on a variety of topics, from 'Gardening' (his great love) to 'Poetry and Music', and in the last-named essay appears his famous sentence: 'When all is done, Human Life is, at the greatest and best, but like a froward Child, that must be play'd with and humoured a little to keep it quiet till it falls asleep, and then the care is over.'

The True Historical Narrative of the Rebellion and Civil Wars in England, by Edward Hyde, 1st Earl of Clarendon (1609–74), was begun in the late 1640s [2] and continued in the early 1670s, when he also wrote the *Life* of himself which he amalgamated piecemeal with the *History*. Nothing was published until his son brought out an imperfect transcript in 1702–4. [3] Clarendon, as a leading statesman and adherent of the royalist cause, had been deeply implicated in the events he recorded, and his noble work has at once the advantages and the defects of history written at close quarters. As literature it has great merits, in the skill with which the material is deployed and the narrative conducted, and in the character-sketches of the leading personalities. Contemplating the situation as it appeared before the calamity, Clarendon wrote:

> Of all the Princes of *Europe* the King of *England* alone seemed to be seated upon that pleasant Promontory, that might safely view the tragick Sufferings of all his neighbours about him. . . .

[1] See above, p. 78.
[2] I treat of Clarendon and Halifax here since their works were first published in the eighteenth century and became part of the literature of that period, though written earlier.
[3] No authentic text appeared until 1888.

32. *Hubidras and the Lawyer* by William Hogarth

33. Isaac Watts by an unknown artist

34. Matthew Prior by Jonathan Richardson

35. Frontispiece to John Philips' *Cyder*, engraved by
Michael van der Gucht

36. Samuel Richardson by Joseph Highmore

37. Tobias Smollett by an unknown artist

38. Laurence Sterne by L. C. de Carmontelle

39. A scene from *Roderick Random* by Tobias Smollett

40. A satirical print *A Just View of the British Stage* by William Hogarth

41. A satirical print *The Rival Printers*

42. A satirical print *Rich's Glory* by William Hogarth

In this blessed Conjuncture . . . a small, scarce discernable
Cloud arose in the North; which was shortly after attended with
such a Storm, that never gave over raging, till it had shaken and
even rooted up the greatest, and tallest Cedars of the three
Nations; blasted all its Beauty and Fruitfulness; brought its
Strength to Decay, and its Glory to Reproach, and almost to
Desolation; by such a Career, and Deluge of Wickedness, and
Rebellion, as by not being enough foreseen, or, in Truth, suspected,
could not be prevented.

Clarendon's is history in the grand manner of high tragedy, and
what his book suffers through absence of the level-eyed detachment cultivated by modern professional historians is more than
compensated by dramatic intensity. And while his judgements
of men may sometimes want true perception or display a
natural partiality, his character-drawing is extraordinarily
vivid. The Cromwell portrait shows honest bewilderment that
this hated man 'could never have done half that mischief
without great parts of Courage, Industry, and Judgement'.

Without doubt, no Man with more wickedness ever attempted
anything, or brought to pass what he desired more wickedly,
more in the face and contempt of Religion, and moral Honesty;
yet wickedness as great as his could never have accomplish'd
those trophies, without the assistance of a great Spirit, an admirable circumspection, and sagacity, and a most magnanimous
resolution.

If what Clarendon wrote of his master and hero Charles I is
overwrought and extravagant, it is nevertheless free from
sycophantic adulation and fulsome compliment. There is tragic
passion in the phrase, 'that very hour when he was thus
wickedly murdered in the sight of the sun'; and defiant
loyalty in the conclusion that

he was the worthiest gentleman, the best master, the best friend,
the best husband, the best father, and the best Christian, that the
age in which he lived had produced. And if he was not the best
king, if he was without some parts and qualities which have
made some kings great and happy, no other prince was ever
unhappy who was possessed of half his virtues and endowments,
and so much without any kind of vice.

Still more belatedly in the eighteenth century appeared 'The
Character of Charles II' by George Savile, Marquess of

M

Halifax (1633–95), published in 1750 among his *Political, Moral, and Miscellaneous Reflections*. Though Halifax was one of the most accomplished prose writers of the Restoration period his style suffers in comparison with Clarendon's, seeming beside his to be more involved and circumlocutory than when measured by the general standard of contemporary prose. It takes him a whole paragraph of nearly twenty lines to inform the reader that Charles II was too good natured or too indolent to say No, yet, immediately after, he lights up brilliantly a less amiable aspect of the king's character in the twenty words which end this very short paragraph:

> It must be allowed he had a little Over-balance on the well-natured Side—not Vigour enough to be earnest to do a kind Thing, much less to do a harsh one; but if a hard Thing was done to another Man he did not eat his Supper the worse for it.

Halifax (in 'A Rough Draft of a New Model at Sea') wrote the well-remembered injunction to the British nation to guard her sea-defences: 'Look to your Moat'; and, taking time off from public affairs, he addressed some attractive essays to his child in *A Lady's Gift; or, Advice to a Daughter* (1688). It is, however, by three political pamphlets, almost sardonically free from political illusion, that he is most frequently recalled: *A Letter to a Dissenter* (1687), *Character of a Trimmer* (1688), and *The Anatomy of an Equivalent* (1688).

From the time it was first published posthumously in 1723, *The History of My Own Times* by Gilbert Burnet (1643–1715), Bishop of Salisbury from 1689, has been much dispraised. Swift condemned the book for what seemed to him its vanity and partiality, and alleged that it was 'generally made up of coffee-house scandals', while a modern historian speaks of the author as 'the debased Burnet'.[1] He was much involved in the tortuous political affairs of the period, but though he has been called a time-server his record appears no more discreditable than that of some of the contemporaries who attacked him; and he sacrificed his office as Royal Chaplain by reproving Charles II for disorderly living. Burnet wrote much, including *The History of*

---

[1] C. V. Wedgwood: *Seventeenth Century English Literature* (Home University Library, 1950), p. 20.

the Reformation of the Church of England (3 vols., 1679, '81, 1714). Whatever its shortcomings as history, *The History of My Own Times* has become a literary classic. Its design was 'to give a history of our affairs for fifty years, from the 29th of May, 1660' but Book I recapitulates affairs from 1603 to 1660. The work is not confined to bare facts, and occasionally turns aside to give some glimpse of secondary matters which show, for example, the state of the public mind. Thus he records that at the time of the Great Fire of 1666 suspicions of a papist plot led to the arrest of one of the Countess of Clarendon's men accused of cutting off London's water supply by turning the cocks at the New River head in Islington and carrying off the keys.

> So when the fire broke out next morning, they opened the pipes in the streets to find water, but there was none. And some hours were lost in sending to *Islington*, where the door was to be broke open, and the cocks turned. And it was long before the water got to *London*.

A House of Commons Committee found that 'many stories, which were published with good assurance, came to nothing on a strict examination', but, already, rumour and panic had brought to the gallows 'one Hubert, a French Papist', a crazed person who had made a confused declaration that he started the fire. It is inevitable that Burnet and Clarendon should be compared, though the two men were very different in temper and cast of mind: Clarendon grave and with an acute sense of the tragedy inherent in the human situation; Burnet assertive and censorious.

But for the attention given him by Pope, to whom he was a stronger irritant than reason should have allowed, John Dennis (1657–1734) would be a still lesser figure than he now seems. His plays are negligible except as period relics, and his pamphlets in defence of the stage against contemporary detractors have only a minor documentary interest. As a literary and dramatic critic he could hit the right nail firmly and cleanly on the head, but he continued to hit it long after it was driven home. Many of the faults he points to in Addison's *Cato* are faults indeed, and could still be noted with interest and profit if Dennis had had the skill to criticize his own criticism and prune it of the excess that leads to absurdity and makes him less a critic than a niggler and natterer. His seven letters containing 'Remarks on Mr. Pope's Rape of the Lock', with their preface, squander thirty quarto pages on a dully ridiculous and ludicrously inappropriate attempt to demolish fantasy with a *pied-à-lettre* bombardment.

The most attractive minor figure in the Swift and Pope circle, John Arbuthnot (1667–1735), physician to Queen Anne, was both genial and witty, and his group of political pamphlets published as *The History of John Bull* (1720) was destined to provide the name since then applied to the typical Englishman. The author described him as 'in the main, . . . an honest plain dealing fellow, cholerick, bold, and of a very unconstant temper; . . . very apt to quarrel with his best friends, especially if they pretended to govern him: if you flattered him, you might lead him like a child'. These lightly allegorical pamphlets are not unamusing at surface level, but if their political significance is to be grasped they require more annotation than most present-day readers would have patience for. With Swift, Pope, Congreve, Gay, Parnell, and others Arbuthnot started (c. 1713) the Scriblerus Club, and apparently he was the principal author of *The Memoirs of the extraordinary Life, Works, and Discoveries of Martinus Scriblerus* which remained uncompleted at his death, and unpublished until it was included in the second volume of Pope's prose works in 1741. The aim of the *Memoirs* was to ridicule 'all the false tastes in learning, under the character of a man of capacity enough, that had dipped into every art and science, but injudiciously in each'. The part actually written gives a humorous account of the birth, upbringing, speculations, and works of Martin. When he set out to investigate the diseases of the mind

. . . he thought nothing so necessary as an inquiry after the seat of the soul; . . . Sometimes he was of opinion that it lodged in the brain, sometimes in the stomach, and sometimes in the heart. Afterwards he thought it absurd to confine that sovereign lady to one apartment, which made him infer that she shifted it according to the several functions of life: the brain was her study, the heart her state-room, and the stomach her kitchen. . . . Thus, in epicures, he seated her in the mouth of the stomach, philosophers have her in the brain, soldiers in their heart, women in their tongues, fiddlers in their fingers, and rope-dancers in their toes.[1]

The most striking of Arbuthnot's works is the still apposite pamphlet *The Art of Political Lying* (1712), which purports to be the prospectus for a full-length treatise on the same subject, to be done as two quarto volumes. In setting out what the imagined book would say, Arbuthnot in fact says it, satirically. His author, he reports, is to show that while people have a right to private truth, 'they have no right at all to Political Truth'; and to the question 'whether the right of coinage of Political Lies be wholly in the government?' he replies that 'the right of inventing and spreading Political Lies is partly in the people' since the exercise of that right is the only means 'left to the good people of England to pull down a ministry and government they are weary of'. The good humour of this pamphlet is Arbuthnot's own; its cynicism is a pointer to the level of contemporary politics; and in part it is perennially applicable.

George Berkeley (1685-1753) and William Law (1686-1761) belong primarily to philosophy and religion, but both were also notable prose writers. Berkeley, born and educated in Ireland, was Bishop of Cloyne from 1734 to 1752. He visited America in connection with his unfulfilled plan for a missionary training college in Bermuda, and also spent some time in London, where he mixed with Steele, Addison, Pope, Swift, and their circle. He expounded a philosophical idealism which holds (in opposition to Locke) that there is no material reality and that things exist only as mental perceptions, communicated to human minds through 'an *omnipresent eternal mind*, which knows and comprehends all things'. His works include *An Essay towards a New Theory of Vision* (1709), *Principles of Human Knowledge* (1710), *Three Dialogues between Hylas and Philonous in opposition to Sceptics and Atheists* (1713), *Alciphron, or the Minute Philosopher* (1732), and *A Theory of Vision* (1733).

William Law was born near Stamford and went to Emmanuel College, Cambridge, of which he became a Fellow after

[1] George A. Aitken: *The Life and Works of John Arbuthnot* (Clarendon Press, 1892), ch. XII.

his ordination in 1711, but, refusing on religious grounds to take the oath of allegiance to George I, he was deprived of his Fellowship. Some years later he became tutor to Edward Gibbon's father and is mentioned in the historian's autobiography. The first of Law's works were controversial (e.g. his attack on Bernard de Mandeville's *Fable of the Bees*); he then wrote *A Practical Treatise on Christian Perfection* (1726), and *A Serious Call to a Devout and Holy Life* (1728), his masterpiece. Whereas his earlier books commend a rational and practical religion, from about 1732 he fell under the influence of the writings of the sixteenth–seventeenth-century German peasant-mystic Jacob Boehme and produced, among other mystical literature, *The Way to Divine Knowledge* (1752). John Wesley and his brother Charles were so powerfully moved by Law that he came to be called 'the father of Methodism'. The *Serious Call*, which brought Johnson to think earnestly about religion, is one of the great Christian classics, an enchanting book not without humour and irony in its vivid word-sketches of typical worldlings, such as the imaginary character he names Matilda:

> Matilda was never meanly dressed in her life; and nothing pleases her in dress, but that which is very rich and beautiful to the eye.
>
> Her daughters see her great zeal for religion, but then they see an equal earnestness for all sorts of finery. They see she is not negligent of her devotion, but then they see her more careful to preserve her complexion, and to prevent those changes which time and age threaten her with.
>
> They are afraid to meet her, if they have missed the church; but then they are more afraid to see her, if they are not laced as strait as they can possibly be. . . .
>
> The eldest daughter lived as long as she could under this discipline, and died in the twentieth year of her age.
>
> When her body was opened it appeared that her ribs had grown into her liver, and that her other entrails were much hurt by being crushed together with her stays, which her mother had ordered to be twitched so strait, that it often brought tears into her eyes whilst the maid was dressing her.
>
> Her youngest daughter is run away with a gamester, a man of great beauty, who in dressing and dancing has no superior.

CHAPTER IX

JOHNSON BEFORE BOSWELL

WHILE English literature would not be seriously poorer if Samuel Johnson's writings were lost and forgotten, the personality of Johnson himself lit up the contemporary scene for the best part of thirty years from the date (1755) of his *Dictionary of the English Language*. He was familiar with statesmen as well as with writers, painters, actors, divines, and bluestockings. If the immense acclaim of his personality were weighed against the relatively slight importance of his literary work, it might be supposed that Johnson in the role of Great Man was a fictional character invented by Boswell in a hero-worshipping biography. But Boswell is no solitary witness. Johnson impressed and frequently overawed the numerous company that moved within his circle or on its circumference, and his familiar friends were generous in affectionate admiration of him.

Physically Johnson was always unprepossessing. At the time of his marriage, when he was twenty-five, he was 'lean and lank, so that his immense structure of bones was hideously striking to the eye, and the scars of the scrophula were deeply visible'; during the years after the age of fifty-three when Boswell knew him

> His figure was large and well formed, and his countenance of the cast of an ancient statue; yet his appearance was rendered strange and somewhat uncouth, by convulsive cramps, by the scars of that distemper [scrofula] which it was once imagined the royal touch could cure, and by a slovenly mode of dress. He had the use only of one eye; . . . so morbid was his temperament, that he never knew the natural joy of a free and vigorous use of his limbs: when he walked, it was like the struggling gait of one in fetters; when he rode, he had no command or direction of his horse, but was carried as if in a balloon.

Though a convinced Christian, Johnson was nevertheless of a melancholic spirit,[1] superstitious, irascible, prejudiced and

[1] Melancholy was a contemporary malady, sometimes a contemporary pose. See above, pp. 27, 158, and below, p. 212 ff.

contradictory, loud-voiced and rough in manner. The recital of these defects of physique and temperament serves only to throw into stronger relief the qualities which more than compensated the defects: his sincerity, piety, and virtue; his humane and benevolent heart; his learning and correctness of taste; the fertility of his imagination; his reasoning powers; his wit and humour. Boswell, who details these aspects of Johnson, not only 'venerated and loved' him but also made possible the veneration and love of successive generations of Johnsonians. Though Boswell's Samuel Johnson was no invention, he was beyond question a creation. From Johnson's letters some portrait of the man could be constructed, but his true genius and the fascination of his personality were most evident in the varied tones and moods of his conversation, richly and uniquely preserved by Boswell with the fidelity of an honest biographer but also with the imaginative insight of a great novelist or playwright.

Only tardy justice has been done to Boswell. The belated discovery of the Boswell Papers (*see below*, p. 225 ff.) brought to view so different a Boswell from the one previously imagined that he can no longer be dismissed as a satellite of the man he honoured with the supreme biography.

For more than fifty of Johnson's seventy-five years he was unknown to Boswell, who was therefore compelled to collect particulars of two-thirds of his life mainly from Johnson himself but partly from other sources. In the published book those fifty years occupied only about one-fifth of the total space, and the greatness of the *Life* depends upon the four-fifths dealing with the last twenty-five years, when Boswell was able to store his own material.

Johnson came from Lichfield in Staffordshire, where his father was a bookseller. Born there on 18 September 1709 he suffered in infancy from the scrofula which afflicted him throughout his life and caused his extremely weak eyesight. In spite of congenital indolence and inertia his memory was phenomenal, and he absorbed knowledge with remarkable rapidity at Lichfield Grammar School and afterwards at Stourbridge, though he attributed his proficiency in Latin to the wholesome effects of sound whipping. On the other hand, he blamed upon his schoolboy fondness for reading romances of chivalry the later 'unsettled turn of mind which prevented his ever fixing in any profession'. He professed to have idled at home for two years after leaving Stourbridge Grammar School when he was sixteen, but it seems that he undertook a great deal of reading of the classics. He went to Oxford in October 1728 as a Commoner of Pembroke College, at the instance, it is said, of a wealthy former schoolfellow who promised but failed to support him. After little more than a year there, he was forced by poverty—'so extreme that his shoes were worn out, and his feet appeared through them'—to return to Lichfield, where the bookselling business was in a poor way. Michael Johnson, his father, died in 1731, leaving Samuel only £20. In the next year he spent a few unhappy months as an usher at Market Bosworth School, Leicestershire, going from there as guest-assistant to a Birmingham bookseller, who paid Johnson five guineas for his first literary work, a translation from the French of *A Voyage to Abyssinia* by a Portuguese Jesuit priest, Jerome Lobo. In the same year (1735) he married Elizabeth Porter, a widow twenty years older than himself. Boswell gives a comical account by Johnson himself of the couple's journey on horseback from Birmingham to Derby for the wedding:

> Sir, she had read the old romances, and had got into her head the fantastical notion that a woman of spirit should use her husband like a dog. So, Sir, at first she told me that I rode too fast, and she could not keep up with me; and, when I rode a little slower, she passed me, and complained that I lagged behind. I was not to be made the slave of caprice; and I resolved to begin as I meant to end. I therefore pushed on briskly, till I was fairly out of her sight. The road lay between two hedges, so I was sure she could not miss it; and I contrived that she should soon come up with me. When she did, I observed her to be in tears.

The marriage, notwithstanding this curious prelude, was a happy one, and Johnson's references to his wife (who died in 1752) were, to the end of his own life more than thirty years later, always marked by affectionate devotion.

A boarding school which he started at Edial, near Lichfield, in 1736 failed, and with one of his very few pupils, David Garrick,[1] he started for London in March 1737. Johnson

[1] See below, pp. 190–1.

worked for Edward Cave, publisher of *The Gentleman's Magazine* —to which he contributed, during the next ten years or so, verse, essays, biographical sketches, and accounts of parliamentary proceedings under the heading *Reports of the Debates in the Senate of Lilliput* (1740–43), sometimes loosely based upon (but certainly not reporting) members' speeches, which he did not attend to hear and at least occasionally fabricated.

His first independent work, *London: A Poem in Imitation of the Third Satire of Juvenal*, published by Dodsley in May 1738, reflects through some 260 lines in rhyming couplets the sorry state of London at that time, politically and otherwise:

> Here malice, rapine, accident, conspire,
> And now a rabble rages, now a fire;
> Their ambush here relentless ruffians lay,
> And here the fell attorney prowls for prey;
> Here falling houses thunder on your head,
> And here a female atheist talks you dead.

Apart from the *Debates in the Senate of Lilliput* and in 1744 *An Account of the Life of Mr. Richard Savage*,[1] Johnson produced nothing important until he addressed to Lord Chesterfield the *Plan of a Dictionary of the English Language* (1747). Chesterfield claimed that his failure to respond was inadvertent when Johnson attacked him in a letter following the publication of the *Dictionary* (1755), which Chesterfield commended in two articles contributed to *The World*. Johnson thereupon wrote:

> When I had once addressed your Lordship in publick, I had exhausted all the art of pleasing which a retired and uncourtly scholar can possess. . . . Is not a Patron, my Lord, one who looks with unconcern on a man struggling for life in the water, and, when he has reached ground, encumbers him with help? The notice which you have been pleased to take of my labours, had it been early, had been kind; but it has been delayed until I am indifferent, and cannot enjoy it; till I am solitary, and cannot impart it; till I am known and do not court it.

[1] Richard Savage (?–1743), who posed as the illegitimate son of titled parents, was a meagrely talented playwright and versifier, author of *The Bastard* (1728) and *The Wanderer* (1729). His origins and life were more commonplace than Johnson's account of them, and he died in squalor, having only narrowly escaped hanging for murder.

With six assistants the task of compiling the *Dictionary* [1] took Johnson eight years instead of the three years he had estimated. His purpose was to make a dictionary 'by means of which the pronunciation of our language may be fixed, and its attainment facilitated; by which its purity may be preserved, its use ascertained, and its duration lengthened'. The Preface, relating largely to the method of dealing with the illustrative quotations and the sources drawn upon for them, remains one of Johnson's best and most characteristic pieces. Its references to the illnesses and other handicaps which beset him during the labour

CANA'RY. *n. f.* [from the *Canary* iflands.] Wine brought from the Canaries; fack.

   I will to my honeft knight Falftaff, and drink *canary* with him.——I think I fhall drink in pipe wine firft with him; I'll make him dance.   *Shak:fpear:.*

To CANA'RY. *v. a.* A cant word, which feems to fignify to frolick. ✕✕✕

   Mafter, will you win your love with a French brawl?—— How mean'ft thou, brawling in French?——No, my compleat mafter; but to jigg off a tune at the tongue's end, *canary* to it with your feet, humour it with turning up your eyelids.
                                              Shakefp. L:ve's Labour Loft.

CANA'RY BIRD. An excellent finging bird, of a green colour, formerly bred in the Canaries, and no where elfe, but now bred in feveral parts of Europe, particularly Germany.

   Of finging birds, they have linnets, goldfinches, ruddock, *canary birds*, blackbirds, thrufhes, and divers other.
                                              Carew's Survey of Cornwall.

Canary was the name of a particular Dance, of this I have met with many Instances in the old Plays.

An entry from the third edition of his *Dictionary* corrected by Johnson

of compilation are moving, though perhaps not free from background whispers of self-pity. Boswell records the stages in the progress of the work and also its completion in the large upper room of the house in Gough Square, off Fleet Street, which is preserved as a Johnson memorial.

The *Dictionary* was indebted in some measure to earlier lexicographers, but a vast amount of the etymological and other material was Johnson's own. Inevitably it has long since been displaced by later dictionaries, but all its successors owe more than a little to Johnson, though his spirited eccentricity in occasionally defining words according to his prejudices is a liberty no longer enjoyed or coveted by philologists.

[1] Published in two folio volumes as *A Dictionary of the English Language, in which the Words are deduced from their Originals, and illustrated in their different Significations by Examples from the Best Writers.*

His other long poem *The Vanity of Human Wishes* (1749) is also an 'imitation' from Juvenal (the Tenth Satire), but more universal in its aim than *London*. It is comprehensively though not profoundly pessimistic; Johnson was not a good enough poet to touch the depths of human experience and here he expresses, a self-indulgent distemper rather than a philosophy. But the poem has well-remembered lines: 'Let observation with extensive view, Survey mankind, from China to Peru'; 'He left the name, at which the world grew pale, To point a moral, or adorn a tale'; 'Hides from himself his state, and shuns to know, That life protracted is protracted woe'. Many of the lines are so well turned that their technical efficiency goes far towards disguising the specious but essentially gimcrack cynicism:

> Should no Disease thy torpid veins invade,
> Nor Melancholy's phantoms haunt thy shade;
> Yet hope not life from grief or danger free,
> Nor think the doom of man revers'd for thee:
> Deign on the passing world to turn thine eyes,
> And pause awhile from letters to be wise;
> There mark what ills the scholar's life assail,
> Toil, envy, want, the patron, and the jail.

Lacking Pope's agility and audacity of wit, Johnson's satire is ponderous and heavy-footed. The absence of genuine satirical conviction from *The Vanity of Human Wishes* leads the poem in its final twelve lines to suffer a kind of death-bed repentance as a concession to formal piety.

While Johnson was hoping in vain for more pupils at Edial in 1736, he began a blank-verse tragedy called *Irene*, and leaving London for a while in the middle of the following year he finished the play at Lichfield. His efforts to get it performed were fruitless until, after more than ten years, it was put on under David Garrick's management at Drury Lane on 6 February 1749, a few days before it appeared in print. When Garrick insisted on certain enlivening changes (such as the strangling of the heroine in sight of the audience) which violated the principles of 'classical' drama, the author strove unavailingly to preserve the integrity of his text. The play had nine performances, helped out with farces and dancing on the last three nights. In spite of a cast which included Garrick himself, Barry, and Mrs. Cibber, and magnificent costumes and staging, the reception was disappointing, but Johnson's £195 from the theatre and £100 from Dodsley, the publisher, was a far more substantial reward than his previous works had brought. *Irene* (renamed *Mahomet and Irene* for the theatre) is totally undramatic, and comprises only a succession of declamatory speeches. There is no breath of life in any character; indeed there are no real characters, only name-labels. The failure of *Irene*, however, was due less to Johnson's ignorance of the elements of a stage play than to the futility of the kind of composition to which it belonged. He himself pointed to the root of the matter when he wrote some thirty years later (*c*.1780) in his essay on Addison in the *Lives of the English Poets*: '[*Cato*] is rather a poem in dialogue than a drama, rather a succession of just sentiments in elegant language, than a representation of natural affections, or of any state probable or possible in human life. . . . The emulation of parties made it successful beyond expectation, and its success has introduced or confirmed among us the use of dialogue too declamatory, of unaffecting elegance, and chill philosophy.'

From 20 March 1750 to 14 March 1752 Johnson was issuing each Tuesday and Saturday *The Rambler*, a periodical after the pattern of *The Spectator* but without the humour and verve of Addison and Steele. He displayed a somewhat lighter touch in 'The Idler' essays which appeared every Saturday in the *Universal Chronicle* from 15 April 1758 to 5 April 1760. In these he introduced himself as Mr. Sober, and other named characters include Tom Tempest, 'a steady friend to the house of Stuart'; Jack Sneaker, 'a hearty adherent to the present establishment'; and Dick Minim, the critic, who inherited a fortune after his apprenticeship to a brewer:

. . . being now at liberty to follow his genius, he resolved to be a man of wit and humour. That he might be properly initiated in his new character, he frequented the coffee-houses near the theatres, where he listened very diligently, day after day, to those who talked of language and sentiments, and unities and catastrophies, till by slow degrees he began to think that he understood something of the stage, and hoped in time to talk himself.

In 1756 Johnson issued his *Proposals for printing the Dramatick Works of William Shakespeare* (*see below*, p. 228). He had been

To Mr Longman Bookseller
Paternoster Row

Sir

The Contract fairly engrossed was sent to me yesterday, I suppose by Mr Knapton's direction who is out of town. I should think it a favour if You and the rest of the Gentlemen would breakfast with me that we may sign. If You will appoint a day and write a note to the rest, the Bearer will take it to each of them, or if any other place be more convenient, the writings shall be brought wherever You shall desire it.

Sir,

Your humble servant

Sam: Johnson

At the golden Anchor near
Holborn Bars

given the honorary degree of M.A. at Oxford the year before, when the *Dictionary* was about to appear, but fortune did not accompany fame and in 1759 he was compelled to labour at *The History of Rasselas, Prince of Abissinia* (written in seven evenings) and to sell the first edition for £100 to pay his mother's funeral expenses and to clear her debts. *Rasselas* is not easy to classify. It has been called 'a didactic romance', and might equally well be called 'a novel with a purpose', or 'an essay in philosophical fiction'. Rasselas, fourth son of the emperor, glutted with luxury and ease, sets out from his native 'happy valley' with his sister and a philosophical old mentor Imlac, who, having told the story of his earlier wanderings about the world, sums up his experience in the conclusion that 'Human life is every where a state in which much is to be endured, and little to be enjoyed'. The three proceed to Cairo and elsewhere in Egypt, observing the state of people in several walks of life and at length returning to their own land:

> The princess thought, that of all sublunary things, knowledge was the best: She desired first to learn all sciences, and then purposed to found a college of learned women. . . . The prince desired a little kingdom, in which he might administer justice in his own person, and see all the parts of government with his own eyes; but he could never fix the limits of his dominion. . . . Imlac was contented to be driven along the stream of life without directing [his] course to any particular port.

The last chapter of *Rasselas*, in which that passage appears, is headed 'The conclusion, in which nothing is concluded' and its final paragraph includes the sentence 'Of these wishes that they had formed they well knew that none could be obtained.' Though the book ends on this seemingly hopeless note, a view of the good life is implicit throughout, even if only negatively, for in the successive statements of the discontents of the philosophers, the great ones, the hermit, the monks of St. Anthony, and others, the deeper needs of humanity are implicit. And while *Rasselas* has little story, and little entertainment value as fiction, it sustains a quiet interest which leads the reader easily through its unexciting prose. A passage in chapter VI has taken on a sharper significance in the present century. When Rasselas discusses with an artist acquaintance ways of escape from the mountain-girt valley, flying is mooted. The artist undertakes to experiment, but only on condition of secrecy:

> If men were all virtuous . . . I should with great alacrity teach them all to fly. But what would be the security of the good, if the bad could at pleasure invade them from the sky? Against an army sailing through the clouds neither walls, nor mountains, nor seas, could afford any security. A flight of northern savages might hover in the wind, and light at once with irresistible violence upon the capital of a fruitful region that was rolling under them.

The next three or four years of Johnson's life were crucial. When *Rasselas* appeared he was nearly fifty, and though he was esteemed and eminent he was also poor and had little expectation of better fortune. George III, however, on coming to the English throne in 1760 desired to recognize and encourage the arts. Among those who benefited was Johnson, a pension of £300 yearly being conferred upon him in 1762 on the understanding from the Prime Minister (Lord Bute) that it did not commit him to become a government propagandist: 'It is not given you for anything you are to do,' said Bute, 'but for what you have done.' In the following year Johnson and Boswell first met (16 May 1763), and in 1764 Joshua Reynolds proposed the foundation of The Club.[1]

Now, at the age of fifty-four, Johnson had an income, a regular audience of distinguished and like-minded friends, and a biographer.

[1] See below, pp. 230–1.

CHAPTER X

THE NOVEL IN MATURITY

THERE is less difficulty in defining 'the Novel' than in fitting novels to an acceptable general definition. 'A fictitious prose narrative of considerable length, in which characters and actions representative of real life are portrayed in a plot of more or less complexity': so runs the Oxford Dictionary definition, and though it cannot easily be bettered many novelists would repudiate it. That a novel should be fictitious few would dispute, yet many novels have drawn extensively upon fact. That the fictitious element, when present, should be representative of real life is a condition violated by thousands of novels warmly approved by multitudes of novel-readers. That there should be a plot is no longer a requirement in 'literary' novels written for an intellectual minority content with a 'situation' requiring no entanglement or unravelling, no intrigue or excitement, only some emanation of circumstance and personality which may have duration but has neither beginning nor end. Orthodox critics faced with a modern novel of that kind are prone to declare that it is no novel at all, though it is in fact a kind that goes back at least as far as Laurence Sterne, who cared nothing for plot and everything for the freedom to wheedle language into giving form to evanescent thought however fantastical and to wandering fancy however profound.

In literary history the Novel has been the arch-rogue and vagabond, stealing into every preserve and establishing illicit relationships in every quarter. There have been novels in verse (e.g. Chaucer's *Troilus and Criseyde* and Browning's *The Ring and the Book*), novels of action, novels of character, biographical novels, historical novels, religious novels, political and sociological novels, psychological and philosophical novels, subjective novels, novels of sentiment, humorous novels, and such unclassifiable 'novels' as James Joyce's *Finnegans Wake*. No single formula could embrace them all, and it would be vain to seek a formula so comprehensive that no 'novel' could be held to contravene it. We can, it seems, ask no more in the twentieth century than that *a novel should treat of some aspect of being, actual or imagined, presented in a manner not exclusively factual, usually at length and usually in prose.* In the English Novel as it was shaped in the eighteenth century, however, there were clearer and firmer outlines.

References have already been made in earlier chapters to tentative approaches to the Novel in the Elizabethan period;[1] by the writers of the seventeenth-century 'Characters'; by Bunyan, Defoe, and Swift; and by Steele and Addison in *The Spectator.* The Elizabethans could conduct a fictional narrative, but they were spellbound by words, and prose became for them like an enchanted wood, delightful to wander in and peopled almost exclusively by figures of romance. *The Pilgrim's Progress, Robinson Crusoe,* and *Gulliver's Travels* have action and adventure and progress, economy and directness of language, but little sense of human character and its development: Christian, Crusoe, and Gulliver retain an umbilical attachment to their literary creators, who saw life in terms of religion or politics far more than in terms of individual personality. Something at least of the missing humanity was provided by Steele and Addison in the de Coverley papers, where Sir Roger himself and his companions have the semblance of creatures of flesh and blood, however formalized in presentation by the requirements of urbane writing.

Up to 1740, the year in which Richardson's *Pamela* appeared, no one had succeeded in doing for the reader of prose what Chaucer had done in poetry three and a half centuries before and Shakespeare had done in the theatre more than a century before: i.e. create men and women in the round and endow them with an independent existence, so that for the reader or spectator they appeared as the masters or as the victims of their own destiny, not puppets dancing on strings in the author's hands. Within little more than thirty years from the date of *Pamela,* the tradition of the English novel of character, action, and humour was fully shaped and virtually settled. The nineteenth-century novelists were to carry the novel to greater heights, but for the most part they built upon foundations laid by Richardson, Fielding, and Smollett, while Sterne was to be

[1] See Ward: I, 128, 153 ff.

taken as master in the twentieth century by novelists so patently unlike as H. G. Wells and Virginia Woolf.

So long as the theatre kept its hold upon polite society, play-going and playreading went far to occupy spare hours unclaimed by the more exacting social activities of the leisured. The decline of the theatre and of its fashionableness in the eighteenth century created something of a vacuum in the lives of many of its former habitués and these formed the substantial nucleus of a new reading public. Women readers had, before long, discovered the attractions of fiction through French novels, such as Mme de Scudery's vast *Le Grand Cyrus* (1649–53) and Mme de la Fayette's *La Princesse de Clèves* (1678), but these had no successful competitors in England though they had numerous rivals, among them *Oroonoko; or The History of the Royal Slave* (*c.* 1678) by Mrs. Aphra Behn (1640–89), which foreshadowed the sentimental humanitarianism of Rousseau and his school in the second half of the eighteenth century.

Among the countless readers of *Robinson Crusoe* and *Gulliver's Travels* must have been many women, but neither of these books, nor *Moll Flanders* and Defoe's other novels, could be taken feelingly to the female heart. It was upon that heart-hungry public that Richardson's *Pamela* descended as an unheralded emotional bounty.

Samuel Richardson

An exceptionally penetrating eye would have been needed to see in Samuel Richardson (1689–1761), before the event, the founder of the modern English novel. His father was a joiner in Derbyshire, where Samuel was born. While still a child, his solemn demeanour appeared to fit him for training as a parson, but no money was forthcoming. He set up as a moralist before he was eleven, writing (in the guise of a grown-up) to rebuke a backbiting and scandal-loving widow of fifty; and in his earliest teens he was providing model love-letters for three young sewing-women who told him, separately and confidentially, of the vagaries of their suitors. Absurd though the boy's situation might appear in such company, it was then that he began to acquire the curious knowledge of the nature of women which was to be the striking feature of his novels. At sixteen he was sent to London as a stationer's apprentice married his master's daughter, became the owner of a printing business in the neighbourhood of Fleet Street, was appointed printer of the House of Commons proceedings, and in due course rose to be Master of the Stationers' Company.

Two fellow printers and booksellers commissioned him to write 'a little volume of letters, in a common style, on such subjects as might be of use to country readers' unable to compose for themselves. This also included letters suitable to be written by 'handsome girls' in domestic service, with guidance on how to avoid 'the snares that might be laid against their virtue'. This volume, *Familiar Letters*,[1] came out in 1741, after the project had borne other fruit in the previous year, for the letters-for-handsome-girls notion led Richardson to a more dramatic presentation of a particular case of Virtue in Peril and Virtue Triumphant in the novel, *Pamela; or Virtue Rewarded*, which took fashionable London by the heart-strings and tear-ducts and was found scarcely less impressive by continental readers.

Rarely has a great novel to surmount so many internal obstacles as are planted in *Pamela*. Ridiculous, incredible, morally repulsive, pompous, tedious, it is nevertheless a fascinating masterpiece, to be read deliberately and at a mature age if its merits are to be seen more readily than its faults. It is ridiculous because of its solemn humourlessness; incredible because no servant girl with work to do would have had time to write so voluminously (nor would she have been articulate enough); morally repulsive because the girl's 'virtue' is little better than a form of calculating prudence; pompous because it strikes so many attitudes; tedious because the style is so frequently without either tone or colour.

Wherein, then, lies the fascination of *Pamela*? wherein its right to rank as a masterpiece? The answer to both questions must be: In its authenticity. Pamela is a *real* person, and a Pamela—a live Pamela—would have been what Richardson's Pamela is: ridiculous, boring, pompous on her own small scale, cunningly chaste. Her incredibility is only apparent if the

[1] Its full title was *Letters written to and for particular Friends, on the most important Occasions. Directing not only the requisite Style and Forms to be observed in writing Familiar Letters; but how to think and act justly and prudently in the common Concerns of Human Life.*

III. *Pamela is married.*

A scene from Richardson's *Pamela* by Joseph Highmore

reader declines to accept the author's chosen convention for the presentation of his story. All the conventions available to a novelist are incredible in some degree to a non-cooperative reader: the novel-in-letters convention is not the most incredible, and the egotism of the principal letter-writer in *Pamela* is only more evident than in most examples of first-person narration because Pamela lacks the sophistication to cover her egotism. Once the ridiculousness and the rest of the obstacles in *Pamela* have been faced (and to face them squarely is to surmount them), the excellence, the authenticity and essential truth, the humanity and understanding, and the curiously touching genuineness of emotion and affection beneath the girl's disingenuous prudence—these qualities predominate.

The faults and the virtues of Richardson's novel were the faults and virtues of Richardson himself. He was mawkishly moral, but his morality was genuine, and his mawkishness was free from guile. He was, for a large part of his life, fussed over by immoderately admiring women who aggravated his inborn disposition towards priggishness, but if this accounts for a certain want of masculine robustness it is compensated by his unique ability to probe to the centre of a woman's nature, whether in the semi-comic situation of Pamela or in the tragic situation of Clarissa Harlowe in his second novel.

The more complex exchange of letters in *Clarissa; or, The History of a Young Lady* (1748)—between Clarissa and her friend Miss Howe on the one part, and her ravisher Lovelace and his friend Bedford on the other—slows the narrative and makes Clarissa's ordeal and fate a drawn-out agony; yet, surprisingly, it does not reduce the tragic intensity nor blur the impression of inevitability. Abduction and seduction (designed or effected) provide the theme for each of Richardson's three novels, but in the third, *The History of Sir Charles Grandison: in a Series of Letters published from the Originals by the Editor of Pamela and Clarissa* (1753-4), he shifts the focus of interest to a male character and succeeds only in demonstrating how much less penetrating was his vision when turned upon the nature of men. His long preoccupation with the protection of female sexual virtue gives an oddly epicene character to his work, and this undoubtedly accounts for the readiness of his male contemporaries to consider him a namby-pamby and a figure of fun.

The magnitude of Richardson's achievement is dwarfed for present-day readers by the greater novels written in the intervening two centuries. He should be judged, however, in the light of what had not been done by his predecessors, rather than by comparison with all that has been done by his successors. As a novelist Richardson had two root-and-branch weaknesses: he could not tell a story and he was insufferably long-winded. Either one of these weaknesses might have been carried off; but, together, they have fatally tried the patience of posterity and relegated Richardson to the company of the masters who are greatly lauded and persistently unread. Yet an age like the present, obsessed as it is by a ceaseless itch for psychological probing, can only through ignorance or through want of mental staying-power neglect the father of the psychological novel.

Henry Fielding

Though Richardson's contemporary popularity was not universal and he was derided by some, he has been excellently avenged. In addition to establishing his own kind of novel he was also instrumental in establishing its opposite kind, the kind which at length reached its height in Dickens. Contemptuous of *Pamela*, a barrister who was also a minor playwright and a journalist set out to parody it. The result was Fielding's novel, *The History of the Adventures of Joseph Andrews, and of his Friend Mr. Abraham Adams*, which purported to be a mocking account of the experiences of Pamela's brother under temptation by his employer, Lady Booby, as Pamela had been by her Mr. B. Happily, before the book was far advanced, the characters took charge of the author and subordinated the original derisive intention. *Joseph Andrews* therefore became far less a parody of Richardson than the first of a new kind of novel which coming generations of writers were to prove inexhaustible and capable of infinite variation.

Henry Fielding (1707–54) was born near Glastonbury, at Sharpham Park in Somerset, and coming of a propertied family he enjoyed advantages of upbringing and education denied to Richardson, who was already working in London at the time of his future tormentor's birth. Fielding went to Eton, where the future statesmen Henry Fox and the elder Pitt were among his schoolfellows, and then to Leyden to study law. At the age of about twenty-one he began to write burlesques of current theatrical fashions,[1] and before long was using the stage as a platform for political satire. This led to the imposition of censorship under the Licensing Act of 1737. His career in the theatre wrecked, Fielding turned back to the law, becoming a barrister of the Middle Temple in 1740, the year of *Pamela*. Whether he had any hand in *An Apology for the Life of Mrs. Shamela Andrews* (1741) is unknown. Richardson believed this burlesque to be by Fielding, but it seems unlikely, since he must already have been busy with the finer parody which became *Joseph Andrews*, published anonymously in the next year. The third edition (1743) was the first to bear the author's name.

Whereas Richardson's novels are largely static, Fielding's are full of movement and bustling life. Richardson's, dedicated to virtue, are unable to exclude vice in ugly forms; while Fielding's, irreverent to prudery and not over-tender to conventional morality, are free from viciousness through their liveliness of spirit and outdoor healthfulness. In Richardson's books there is always some sense of an enclosed laboratory where a section of humanity is under microscopic observation. Fielding, on the contrary, flings the doors of the world wide open, and life—rude and gentle, gay and drab, generous and mean—comes tumbling in. His world is Vanity Fair on the largest scale and he is its enthusiastic and talkative showman, not only moving among the characters but stepping up at intervals to address the audience directly on this and that. In *Joseph Andrews* the first chapters of Books I, II, and III, like the opening chapters of all eighteen Books of *Tom Jones*, are literary essays such as *The Tatler* or *The Spectator* might have printed and are completely detachable from the novels. But to detach them, or to pass them over unread, would detract from the total effect, for though Fielding, unlike Richardson, was an outward-looking, extroverted man, he was nevertheless *in* his novels from beginning to end—enthusiastically running the show, as it were, and not (as Jane Austen was to do) withdrawing to the wings and letting the show appear to run itself. The world is so full of a number of things, Fielding seems aware, that he

[1] See below, pp. 200–201, for further reference to Fielding's plays.

cannot refrain from buttonholing his audience at intervals and pouring into their ears some matter that interests him. Thus, in the first chapter of Book III of *Joseph Andrews* he discourses on biography, on romances, and on his own methods as a novelist. In that last connection he writes:

> . . . I declare here once for all, I describe not men, but manners; not an individual, but a species. Perhaps it will be answered, are not the characters then taken from life? To which I answer in the affirmative; nay I believe I might aver, that I have writ little more than I have seen.

Fielding in fact did more than he here proclaims, more perhaps than he was aware. He certainly drew upon life and wrote of what he knew; it may be the case that he described species; but what went far towards making him a great novelist was his then unprecedented gift for individualizing characters so that they behave as persons, not stand as types. His novels may be novels of manners, but it is incomparably more important that they are novels of humanity, of men and women in character and action. He was not without bias, for he had a satirically humorous eye and delighted more in oddity than in the ordinary. The virtuous heroine of his last novel, *Amelia*, is too good to be true, and though Squire Allworthy and Sophia Western in *Tom Jones* are normally good and also likeable, the Fielding characters most enjoyed and best remembered are the good but eccentric Parson Adams and the schoolmaster Partridge, Tom Jones's companion. His unpleasant characters—notably Thwackum, Square, and Blifil in *Tom Jones*—are little less memorable; and he has great comic characters in Mrs. Slipslop, Mrs. Tow-wouse, Parson Trulliber (*Joseph Andrews*), and Molly Seagrim, whose Homeric battle with the mob in the churchyard is one of the immortal passages in *Tom Jones*.

When Joseph Andrews lost his situation after evading the amorous advances of Lady Booby and Mrs. Slipslop and set out from London for the village where his sweetheart Fanny lived, he started on a series of wanderings and varied experiences which, though they are presented dramatically, enabled Fielding to bring into the novels much implicit criticism of contemporary conditions and standards. Joseph is set upon, robbed, and stripped by footpads; the stage coach which (against the will of most of the passengers) picks him up is waylaid by highwaymen; while subsequent chapters introduce conversational discourses on morals, education, religion, and other matters of public interest. One of the ironies of literary history is that Fielding has often been, and in some places is still, regarded askance as a writer of improper novels. Not only is this a crass misconception of his purpose as a writer but, also, it obscures the fact that Fielding was an active social reformer. Appointed a justice of the peace for Westminster in 1748, he conducted a successful campaign for the suppression of the gangsterism which was rife in the metropolis, and attacked among other public evils the appalling drunkenness which Hogarth's pictures were simultaneously exposing. In *The Life of Jonathan Wild the Great* (1743) Fielding employed the novel to depict with devastating satire the career, the companions, and the end of a rogue who achieved his evil brand of greatness by reversing all the decencies of human behaviour, and continued 'great' to the last by picking the chaplain's pocket a moment before he is himself hanged.

The charges of impropriety brought against Fielding are on account of his masterpiece *The History of Tom Jones, a Foundling* (1749), and arise from the hero's relationship with the elderly Lady Bellaston. Tom, abandoned when a baby and brought up in Somerset by Squire Allworthy, falls in love with Sophia Western, daughter of a neighbouring squire, but through his association with Molly Seagrim, a gamekeeper's daughter, and the illwill of Thwackum, Square, and Blifil he loses his benefactor's confidence and affection and departs for Bristol intending to go to sea. After varied adventures he encounters a philosophical barber known as Little Benjamin, whom he discovers to be Partridge the schoolmaster who had left his home after a false accusation of being Tom's father. The two travel together to Gloucester and elsewhere, at last reaching London by a roundabout route through Coventry and St. Albans. Sophia had also gone to London to avoid marriage with the odious Blifil, and she and Tom (who is found to be Squire Allworthy's nephew) come together through Lady Bellaston, who had before caused trouble to both.

While the story might seem to be the least part of *Tom Jones*, it does serve as a spine to the novel, providing an articulated form and a structural anchorage for the many incidents and episodes in which the characters are involved. For the most part the book takes a refreshingly kindly view of humanity. If Tom has few bedroom scruples he also has no mean vices. He is a whole person, generous in nature, healthy in spirit, and a worthy mate for the wholesome and pleasing Sophia. Fielding lived up to the claim made in the first pages of *Tom Jones*: 'The provision . . . we have here made is no other than *Human Nature*', and there is no English novel for which that admirable and ambitious claim could more confidently be made.

Tobias Smollett

Fielding presented Human Nature in his novels, but he did not exhaust the subject nor display all its aspects. When the full horror beneath the satirical surface of *Jonathan Wild* is recognized, there might seem to be little else to reveal of humanity on its darker side. But *Jonathan Wild* is not a realistic novel. It does not aim to show roguery and crime 'in the raw'. It is, on the contrary, a highly intellectualized and carefully finished exercise in literary artistry which makes its shattering effect largely by contrast between the medium and the subject. It has neither the filth of the stews nor the stink of the gaol.

With Smollett it is otherwise. His account of Bridewell in *Roderick Random* reproduces the hero's own impression of the place—that it 'approaches nearest the notion I had always entertained of the infernal regions'; while in the account of conditions on board the *Thunder* the nauseating stench of the sick berth and the brutalities of naval life are conveyed without verbal gloss. Smollett's novels survive by the power of his writing, naked and raw, not by literary effects. The naval passages have in them the surge and thunder, the blood and dirt, of barbarous necessity.

Tobias Smollett (1721–71) was the son of Sir James Smollett, provost of Dumbarton. He went to Glasgow University, but, having no money, embarked at the age of twenty as surgeon's mate on the *Cumberland*, was at the Carthagena battle, and married in Jamaica. Returning to London in 1744 he practised as a surgeon in Downing Street and, influenced by Le Sage's picaresque novel *Gil Blas*, wrote *Roderick Random* (1748), which describes the adventures and hardships of the impoverished

Roderick first as a pressed man in the British navy, afterwards in the French army, and still later as a ship's surgeon. There is a great deal of rumbustious adventure and not a little that is disgusting; but the tang of actual experience is everywhere present, and the rip-roaring Tom Bowling has passed into fancy as a representative old-time British naval officer: '. . . He was a strong-built man, somewhat bandy-legged, with a neck line like that of a bull, and a face which (you might easily perceive) had withstood the most obstinate assaults of the weather', and his language matched his appearance.

Smollett's output during the next twenty years included four more novels; a translation of *Don Quixote* (1755); a *History of England* (1757); a considerable quantity of political journalism (he was imprisoned in 1759 for uttering a libel in *The Critical Review*, which he edited); a farcical play, *The Reprisal* (1757); *The History and Adventures of an Atom* (1769), an indecent political satire. A health journey to the Continent in 1763 produced his *Travels through France and Italy* (1766), in a series of letters dated mainly from Nice. Sterne, who met him abroad, refers to him in *A Sentimental Journey* as 'the learned Smelfungus' who 'set out with the spleen and the jaundice, and every object he pass'd by was discoloured or distorted. He wrote an account of them, but 'twas nothing but the account of his miserable feelings.'

Of Smollett's novels after *Roderick Random*, the best are *The Adventures of Peregrine Pickle* (1751), which has in Commodore Hawser Trunnion a fuller portrait of the 'sea-dog' type than Tom Bowling, and *The Expedition of Humphry Clinker* (1771), a novel in letters which is politer in style than the rest of Smollett's work. *Ferdinand Count Fathom* (1753) and *Sir Lancelot Greaves* (1760–2) have little merit.

Laurence Sterne

If anyone can be said to have made an implicit declaration of independence for the Novel, Sterne is that one. Twenty years after *Pamela* he began to publish *Tristram Shandy*, which is mainly a vast digression; and *A Sentimental Journey* (1768) which would rarely be called a novel if it could by any stretch be fitted into another category.

An unlikely novelist, Laurence Sterne (1713–68) was a still more unlikely clergyman. Born at Clonmel in Ireland, where his father was at the time a serving officer in the English army, he went to school in Halifax before going to Jesus College, Cambridge; then, entering the Anglican Church, he became vicar of Sutton-in-the-Forest, near York, from 1738 to 1759. In 1741 he married Elizabeth Lumley—cousin of Lady Mary Wortley Montagu—to whom he wrote during the two years of their courtship the *Letters to Eliza* (published 1775). The marriage was unhappy, principally because of Sterne's unstable affections, and his wife became insane in 1758. An allegory he published in 1759, on a local ecclesiastical dispute, hit the centre of the target so forcibly that, in spite of his agreeing to withdraw and destroy the pamphlet, the attention it received persuaded him to take to authorship. The first product of the new activity was volumes I and II of *The Life and Opinions of Tristram Shandy, Gentleman* (1760; III–VI, 1761–2; VII–VIII, 1765; IX, 1767). Tristram hardly gets into the book at all. He is not born until volume IV, and he makes no further appearance after volume VI, being at that point no more than breeched. It is for the most part a wonderfully entertaining conversation-piece which rambles over the strange assortment of topics that heterogeneous reading had packed into Sterne's brain. Much of the material may be secondhand and irrelevant, but in its new presentation it becomes one of the most original books of all time, and its characters—Walter Shandy, Mrs. Shandy, Uncle Toby, Corporal Trim, Dr. Slop, Parson Yorick, the Widow Wadman—are a joy. Sterne's taste for sly indecencies is as organic in his writings as the excretory apparatus is in human beings, and is as inevitably to be accepted without vain disgust. There are, indeed, moments when he effects a surprising union between impropriety and wisdom.

Sterne adopted the pseudonym Mr. Yorick on the title-page of *A Sentimental Journey through France and Italy* (1768), which he left unfinished. Here, more than a century before psychologists invented the phrase, 'free association of ideas' has its fling. The book is more a journey around a mind than a journey in space and therefore nothing is incongruous, whether it be such an aside as 'if I am a piece of a philosopher, which Satan now and then puts it into my head that I am', or the reflections on liberty and captivity promoted by the sight of a caged starling, or the praise of the *Pont Neuf* as 'the noblest, the finest, the grandest, the lightest, the longest, the broadest that ever conjoin'd land and land together upon the face of the terraqueous globe'. Sterne had invented a literary hold-all which could be enlarged or contracted at will, and into which could be dropped alike the relevant and the irrelevant with the assurance of congruity.

CHAPTER XI

EIGHTEENTH-CENTURY DRAMA

BETWEEN 1707 and 1773—i.e. between Farquhar's *The Beaux'
Stratagem* and Goldsmith's *She Stoops to Conquer*—not a play
was written that continues to live by its merits as spoken drama.
The Beggar's Opera (1728) has outstripped all other eighteenth-
century stage pieces in the favour of twentieth-century
audiences, but without the new artful aids of stylized scenery
and costumes and new 'arrangements' by modern composers
or orchestrators, Gay's dialogue and verses would have been
less sure of continued favour.

Garrick and Others

Paradoxically, the sixty or seventy years which were barren of
plays with the vitality to survive, were years when the theatre
was vigorously alive. What are still the leading London
theatres were either founded or first made famous in the
eighteenth century: Covent Garden theatre was built in 1732,
preceded by the Haymarket theatre in 1720; while Drury Lane
theatre, opened in 1663, established itself as a national institution, after many vicissitudes, round about the middle of the
eighteenth century when Garrick brought into its chaos not
only his acting genius but also his organizing skill and sense
of discipline. The traditional belief that David Garrick
(1717–49) was the greatest of English actors cannot be either
proved or disproved. Too little can be gathered of the abilities
of such predecessors as Richard Burbage (1567–1619) and
Thomas Betterton (?1635–1710) to permit us to judge the
comparative rank of the three; nor is it possible to measure
Garrick's stature against Kean's or Irving's in the nineteenth
century. Contemporary references show that his style was more
naturalistic in speech and bearing than was usual in his time,
and his acknowledged authority and influence must therefore
have militated against the formal mannerisms of the pseudo-
classical mode which brought to birth, as well as others of the
kind, Addison's *Cato* and Johnson's *Irene*.

The autobiographical *Apology for the Life of Mr. Colley Cibber, Comedian* (1740) and the early biographies of Garrick [1] give a close view of the eighteenth-century theatre and its personalities, though no convincing explanation is yet forthcoming of the puzzling fact that ages of great acting do not coincide with ages of great playwriting. Neither Garrick nor Irving in their respective centuries found writers to provide great plays for them, and the fame of both was achieved in revivals of earlier masterpieces and superb performances in negligible pieces.

Garrick's own plays are of small literary interest. He made numerous adaptations of Shakespeare and others, wrote farces, and, most notably, collaborated with George Colman the elder (1732–94) in *The Clandestine Marriage* (1766). Colman, the son of a diplomat, was educated at Westminster and Oxford and studied law. Friendship with Garrick led him to play-writing, first with a farcical satire, *Polly Honeycombe* (1760), followed in the next year by *The Jealous Wife*, which Colman acknowledged to be indebted to Fielding's *Tom Jones*, *The Spectator*, and the *Adelphi* of Terence, as well as to Garrick, a multiple parentage which had only commonplace issue. In the five years between this play and *The Clandestine Marriage* either Colman's talent developed remarkably or he owed much to Garrick, who appears, indeed, to have worked at the character of Lord Ogleby, a decrepit old rake clinging to the illusion that he is still an acceptable lover for young women. The scenes between Ogleby and Fanny, which might easily have been disgusting, have both humour and pathos; and though Ogleby is a decayed ruin of a man, sustained by pills and cordial waters and palsy drops, rouged and requiring, as his valet says, 'a great deal of brushing, oiling, screwing, and winding up to set him going for the day', he is nevertheless a gentlemanly ruin with marks of breeding still upon him.

Steele's plays and Addison's *Cato* have already been discussed (*see above*, p. 126 ff.). Those of Mrs. Susannah Centlivre (?1667–1723)—the wife of Queen Anne's cook, who first met her when she was with a company of strolling players at Windsor—are mainly comedies of intrigue, among which

---

[1] Thomas Davies: *Memoirs of the Life of David Garrick* (1780); Arthur Murphy: *Life of David Garrick* (1801).

The Busy-Body (1709) had a fairly long stage-life after its first production at Drury Lane; Don Felix in *The Wonder! A Woman Keeps a Secret* (1714) was one of Garrick's successful parts; and *A Bold Stroke for a Wife* (1718), which shows in its London scenes Mrs. Centlivre's occasional talent in representing the bustle of working life, is the source of a familiar saying, 'the real Simon Pure', from the name of a Quaker character in the play.

Colley Cibber (1671–1757) survives only in the historically valuable autobiography mentioned above, but in his lifetime he achieved both fame and notoriety. He was Poet Laureate from 1730 and actor-manager at Drury Lane for a long period; but he was pompous and unpopular with the intellectuals, exciting the derision of Fielding and others, including Pope, who made him (in place of Lewis Theobald[1]) the hero of *The Dunciad* in its final version. Cibber's many plays, mostly comedies of sentiment which served their turn as acting pieces with a temporary appeal, included *Love's Last Shift* (1696), *The Careless Husband* (1705), and *The Provok'd Husband* (1728).

Farquhar

The playwriting career of George Farquhar (1677–1707) lasted less than ten years, and his best play, *The Beaux' Stratagem*, written in six weeks, was finished on his death-bed. He was then barely thirty, with three outstanding stage-pieces to his credit. Taking the dead material of Restoration comedy— upon which the plays of Congreve, Wycherley, and Vanbrugh had sprouted a bright fungus of wit—Farquhar injected new life into it, by degrees refined it, and substituted for the heartlessness of Restoration fashion the humour and humanity of a more democratic age. Though two generations and accelerated changes of taste divided them, Goldsmith as a playwright was the natural heir of Farquhar, who, even in his indifferent first play, *Love and a Bottle* (1698), had shown that he approached dramatic composition with a craftsman's care, not with the airy flourishes of an improvisator. He issued in 1702 *A Discourse . . . upon Comedy in reference to the English Stage*, developing points which Lyrick makes in conversation in *Love and a Bottle*:

---

[1] See above, pp. 147–8.

IV. A scene from Colman and Garrick's *The Clandestine Marriage* by Johann Zoffany

First, there's the decorum of time. . . . Then there's the exact-
ness of characters. . . . Then there's laying the drama. . . .
Then there are preparations of incidents, working the passions,
beauty of expression, closeness of plot, justness of place, turn of
language, opening the catastrophe. . . . As the catastrophe of
all tragedies is death, so the end of comedies is marriage.

Farquhar had had about a year's experience as an actor in
Dublin before he moved to London. He was born in London-
derry (the son of an Irish clergyman and of a probably English
mother) and educated there and at Trinity College, Dublin.
While still an undergraduate he developed a passion for the
theatre and, leaving college without a degree, began his stage
career as Othello about 1696, after a short spell as a printer's
reader. An accident during a performance of Dryden's *The
Indian Emperor*, in which he wounded another player, led him
to give up acting, and he left Dublin for London in 1697,
turned to playwriting, and was moderately successful with
Love and a Bottle, produced at Drury Lane in December 1698.
The central character, Roebuck, a devil-may-care young
Irishman, has been taken as 'probably a piece of idealised self-
portraiture . . . a certain rollicking good-nature distinguishes
this Irish adventurer from the fine-gentleman libertines of
Wycherley or Congreve. Thus early does Farquhar's individuality assert itself.'[1]

A year later *The Constant Couple, or a Trip to the Jubilee* (performed at Drury Lane on 28 November 1699) gave Farquhar
an assured place in the theatre. Described as 'an unprecedented
success', it had numerous performances—possibly as many as
the fifty-three in the opening season which Wilks (the first
to play Sir Harry Wildair, and Farquhar's good friend from the
Dublin days) claimed for it—and was frequently revived.
Wildair, 'an airy gentleman, affecting humorous gaiety and
freedom in his behaviour', became a favourite 'breeches part'
for Peg Woffington and other actresses with a bent for male
impersonation. Neither in vocabulary nor in incident does the
play make any revolutionary break with Restoration custom,
and there is nothing to admire in Wildair's character; but by
the end of *The Constant Couple* decency and affection in the

[1] See William Archer's introduction to the Mermaid edition of Farquhar's plays (Benn, London, 1949).

women have prevailed and the cynical presumption of rooted debauchery commonplace in late seventeenth-century comedy is abandoned.

Four minor plays followed: a sequel, *Sir Harry Wildair* (1701), *The Inconstant* (1702), *The Twin-Rivals* (1702), and *The Stage Coach* (1704). Then came *The Recruiting Officer* (1706) and *The Beaux' Stratagem* (1707), both with provincial settings, the first at Shrewsbury (dedicated 'To all my friends round the Wrekin'), the other at Lichfield, Farquhar having been stationed in turn at both places as a recruiting officer after joining the Grenadiers in 1704.

Unusually and refreshingly, *The Recruiting Officer* begins in the market place, with Serjeant Kite and a drummer 'and Mob following'. The Serjeant's first speech sets the play on its lively course and it never loses momentum:

> If any gentlemen soldiers, or others, have a mind to serve her Majesty, and pull down the French king; if any prentices have severe masters, or any children have undutiful parents: if any servants have too little wages, or any husband too much wife: let them repair to the noble Serjeant Kite, at the sign of the Raven in this good town of Shrewsbury, and they shall receive present relief and entertainment.

The love affairs of Silvia and Melinda, the backbone of the plot, are of small interest compared with the country humours of the recruits, Permain and Appletree, of the clownish Bullock and his sister Rose, and of Serjeant Kite, who poses as a fortune-teller to bamboozle his clients into enlisting. Most of the characters are drawn with vigour, the most remarkable being Silvia, who dresses up as a young man to enable her to join the company of Captain Plume, whom she loves but has promised not to marry without her father's consent. The device is no more credible with her than with any other young woman in man's clothes on the stage, but Farquhar does go some way towards providing her with an effective psychological disguise. The part of Sylvia was first played by beautiful Anne Oldfield (1683–1730), whom Farquhar had introduced to the stage when she was sixteen, after he had overheard her reading aloud in a tavern. She became one of the finest actresses in the London theatres throughout the next quarter of a century, creating major roles in many plays, including Mrs. Sullen in *The Beaux'*

Stratagem. This last and best of Farquhar's comedies is an affair of complicated intrigue starting with an excellent scene in a Lichfield inn, which introduces the landlord Boniface, his daughter Cherry, and the two curiosity-arousing strangers from the London coach, Aimwell and Archer, adventurers seeking to mend their fortunes, Archer masquerading as the other's footman. The scene is a model of the play-writing art, for comedy, characterization, dialogue, and for the natural ease with which essential information is conveyed to the audience through Boniface's chatter and the banter of the visitors. Mrs. Sullen, married to the dull and boorish son of Lady Bountiful, falls in love with Archer, and her sister-in-law Dorinda with Aimwell, when they see the men in church. Their affection is returned, and Archer and Aimwell contrive to become guests at the Sullens' house, where they rescue the girls from housebreaking highwaymen. Sullen agrees to a divorce and the quartet of lovers is satisfied. Amoral without indecency and disillusioned without cynicism, *The Beaux' Stratagem* is also without the scintillating wit of *The Way of the World*, though it belongs to that genre; but what it lacks of Congreve's brilliance is compensated by its humanity and variety and ease of manner. Farquhar's characters are people of the common world; Congreve's are superb creatures of intellectual fantasy. Mrs. Sullen is half-sister to Sheridan's Lady Teazle, but no closer than third cousin to Millamant when she talks (II, i) to Dorinda of her experience of matrimony:

Dost think, child, that my limbs were made for leaping of ditches, and clambering over stiles? or that my parents, wisely foreseeing my future happiness in country pleasures, had early instructed me in the rural accomplishments of drinking fat ale, playing at whisk, and smoking tobacco with my husband? . . .

. . . 'tis a standing maxim in conjugal discipline, that when a man would enslave his wife, he hurries her into the country; and when a lady would be arbitrary with her husband, she wheedles her booby up to town.—A man dare not play the tyrant in London, because there are so many examples to encourage the subject to rebel. O Dorinda! Dorinda! a fine woman may do anything in London: o' my conscience, she may raise an army of forty thousand men.

The Shakespeare Incubus

Scant respect had been accorded to Shakespeare by his seventeenth-century adapters, and in some instances his plays had been treated as little better than raw material for opera. Actors in the eighteenth century continued the seventeenth-century stage practice of making free and playing fast and loose with the text of Shakespeare's plays, while, on the other hand, poets and scholars strove with varying perception and skill to clear the text of errors.[1]

The first of the eighteenth-century editors of Shakespeare, Nicholas Rowe (1674–1718), earned contemporary repute as translator (of the first-century Roman poet Lucan) and tragic playwright. The son of a barrister, Rowe was born in Bedfordshire. From a private school at Highgate he went as a King's Scholar to Westminster, and afterwards studied law until a legacy from his father set him free to write plays. His first piece, *The Ambitious Stepmother* (1700), performed at the Lincoln's Inn Fields theatre, was followed by *Tamerlane* (1701), which is so far from imitating Marlowe's *Tamburlaine* that it presents the Scythian tyrant as an admirable heroic figure. Though it is allowable for a dramatist to manipulate history for the purposes of imaginative creation, Rowe was outrageously indifferent to probability and impotent to establish any likeness between stage characters and human beings.

For his two most successful tragedies, *The Fair Penitent* (1703) and *Jane Shore* (1714), Rowe had the services of the outstanding players of the period, and Calista and Jane Shore later became renowned parts in Mrs. Siddons's repertoire. The plot of *The Fair Penitent*—borrowed in part from *The Fatal Dowry* (c. 1630) by Philip Massinger and Nathan Field—is the very familiar one of an apparently chaste young woman, Calista, daughter of Sciolto, a Genoese nobleman, given in marriage to a worthy young man, Altamont, to whom it is shortly revealed that she has been the mistress of the libertine Lothario. At length, Lothario and Sciolto are killed, Calista stabs herself to death, and the final curtain falls after one of those rhymed passages of commonplace moralizing used by Rowe to give

---

[1] See below, pp. 227–8, on eighteenth-century editions of Shakespeare.

tone to his plays and offset the Restoration immoralism
lingering in the theatres.

> By such Examples are we taught to prove,
> The Sorrows that attend unlawful Love;
> Death, or some worse Misfortunes, soon divide
> The injur'd Bridegroom from his guilty Bride:
> If you wou'd have the Nuptial Union last,
> Let Virtue be the Bond that ties it fast.

In the Prologue to *Jane Shore*, Rowe, having referred to the
poets of an earlier age, says:

> Our Numbers may be more refin'd than those,
> But what we've gained in Verse we've lost in Prose.
> Their Words no shuffling, Double-meaning knew,
> Their Speech was homely, but their Hearts were true.
> In such an Age, immortal *Shakespeare* wrote,
> By no quaint Rules, nor hampering Cricks taught;
> With rough majestic Force he moved the Heart,
> And Strength and Nature made amends for *Art*.
> Our humble Author does his Steps pursue,
> He owns he had the mighty Bard in view;
> And in these scenes has made it more his Care
> To rouse the Passions, than to charm the Ear.
> Yet for those gentle Beaux who love the Chime,
> The Ends of Acts still jingle into Rhyme.

Rowe's unconscious self-deception was boundless. He failed
precisely in the qualities he professed to imitate from Shakespeare—force, strength, nature, passion—though the contemporary style of acting, rhetorical and declamatory, doubtless
played upon the nerves and senses of the audience and roused
feelings beyond the playwright's scope. An Elizabeth Barry
or a Sarah Siddons might, even today, fill Calista's bombinat-
ing oratory with the force, strength, nature, and passion which
were only deluding marsh-lights to Rowe.

> Death! and Confusion! Have I liv'd to this?
> Thus to be treated with unmanly Insolence!
> To be the Sport of a loose Ruffian's Tongue!
> Thus to be us'd! thus! like the vilest Creature,
> That ever was a Slave to Vice and Infamy. . . .
> Religious Hardships will I learn to bear,
> To fast, and freeze at Midnight Hours of Pray'r;

Nor think it hard, within a lonely Cell,
With melancholy, speechless Saints to dwell;
But bless the Day I to that Refuge ran,
Free from the Marriage Chain, and from that Tyrant, Man.
[Exit Calista.[1]

These passages and many more in Rowe's tragedies are magnificently ridiculous histrionics. How far short they come of having 'the mighty Bard in view' can be gauged by comparison even with Shakespeare's verse before he reached maturity—with, say, the women's speeches in *Richard III*, where the language at its most extravagantly histrionic is still the vehicle of genuine feeling.

Of the half-dozen tragedies of John Home (1722–1808), *Douglas* (1756) alone is remembered, mostly on account of a few lines from one of the hero's speeches which, without obvious cause, have amused posterity:

My name is Norval; on the Grampian hills
My father feeds his flocks; a frugal swain,
Whose constant cares were to increase his store.

Born at Leith and educated there and at Edinburgh University, Home forsook the Scottish ministry when his early playwriting activities were censured by theatre-hating co-religionists. He moved to London, becoming secretary to the Prime Minister, Lord Bute, and then tutor to the Prince of Wales (afterwards George III). Except in *Douglas* (suggested by the Scottish ballad 'Childe Maurice') and *The Fatal Discovery* (1769), a product of his enthusiasm for Macpherson's *Ossian* (*see below*, p. 216), Home turned to obscure classical sources, to Spanish history, and to English history for themes. He failed to persuade Garrick to produce his first two plays at Drury Lane, but after *Douglas* had been acclaimed as a national masterpiece at the Canongate Theatre, Edinburgh, in December 1756, Garrick put on that and Home's other works, but they were received with dwindling public interest until the complete failure of *Alfred* (1778) caused Home to abandon playwriting. *Douglas* owes its repute partly to Scottish fervour and partly also to the wild ballad theme, which breaks through the flat literaryness of Home's blank verse. But, fervently though it may from time

[1] *The Fair Penitent*, III, i, 127–31; 226–31.

to time be resurrected as evidence of northern achievement, *Douglas* is little more than a relic of the false devotion to Shakespearean blank-verse drama which led Home to scribble in Westminster Abbey:

> Image of Shakespeare! to this place I come
> To ease my bursting bosom at thy tomb. . . .

The conviction that seriousness of purpose imposed upon verse playwrights the duty of following in the steps of Shakespeare, the supreme model, was a fallacy maintained throughout the eighteenth and nineteenth centuries and not abandoned until the dramatic works of W. B. Yeats, J. M. Synge, and Sean O'Casey in the first quarter of the present century showed that essential poetry can inhabit many forms. It came at last to be appreciated that the genius of Shakespeare, unique and therefore inimitable, had cast over English poetic drama a shadow in which lesser talents withered. The *réclame* that followed T. S. Eliot's *Murder in the Cathedral* (1935) appeared to dissipate finally the Shakespeare obsession, though, as is natural when creative ability is in a minor phase, a new imitative obsession immediately took its place.

Minor Comedy and Tragedy

With its first run of more than sixty performances at Lincoln's Inn Fields in 1728, *The Beggar's Opera* by John Gay (1685–1732) brought a substantial sum to the author and a fortune to the producer, John Rich, after it had been refused by Cibber for Drury Lane. Nearly two centuries later, when put on by Nigel Playfair at the Lyric Theatre, Hammersmith, it ran for close on 1,500 performances from 5 June 1920. Swift had suggested that Gay might write 'a Newgate pastoral', but *The Beggar's Opera* became a very different thing, a musical satire which mocked by implication the growing fashion for opera and at the same time obliquely satirized leading politicians in the characters of Lockit the corrupt jailer and Peachum the informer.

Gay, born poor at Barnstaple in Devon and orphaned at the age of ten, became miserably apprenticed to a London silk-merchant. He turned to writing, published in 1708 a blank-verse poem, *Wine*, and thereafter for the rest of his life was a copious author of verse and plays. His most successful non-dramatic writings were *Trivia, or The Art of Walking the Streets of London* (1716), a kind of rhymed guide to the customs, sights, and dangers of the metropolis; and *Fables* (1727, '38, '50), in which he became a modern Æsop with a sardonic bite.

The Beggar's Opera earned much censure from moralists as well as popularity with the town and is one of the curiosities of literature, for it gives a horrifying picture of life on its lowest level (doing with crude realism what Fielding, using a very different technique, was to do again fifteen years later in *Jonathan Wild*[1]), yet its fundamental beastliness is freed of offence by translation into the operatic mode, where vice becomes a form of comedy, harlotry and bigamy material for charming lyrics and music, and hanging a light jest. As an ethical feat, it persuaded Johnson that no man would be made a rogue by seeing it; but he added: ' ". . . At the same time I do not deny that it may have some influence, by making the character of a rogue familiar, and in some degree pleasing." Then [says Boswell] collecting himself as it were, to give a heavy stroke: "There is in it such a *labefactation* of all principles, as may be injurious to morality."' As a literary feat *The Beggar's Opera* can hardly be overpraised. It has a coherent story which moves smoothly and swiftly; the characters are modelled three-dimensionally and differentiated with remarkable economy of means; and many of the lyrics for the sixty-nine songs are poems in their own right, not merely singable words.

There is little need to dwell upon Fielding's contributions to the theatre, numerous though they were and amusing as some of them are still to those with enough background knowledge of the period to catch the satirical point of his burlesques and to enjoy the wit and humour continuously present in their wildest hilarities and maddest absurdities. But for his eminence as a novelist, however, Fielding would probably receive less than the little attention now given to his plays, mainly as museum pieces, though *The Tragedy of Tragedies; or the Life and Death of Tom Thumb the Great* (1730) is as uproariously funny as the playlet embedded in Max Beerbohm's '*Savonarola*' *Brown*.[2]

[1] See above, pp. 185, 186.
[2] One of the pieces in *Seven Men* (1919).

Much of the fun is illegitimate to *Tom Thumb* as a stage play,
for the printed text is elaborately footnoted with literary jokes
which could not by any means be preserved in performance.
Nevertheless the spoken dialogue abounds in passages parody-
ing current types of 'heroic' tragedy and laughing them into
inflated nonsense. It may be thought irreverent that Fielding
should provide King Arthur with a wife named Dollallolla and
with a daughter Huncamunca thus apostrophized (II, v) by a
suitor, Lord Grizzle:

> Oh! *Huncamunca, Huncamunca,* oh!
> Thy pouting Breasts, like Kettle-Drums of Brass,
> Beat everlasting loud Alarms of Joy;
> As bright as Brass they are, and oh, as hard;
> Oh Huncamunca, Huncamunca! oh![1]

but Fielding, though no respecter of pretentious solemnity in
any quarter, was a well-tempered parodist whose comically
feathered arrows went more surely to the mark than the
grape-shot of embittered satirists.

George Lillo (1693–1739) attempted with *The London Merchant, or the History of George Barnwell* (1731) to do for the
eighteenth-century theatre what the unidentified author of
Arden of Feversham had set out to do in the 1590s, namely (in
words from Lillo's Prologue) 'to show, In artless Strains, a Tale
of private Woe' as a departure from the customary drama in
which
> The Tragic Muse, sublime, delights to show
> Princes distress'd, and Scenes of royal Woe.

Taking the old ballad of George Barnwell, Lillo adapted and
extended it to a five-act prose tragedy on the fate of the
apprentice Barnwell, who is instigated by his inamorata,
Millwood, to rob his master and murder his uncle; she thereupon betrays him and he is arrested and executed. Millwood's
declared motive is to avenge herself on men for their general
ill-treatment of women, but her scheme recoils upon herself;
betrayed by her maid Lucy, she also is condemned to death.
The play is not unimpressive, nor is it genuinely tragic, its

---

[1] Mocking James Thomson's *Sophonisba*: see below, p. 212.

potential effect being ruined by the uniformly bookish language used by all the characters. Indeed, the failure of innumerable otherwise worthy plays is due to the dramatists' failure
of ear and consequent inability to create for stage purposes the
illusion of natural speech.

Of the other minor playwrights of the century, passing
mention need be made only of Isaac Bickerstaffe (*c*. 1724–
c. 1812) for his light operatic comedies, including *Love in a
Village* (1762) and *Lionel and Clarissa* (1768); Arthur Murphy
(1727–1805) for his lesson to wives (and husbands) *The Way to
Keep Him* (1760); Thomas Morton (?1764–1838) for his drama
Speed the Plough (1798), through which the often-mentioned but
never-seen Mrs. Grundy has become the symbol of English
prudery; and Richard Cumberland (1732–1811)—author of
tragedies and of sentimental comedies, including *The Brothers*
(1769) and *The West Indian* (1771)—ridiculed in Sheridan's
The Critic as Sir Fretful Plagiary.

Goldsmith and Sheridan

The comedy of sentiment introduced by Steele at the beginning
of the eighteenth century as an antidote to the Restoration
drama of wit and intrigue and indecency, set a fashion followed
by numerous hack-writers for the stage. As the century proceeded, the hunger for sentiment was gratified through the
new medium of the novel more than from the stage, and sentiment degenerated into languishing sentimentality which the
sillier types of romance-struck girls and women of fashion
absorbed avidly in the course of boudoir reading and theatre-
going.

When Oliver Goldsmith (1730–74), after more than ten
years of miscellaneous writing,[1] had his first play put on at
Covent Garden in 1768, his intention was to counter sentimental excess and to break with what he called (in the preface
to the printed play) 'genteel comedy', by concentrating upon
'nature and humour' and the delineation of character. He
added:

> The author . . . hopes that too much refinement will not
> banish humour and character from ours, as it has already done

[1] Goldsmith's non-dramatic works are discussed below, pp. 234–5.

from the French theatre. Indeed the French comedy is now become so very elevated and sentimental, that it has not only banished humour and Molière from the stage, but it has banished all spectators too.

The plot and sub-plot of *The Good-Natur'd Man* are tediously complicated and drawn out, with mistaken identities and misinterpreted proposals and much paraphernalia of story neither original nor credible; but what Goldsmith aimed particularly to do he did admirably: there is effective delineation of character within the handicapping limits of the plot; there is humour of incident (as in the scene where young Honeywood gets the bailiff's men to pose as his guests and friends) and of character (as in the impostor Lofty and the pessimist Croaker); while the 'lesson' of the play is palatably presented through young Honeywood, the good-natured man, who, in the final scene, admits the justice of his uncle's rebuke:

> . . . I saw with indignation the errors of a mind that only sought applause from others; that easiness of disposition, which though inclined to the right had not courage to condemn the wrong . . . your charity, that was but injustice; your benevolence that was but weakness; and your friendship but credulity.

There were few signs in *The Good-Natur'd Man* that Goldsmith would go on to write a play that would out-do the scores of comedies written in the first three-quarters of the century. Nor when it was done did theatre managers recognize a masterpiece, for it was well over a year before *She Stoops-to Conquer, or The Mistakes of a Night* was hesitantly staged by Colman at Covent Garden, after Garrick lost the chance to take it for Drury Lane. In the dedication to Johnson, who had persuaded the reluctant manager, Goldsmith recorded: 'The undertaking a Comedy, not merely sentimental, was very dangerous; and Mr. Colman, who saw the piece in its various stages, always thought it so.' Two at least of the actors engaged for it shared Colman's opinion and withdrew, but the public thought differently and the play was immediately successful. The device of misunderstanding, incidental in *The Good-Natur'd Man*, is central in *She Stoops to Conquer*. Here again, however, as in the earlier play, the interest of the plot is secondary to that of the characters, of the several episodes, and of the humour. In Tony Lumpkin Goldsmith created one of the great English comic characters, even though he is boorish and unlikeable. Yet *She Stoops to Conquer* is an uncommonly likeable play, through its gaiety of tone and sunny sweetness of temper, which nevertheless has subtle undertones of astringency precisely calculated to prevent cloying. The dialogue is agile; the young men, Marlow and Hastings, are intelligent enough not to be either fops or prigs; the girls, Kate Hardcastle and Constance Neville, have common sense as well as charm; Mr. Hardcastle and Mrs. Hardcastle—the one kindly but with a trace of the sardonic, the other amiably foolish—might well have been taken by Jane Austen as models for certain of her elderly characters.

Less than two years after Goldsmith's second and last play appeared, and some nine months after his death, the Covent Garden audience saw the first play of a new dramatist who, consciously or not, followed the path that Goldsmith had made, and with *The Rivals* (1775) started the brilliant playwriting career that was to last only four years.

Richard Brinsley Sheridan (1751–1816), whose parents were Thomas Sheridan an actor and Frances Sheridan a novelist and playwright, was born in Dublin and educated at Harrow. His mother died when he was fifteen and a few years later his father settled in Bath, whence Richard eloped in 1772 to France with Elizabeth Linley (famously beautiful daughter of the composer and vocalist, Thomas Linley) after fighting two duels with Captain Matthews, a troublesome suitor. Elizabeth also was a singer, and her father became master of the music at Drury Lane when Sheridan took over the theatre. *The Rivals* was produced on 17 January 1775, the short farce *St. Patrick's Day* on 2 May, both at Covent Garden; in 1777 *A Trip to Scarborough* on 24 February and *The School for Scandal* on 8 May, at Drury Lane; in 1779 (30 October), also at Drury Lane, *The Critic*. Sheridan's career as a playwright may be said to have ended with that burlesque piece, since his tragedy *Pizarro* (adapted from Kotzebue's German play) put on at Drury Lane in 1799 added nothing to his reputation. Having bought out Garrick, Sheridan began to manage Drury Lane theatre in 1776. The new theatre he built there and opened on 12 March 1794 was burnt down on 24 February 1809, after which Sheridan's management ended. In the meantime he had become M.P. for Stafford (1780) and the rest of his life was given to politics, in which he played a prominent part, most memorably with his famous orations at the impeachment of Warren Hastings (1787, '88, '94). He was arrested for debt in 1813, and most of the short remainder of his life was clouded by brain disease. He received a spectacular public funeral and was buried in Westminster Abbey.

Sheridan's two great plays, *The Rivals* and *The School for Scandal*, are classified as Artificial Comedies of Manners yet it is their relative freedom from artificiality that puts them above the rest of their kind. The opening moments of *The Rivals*, when the Coachman and Fag meet in a street in Bath, catch at once the tones of 'nature', the illusion of naturalness, that Goldsmith just failed to master; while the second scene (a dressing-room in Mrs. Malaprop's lodgings) introduces convincingly the theme of romantic sentimentality, mocked in the character of Lydia Languish, whose lending-library fare consists of such novels of 'sensibility' as *The Reward of Constancy*, *The Fatal Connexion*, *The Mistakes of the Heart*, *The Delicate Distress*, *The Tears of Sensibility*, *The Innocent Adultery*, and *The Man of Feeling* —the kind of fiction that causes Sir Anthony Absolute to declare to Lydia's aunt, Mrs. Malaprop, that 'a circulating library in a town is as an ever-green tree of diabolical knowledge! . . . And depend on it . . . they who are so fond of handling the leaves will long for the fruit at last.'[1] Less skilfully managed, the immortal Mrs. Malaprop would have become an insufferable bore, but though Sheridan exploits to the full her habit of misapplying words, the trick is never overdone and is used to build up a truly comic human being who claims and retains our liking and never slides wholly into caricature. The young men, Captain Absolute and Falkland, appear less natural than Goldsmith's Young Marlow and Hastings, but Bob Acres is an excellent and agreeable successor to Tony Lumpkin; while there are few scenes in English comedy more amusing than Sir Lucius O'Trigger's conversation when he enters with pistols in the last scene to second Bob in the never-to-be-fought duel with Absolute.

[1] Matthew Green (1696–1737) was more outspoken in *The Spleen* (1737), l. 269: 'Novels (receipts to make a whore)'.

The School for Scandal is more brilliant and substantial and an altogether weightier play than *The Rivals*, which is mostly a frivolity, whereas the other is a morality and more rather than

---

PERFORMED but ONCE.

At the Theatre Royal in Drury-Lane,
This prefent Friday, the 9th of May, 1777,
Will be prefented a NEW COMEDY, call'd THE

School for Scandal.

The PRINCIPAL CHARACTERS by
Mr.   K I N G,
Mr.   Y A T E S,
Mr.   D O D D,
Mr.   P A L M E R,
Mr.   P A R S O N S,
Mr. B A D D E L E Y,   Mr.   A I C K I N,
Mr. P A C K E R,   Mr.   F A R R E N,
Mr. L A M A S H,   Mr.   G A U D R Y,
Mr. R. PALMER, Mr. NORRIS, Mr. CHAPLIN,
And   Mr.   S M I T H.
Mifs   P O P E,
Mifs   P. H O P K I N S,
Mifs   S H E R R Y,
And   Mrs.   A B I N G T O N.
The Prologue to be fpoken by Mr. K I N G,
And the Epilogue by Mrs. ABINGTON.
With NEW SCENES and DRESSES.
To which will be added a Mufical Drama, call'd

The   D E S E R T E R.

Henry by Mr. D A V I E S,
Ruffet by Mr. BANNISTER, Simkin by Mr. CARPENTER,
Skirmifh by Mr. PARSONS,   Flint by Mr. WRIGHT,
Soidiers by Mr. Legg, Mr. Kear, Mr. Griffith. Mr Chaplin Mr. Follit,
Jenny by Mrs. D A V I E S,
Margaret by Mrs. L O V E
Louifa by Mifs C O L L E T T,
The Doors will be opened at Half after Five, to begin exactly at Half after Six o'Clock.

---

less entertaining. It arraigns heartless and malicious scandal-mongering, moralizing sentiment that is no better than a cloak for hypocrisy, current standards of marital conduct, and irresponsible *bonhomie*. Charles Surface is drawn sympathetic-ally as a goodhearted spendthrift whose nature is sound at bottom, but he is censured by implication no less certainly than his hypocritical brother Joseph is in plain terms. Sir

Peter Teazle suffers for his elderly amorous folly in taking a young wife, and Lady Teazle pays in humiliation for her toying beyond the bounds of marriage: justice is dealt all round. The scenes and characters of *The School for Scandal*—the greatest achievement in comedy since Shakespeare—are universally familiar, and its permanent appeal is due chiefly to the fact that, although specifically a period piece, a 'costume play' in the strict sense, it transcends the period 'quaintnesses' of powdered wigs and panniered dresses, flowered suits and buckled shoes, and in such episodes as the screen scene and Charles's auctioning of his ancestors touches the core of human nature.

The farcical *St. Patrick's Day*, the light operetta *The Duenna* (for which Thomas Linley wrote the music), and *A Trip to Scarborough*, which some have regarded as a plagiarism rather than an adaptation of Vanbrugh's *The Relapse*, are of little importance. *The Critic*, however, is the peak achievement in a type of dramatic entertainment which has produced very few masterpieces. Burlesque might at a stretch be traced back to Aristophanes, but Buckingham's *The Rehearsal* (1672), guying 'heroic' tragedy, is the first accredited example in English. Fielding's *Tom Thumb* (*see above*, p. 200) aims in the same direction, and so also does *The Critic*, but Sheridan enlarged the target and made fun not only of stage absurdities but also of the imbecilities of drama critics and of the touchiness of authors. Burlesque flourishes on extravagance, and, being subject to no laws other than those of the author's own making and the discipline to avoid excess, it eludes critical comment. *The Critic*, however, is burlesque and something more. The interpolated 'tragedy', *The Spanish Armada*—pure burlesque of the headiest vintage—is less important than the framework in which Puff, Sneer, Dangle, Sir Fretful Plagiary, and others discuss the theatre and its sycophants. This embodies satire of the most penetrating order and, incidentally, a good deal of oblique criticism, literary and social, as (for example) when Sneer mentions a comedy, *The Reformed Housebreaker*, written by a particular friend of his

> . . . who has discovered that the follies and foibles of society are subjects unworthy the notice of the Comic Muse, who should be taught to stoop only at the greater vices and blacker

crimes of humanity—gibbeting capital offences in five acts and pillorying petty larcenies in two. In short, his idea is to dramatize the penal laws, and make the stage a court of ease to the Old Bailey.

Sneer's friend is reborn in every generation, protesting always that the theatre should function as a reformatory in which the social conscience rules and the spirit of legitimate entertainment is overruled.

43. Colley Cibber as Lord Foppington in Vanbrugh's
The Relapse by Guiseppe Crisoni

44. Scene from *She Stoops to Conquer* by Oliver Goldsmith

45. Illustration by H. Gravelot to The Baboon and the Poultry
for John Gay's *Fables*

46. View of the library at Strawberry Hill

47. Illustration by Isaac Taylor for Goldsmith's *The Deserted Village*

48. *Despair offering a bowl of poison to Thomas Chatterton* by John
Flaxman

49. Illustration by Richard Bentley for Gray's *Ode on the Death of a
Favourite Cat*

50. Frontispiece by Francis Hayman for Smart's *Poems on Several Occasion*

51. Edmund Burke
    Sir Joshua Reynolds

52. Self-portrait of Sir
    Joshua Reynolds

53. Dr. Samuel Johnson
by Sir Joshua Reynolds

. David Garrick as Kitely
by Sir Joshua Reynolds

55. James Boswell as a Corsican Chief
by Samuel Wale

56. Boswell and Johnson in Edinburgh by Samuel Collings

CHAPTER XII

GRAY, SMART, AND OTHERS:
LESSER VERSE AND PROSE 1725-75

MUCH of the massive outpouring of verse in the eighteenth century has lost all but the historical interest of illustrating a certain uniformity of spirit and temper. Perfection of verse-technique and a slightly constipated genius have been enough to give Gray a high place among the poets of his generation; Collins had a genuine and original talent, however small; Smart, potentially greater than either, went mad, a handicap which saved him from undistinguished conformity with the prevailing mental pattern. James Thomson, who was for long ranked as little less than a major poet on account of *The Seasons* and *The Castle of Indolence*, displays in fact most of the mid-eighteenth-century misconceptions of Nature in the former and, in the latter, burdens the Spenserian stanza with incongruities of sophisticated poetic diction and contrived archaism.

The paucity of individual high talent made most verse writers in the half-century covered by this chapter both intellectually and technically unadventurous, and the general absence of originality is reflected in the monotony of tone and outlook. Some such monotony may of course appear when the poetry of any age is viewed in mass, but the buoyancy and freshness of vision of the Elizabethans and the fervour of the seventeenth-century Metaphysicals contrast invigoratingly with the dispirited uniformity of mood which produced in the eighteenth century so much reflection upon Melancholy ('How sweet thy Diapason, Melancholy![1]) and bred that homesickness for the past which had valuable results in archæology, but in literature was responsible for a spurious cult of antiquity which culminated in the forgeries of Chatterton and·the later excesses of the Novel of Terror, even while, on the credit side, it was accompanied by the recovery of the traditional ballads.

Much dwelling on the 'return to Nature' commonly and in its special sense rightly associated with Wordsworth, has drawn away attention from the eighteenth-century type of

[1] John Dyer: *The Ruins of Rome* (1740).

P

poetry, among which Thomson's *The Seasons* was remarkable chiefly on account of its length. In their attitude to and treatment of Nature in poetry, Thomson and his contemporaries paid the penalty exacted for the century's cultivation of urbanity. They had lost the innocent eye and the pellucid tongue of the Elizabethans without acquiring the command of significant imagery and the philosophical penetration which the Romantics were to exercise; they could only present Nature puffed-up and with the wild branches pruned away.

> One would think she might like to retire
>   To the Bow'r I have labour'd to rear;
> Not a Shrub that I heard her admire,
>   But I hasted and planted it there.
> Oh how sudden the Jessamine strove
>   With the Lilac to render it gay!
> Already it calls for my Love,
>   To prune the wild Branches away.[1]

Nature à la Mode

Poetical allusions to Nature, if not Nature poetry, were common in the eighteenth century from the beginning. Pope's 'Ode on Solitude' (*c.* 1700) speaks nostalgically of herds and fields and flocks and trees; while his 'Windsor Forest' (1713) foreshadows—or might be held to have set the measure for—the next half-century or so of mannered versifying on natural scenery, for Pope lets scarcely a feature go without its companion adjective: the trees are thin or tufted or balmy, the plains russet, the hills blueish, the fields fruitful, the corn springing, the amber weeping, the pheasant whirring, the winter groves naked. All the adjectives can be justified and would excite little remark if they did not now seem a portent of what was to come when later writers, intent upon a more refined poetic diction, turned breezes into 'winged Zephyrs', an echo into a 'propagated Cry', a nearby mound into 'yon little Eminence', fish into 'the finny race', a young trout into a 'speckled infant', winter storm clouds into a 'fleecy world' holding a 'vapoury deluge'.[2] Nature poetry without an

---

[1] William Shenstone: *Pastoral Ballad*, 1743.

[2] The first three of these examples come from William Somerville's *The Chace* (1735), the others from Thomson's *The Seasons* ('Spring', 1728; 'Winter', 1726).

incrustation of picturesque epithets and similes was accounted
language crudely impoverished, but such loaded verse at
length appeared to be in its artificiality the very antithesis of
Nature; a rigid barrier between Nature and the poet, who
neither observed nor transmitted, but simply performed
a mental exercise according to a fashionably approved
formula.

It is needless here to follow the progress of the formula
through its manifestations in such works as *The Schoolmistress*
(1737; revised 1742) of William Shenstone (1714–63), much of
it attractively couched in Spenserian stanzas but disfigured in
places by coy simplicity and false archaisms rather than by
modish elaboration. Among the lesser Nature poems of the
time, *Grongar Hill* (1726) by John Dyer (1700–58) is almost
alone in giving evidence that the writer had trusted his own
eyes and senses some of the time. It is plentifully spattered with
conventional poetic diction, but Dyer does at least create the
impression that he actually climbed the hill and recorded (with
additions) what he saw. But, like the great majority of contemporary verse-writers, he was denied the ability to find a
philosophy of Nature and could do no more than moralize the
view:

> O may I with my self agree,
> And never covet what I see:
> Content me with an humble Shade,
> My Passions tam'd, my Wishes laid;
> For while our Wishes wildly roll,
> We banish Quiet from the Soul. . . .

The failure of James Thomson (1700–48) to take a place
among the great poets seems chiefly due to his failure to be
born in another century, for in many passages his work appears
to be hindered from the heights of poetic achievement by the
insufficient imaginative range of current verbal usage. *The
Seasons* was published in four parts: 'Winter', 'Summer',
'Spring' in successive years from 1726; 'Autumn' in 1730,
when the whole was republished with the collective title. It is
often credited with being the first work to challenge the arti-
fices of contemporary poetry and with having 'inaugurated a
new era' by its 'sentiment for Nature'; and notwithstanding

its own crop of artificialities there are signs of an attempt to
break through to simplicity:

> Fair-handed Spring unbosoms every Grace:
> Throws out the Snow-drop, and the Crocus first;
> The Daisy, Primrose, Violet darkly blue,
> And Polyanthus of unnumber'd Dyes;
> The yellow Wall-Flower, stain'd with iron Brown;
> And lavish Stock that scents the Garden round: . . .

Yet the root weakness of the time remains—failure to communicate. Thomson's verse reaches the limit of its capacity
when it has achieved description and statement: the descriptions are attractive and often charming, the statements are
interesting, but no emotional sensation, no sense of the nature
of Nature—if it may be so expressed—gets through to the
reader.

Apart from a line in one of his several tragedies (*Sophonisba*,
1730)

> Oh! Sophonisba! Sophonisba! oh!

parodied by Fielding in *Tom Thumb* (*see above*, p. 201) and still
quoted in ridicule, Thomson's memory rests upon 'Rule,
Britannia', a song in the final scene of *Alfred* (1740), a masque.

The Cult of Melancholy

John Dyer's apostrophe to Melancholy has been quoted above
(p. 209), and some further attention needs to be paid to the
mood which gave rise in the 1740s and after to poems on that
and cognate themes. *The Complaint, or Night Thoughts* by Edward
Young (1683–1765) came out in 1742; *The Grave* by Robert
Blair (1699–1746) in 1743; *The Pleasures of Melancholy* by
Thomas Warton (1728–90) in 1747. The mood prevails also in
Gray and Collins, whose poetry is considered separately below,
as well as in Johnson's *The Vanity of Human Wishes* (*see above*,
p. 172) and Goldsmith's *The Traveller* and *The Deserted Village*
(*below*, p. 235).

Young, who married Lady Elizabeth Lee, daughter of the
Earl of Lichfield, was for the last thirty-five years of his life
rector of Welwyn in Hertfordshire. His extensive writings,
spread over nearly half a century, included poems, tragedies,
and miscellaneous prose, but only *Night Thoughts* has survived.

Despite its gloomy tendency it was immediately and long popular, and Johnson wrote of its 'deep reflections and striking allusions', its 'fertility of fancy', 'vast extent and endless diversity'. This praise may be excessive, yet the poem professes no less than to survey in its ten thousand lines 'Life, Death, and Immortality'. Much of the earlier part is suffused with the melancholy of sleepless nights, but the later stages essay to combat infidelity and the poem ends with an impressive affirmation of faith. Long before he wrote *Night Thoughts*, which has at least spasmodic intimations of greatness, Young published (1725) a group of satires with the general title *Universal Passion* (reissued as *Love of Fame*, 1728). These show him in a brighter aspect, for while the 'Characters of Women' included among them are disillusioned and sardonic they also have wit and humour.

Robert Blair (1699–1746), a Scottish minister, published nothing of note but *The Grave* (1743), a blank-verse poem of some 800 lines which is rather more than the reference-book description of it as 'a celebration of death, the solitude of the tomb, and the anguish of bereavement'. The smell of the charnel house is on it, but it also has livelier points of interest: its Nature passages are less solidly artificial and more genuinely felt than was customary; and it is one of the earliest portents of that preoccupation with romantic decay and morbidly imaginative supernaturalism which was insistent in the second half of the century and led, by way of Horace Walpole's *The Castle of Otranto* (*see below*, p. 216), to the Gothic novels of terror and the architectural curiosities contemporary with them. In Blair's churchyard

> The Wind is up: Hark! how it howls! Methinks
> Till now, I never heard a Sound so dreary:
> Doors creak, and Windows clap, and Night's foul bird
> Rook'd in the Spire screams loud: . . .
>   . . . Rous'd from their Slumbers
> In grim Array the grizly Spectres rise,
> Grin horrible, and obstinately sullen
> Pass and repass, hush'd as the Foot of Night.
> Again! the Screech-Owl shrieks: Ungracious Sound!
> I'll hear no more, it makes one's Blood run chill.

Strange Things, the Neighbours say, have happen'd here;
Wild Shrieks have issu'd from the hollow Tombs,
Dead men have come again, and walk'd about,
And the Great Bell has toll'd, unrung, untouch'd.

This is whole-hearted gothic tushery, despised by the normal mind, yet the mind is powerless to render the imagination and emotions invulnerable to it. The later gothic novelists [1] went headlong into the utterly ludicrous and the disgustingly horrific, but who can withstand the fascination of mysteriously creaking doors and clapping windows, of grisly spectres that rise and grin horribly, of shrieks from hollow tombs, of great bells that toll without human agency? Blood-chilling passages of this order occur in Shakespeare (e.g. *Romeo and Juliet*, IV, iii, 36-54; *Richard III*, I, iv, 20 ff.), and the twentieth-century appetite for crime novels, *alias* 'thrillers', is basically related to the gothic impulse, which is itself more nearly perennial and universal in man than original to eighteenth-century Britain.

The brothers Warton (Joseph 1722-1800; Thomas 1728-90) figure more prominently in histories of literary scholarship than as creators. Both were critics of some importance: Joseph for his essays on *The Genius and Writings of Pope* (I, 1756; II, '82); Thomas for his *History of English Poetry* (I, 1774; II, '78; III, '81), the first work of its kind. Joseph's blank-verse *The Enthusiast: or the Lover of Nature* (1744), although lamenting that 'taste corrupt . . . Should proudly banish Nature's simple charms', itself fails to treat Nature naturally. His *Odes* (1746) are relieved by occasional lines of a fresher tone:

When young-ey'd *Spring* profusely throws
From her green lap the pink and rose;

but a simple wood-pigeon is still fancified as 'the soft turtle of the dale'. Thomas Warton's *The Pleasures of Melancholy* (1747) and even his *Verses on Sir Joshua Reynolds's Painted Windows at New College, Oxford* (1782) are further pointers in the direction to which *The Grave* was oriented. The former has the gothic trappings of ruined abbey, screech owl, mouldering caverns, cloistered brothers, awful solitude, *et al*:

[1] See Vol. III of the present work.

. . . when the world
Is clad in Midnight's raven-colour'd robe,
'Mid hollow charnel let me watch the flame
Of taper dim, shedding a livid glare
O'er the wan heaps; while airy voices talk
Along the glimm'ring walls, or ghostly shape
At distance seen, invites with beck'ning hand
My lonesome steps, thro' the far-winding vaults.

In the verses on the New College windows the poet declares:

Long have I lov'd to catch the simple chime
Of minstrel-harps, and spell the fabling rime;
To view the festive rites, the knightly play,
That deck'd heroic Albion's elder day;
To mark the mouldering halls of Barons bold,
And the rough castle, cast in giant mould;
With Gothic manners Gothic arts explore,
And muse on the magnificence of yore.

The Cult of Antiquity

Before 1750 the stage was prepared, the scenery set, and the
thunder and blood-curdling effects ready in the wings for the
remarkable display of literary theatricals that was to follow
at intervals during the next three-quarters of a century,
drawing in Horace Walpole, Macpherson, Chatterton, Clara
Reeve, Mrs. Radcliffe, 'Monk' Lewis, Charles Maturin, and
others, merging at length through such works as Mary Shelley's
Frankenstein into the nineteenth-century sociological and
humanitarian novels, and itself dissolving in the laughter of
Jane Austen's *Northanger Abbey* and Peacock's *Nightmare Abbey*—
all three published in 1818.

The gothic novel of terror and what is here called the cult
of antiquity were linked by the curious brand of romanticism
which saw the past as a louring landscape scattered with picturesque ruins of abbeys and castles meet for sinister supernatural happenings. Not content with romancing about such
places, the addicts set up artificial ruins, built private mansions
in the guise of ancient ecclesiastical buildings (e.g. Horace
Walpole's Strawberry Hill, William Beckford's Fonthill Abbey,
and Sir Walter Scott's Abbotsford), and even decorated their

estates with mock structures, e.g. Sham Castle (overlooking the city of Bath), which is the façade of a non-existent edifice.

Walpole's *The Castle of Otranto* (1764) gets no farther than its second page before mystery and calamity enter with the destruction of Prince Manfred's son, Conrad:

> . . . dreading he knew not what, he advanced hastily—but, what a sight for a father's eyes!—he beheld his child dashed to pieces, and almost buried under an enormous helmet, a hundred times more large than any casque ever made for a human being, and shaded with a proportionable quantity of black feathers.

Since Walpole had no gift for novel-writing, *The Castle of Otranto*, apart from its pioneer status in the gothic movement, is a mere literary curiosity and requires no fuller mention until the Novel of Terror is discussed as a genre in its chronological place.[1]

A much more important phase of the return to the past was the collection of old songs and ballads by amateur antiquarians:[2] in 1764 came Evan Evans's *Specimens of the Poetry of the Antient Welsh Bards, translated into English*; in 1765 Thomas Percy's *Reliques of Ancient English Poetry*; in 1770 Sir David Dalrymple's *Ancient Scottish Poems, published from the Manuscript of George Bannatyne, 1568*. Percy's collection (*see* Vol. I of the present work, p. 47) cannot easily be over-valued, for it not only recovered and preserved many priceless ballads, but, also, the resulting new knowledge of early popular poems fertilized English poetry for generations thereafter.

Before these genuine recoveries were published, however, James Macpherson (1736–96) had produced in 1760 *Fragments of Ancient Poetry collected in the Highlands of Scotland, and translated from the Gaelic or Erse Language*, following this with *Fingal: An Ancient Epic Poem in Six Books* (1762) and *Temora* (1763). He alleged that the original author of these latter was the Gaelic bard Ossian, but while Macpherson had used fragments of old Gaelic verse, the 'epics' were mainly his own. The oddest feature of the cult of antiquity was that writers were eager to forswear their own creative talents in favour of spurious

---

[1] See Vol. III of the present work.
[2] Anticipated to some extent by Allan Ramsay's collections: see above, pp. 158–9.

ancestors; and that those who at first received such works with
enthusiasm and unstinted admiration rejected them at once as
worthless when their actual authorship was revealed.

The Ossian poems have little interest and no value now, but
their influence was considerable at the time, and they provided
some incentive to Thomas Chatterton (1752–70) who proceeded to hide his own poetic light under the bushel of an
invented Thomas Rowley. He described Rowley as a fifteenth-
century monk of Bristol, where Chatterton himself was born
and lived until he ventured to London in 1770, only to commit
suicide in his Holborn lodging a few months later. Folly, more
than forgery, was the cause of his misfortune. He persisted in
trying to deceive Horace Walpole [1] (whose interest he sought)
far beyond the point where it became plain that the attempt
had failed; and though neglect and poverty are the usually
ascribed causes of his drinking poison, pique must also have
been a prime cause, for Chatterton suffered from the common
delusion of the artist *manqué*—that as a matter of course society
owes him both indulgence and support. The psychological
interest of Chatterton's case is considerable, for it is clear that
the Rowley poems gain nothing by being decked out in mock
fifteenth-century idiom and orthography and would have lost
nothing by using eighteenth-century spelling. Nevertheless
there is the paradox that the Rowley poems are superior to
those Chatterton wrote in his own name, as though a certain
inner excitement and zest stirred by the assumption of a false
identity stimulated his feeble natural talent and gave it new
energy.

Gray, Collins, and Smart

No poet has so high a reputation on so small an output as
Thomas Gray (1716–71). His fame rests, indeed, upon the
128 lines of the *Elegy written in a Country Churchyard* (1751), for
his place among the English poets is unaffected by the rest of
his work. The *Elegy* is a triumph of poetic art and atmosphere:
every word appears both inevitably right and in its inevitably

---

[1] Chatterton turned abusively upon Walpole when the latter doubted
the authenticity of a history of painting (*The Ryse of Peyncteynge yn Englande,
wroten bie T. Rowleie, 1469, for Mastre Canynge*) which the boy sent him from
Bristol.

right place; and its muted melancholy music is in complete harmony with the oncoming of night across the English land-scape. By no means the least of its remarkable features is that the mannered poetic diction which in other poets seems arti-ficial and a blemish, here appears natural and exact: the moping owl; incense-breathing morn; straw-built shed; the cock's shrill clarion; the madding crowd; old fantastic roots; the brook that babbles by. The *Elegy* is a miniature com-pendium of those elements of eighteenth-century poetry discussed above, but now they are unified, given a *rationale*, and made acceptable by being freed from excess. There is the characteristic view of Nature:

> Now fades the glimmering landscape on the sight,
> And all the air a solemn stillness holds,
> Save where the beetle wheels its droning flight,
> And drowsy tinklings lull the distant folds;

the melancholy:

> Can storied urn or animated bust
> Back to its mansion call the fleeting breath?
> Can Honour's voice provoke the silent dust,
> Or Flatt'ry sooth the dull cold ear of Death?

the picturesque antique:

> . . . from yonder ivy-mantled tow'r
> The mopeing owl does to the moon complain
> Of such, as wand'ring near her secret bow'r,
> Molest her ancient solitary reign.

And interwoven with these elements is the rising humani-tarianism which was to swell into the chorus of Rousseau and his English disciples before the century ended.

However inevitable in their places the components of the *Elegy* appear, it was far from being a spontaneous poem. Begun in 1742, the main part was written in the years 1746–50. Gray worked with extreme care and deliberation, achieving finally a masterpiece of verbal craftsmanship with all the appearance of inspired art. Except for the *Ode on a Distant Prospect of Eton College* (1742) and the *Ode on the Death of a Favourite Cat* (c. 1747), which have individual excellences, the rest of his poetry is little above the average eighteenth-century level, though he was more than most an accomplished deviser of felicitous phrases.

Gray was born in London and educated at Eton and Cambridge, travelled on the Continent with Horace Walpole, declined the Poet Laureateship, lived in Cambridge, became Professor of History and Modern Languages there, and died in the Buckinghamshire village of Stoke Poges, possibly the setting for the *Elegy*. Like his friend Walpole,[1] Gray was an excellent letter-writer and his published correspondence gives him a distinguished place among the writers of familiar prose.

William Collins (1721–59) was born at Chichester, Sussex, and educated at Winchester and Oxford. His poems are fewer even than Gray's, the finest being the short 'Ode to Evening' (in *Odes on Several Descriptive and Allegorical Subjects*, 1746) in unrhymed verse with Miltonic echoes. The fact that it was published before the *Elegy written in a Country Churchyard* was completed puts any debt against Gray's account if there are resemblances between the two in this passage from Collins's *Ode*:

> . . . be mine the Hut,
> That from the Mountain's Side,
> Views Wilds, and swelling Floods,.
> And Hamlets brown, and dim-discover'd Spires,
> And hears their simple Bell, and marks o'er all
> Thy Dewy Fingers draw
> The gradual dusky Veil.

In Christopher Smart (1722–71) we face 'the paradox of a man who seems to have lived a sordid existence and yet produced [in the *Song to David*] one of the greatest religious lyrics in English poetry'.[2] Born at Shipbourne Fairlawn, Kent, the son of Lord Vane's steward, he was taught at home until his father's death, when (at the age of eleven) he was taken to Durham and attended the Grammar School there. He fell in

---

[1] Walpole's letters, which (with those written to him) will fill fifty or more printed volumes, occasioned the great quest described by their collector and editor, Wilmarth Lewis, in *Collector's Progress* (Constable, London, 1952). Up to 1957 twenty-one volumes had appeared in the Yale edition.

[2] *The Collected Poems of Christopher Smart*, edited by Norman Callan (2 vols. The Muses Library, Routledge, London, 1949), p. xviii.

love—and eloped temporarily when he was only about thirteen —with Anne Vane, through whose grandmother he was enabled to complete his education at Cambridge, becoming in 1745 a Fellow of Pembroke College. He is mentioned disparagingly in Gray's letters, and being arrested for debt left Cambridge for London, where he worked as a publishers' editor and hack-writer and married the daughter of one of his employers. He fell ill and needy and was helped by Samuel Johnson, who wrote of him as 'my poor friend Smart' when describing his condition after he had been committed in 1756 to an asylum. Released in 1763, he turned again to miscellaneous writing, which met his needs for only a few years. About 1769 he was confined in one of the debtors' prisons and wrote his last poems there.

Until recent years Smart was little mentioned apart from his influence on Browning, whose *Saul* was inspired by Smart's *Song to David* (1763), and he appears in Browning's *Parleyings with Certain People of Importance*. Smart's poetry falls into several categories—Odes and Addresses, Epigrams and Epitaphs, Fables, Religious and Devotional, Occasional and Miscel-laneous. It is considerable in bulk, and some part of it raises problems of interpretation still to be solved. The longest, most remarkable, but most difficult is *Jubilate Agno*, the obscurities of which rival those of Blake's Prophetic Books.[1] It does, how-ever, embrace in sections XIX (lines 51–60) and XX (1–65) one of the most endearing of animal poems, beginning 'For I will consider my Cat Jeoffrey' and containing such delightful lines as 'For he purrs in thankfulness, when God tells him he's a good Cat'. A *Song to David* is relatively simple and rises in the last few of its eighty-six stanzas to an exultant climax:

> Glorious the sun in mid career;
> Glorious th' assembled fires appear;
>   Glorious the comet's train:
> Glorious the trumpet and alarm;
> Glorious th' almighty stretched-out arm;
>   Glorious th' enraptur'd main: . . .

---

[1] See *Jubilate Agno. Re-edited from the Original Manuscript* (Hart-Davis, London, 1954) for a rearrangement of the confused MS. This edition elucidates much that was hitherto baffling, but many obscurities remain for interpretation.

Miscellaneous Verse and Prose

It is impracticable to do more than catalogue summarily certain other works in verse and prose belonging to this period.

Among the versifiers Mark Akenside (1721–70) should be noted for *The Pleasures of Imagination* (1744); William Mason (1724–97) for *The English Garden* (1772, '77, '79, '82); Charles Churchill (1731–64) for *The Rosciad* (1761); James Beattie (1735–1803) for *The Minstrel* (1774); John Byrom (1692–1763) for an extraordinary variety of work, from such hymns as 'Christians awake!' to a narrative of a prize-fighters' encounter with cudgels, broadswords, and quarter-staffs ('Extempore Verses upon a Trial of Skill'), and from an 'Epigram on Handel and Bononcini' ending

> Strange all this Difference should be
> 'Twixt Tweedle-*dum* and Tweedle-*de*!

to 'A Jacobite Toast' ending

> But who Pretender is, or who is King,
> God bless us all!—that's quite another thing.

Outstanding minor novels are Robert Paltock's *Peter Wilkins* (1751), a Crusoe-cum-Gulliver adventure story with winged men and women; Charlotte Lennox's *The Female Quixote* (1752); Henry Brooke's *The Fool of Quality* (1766), a Rousseau-esque work which John Wesley later abridged; Henry Mackenzie's *The Man of Feeling* (1771), an episodic novel of sentiment; Richard Graves's *The Spiritual Quixote* (1772), a satire on the Methodists and on their Calvinistic leader White-field in particular. Fanny Burney's *Evelina* (1778), *Cecilia* (1782), and *Camilla* (1796) belong to a later section (in Vol. III of the present work) on domestic fiction, which was to become the special province of women novelists.

Religious works of literary merit include *The Analogy of Religion* (1736) by Joseph Butler, Bishop of Durham, and the *Journal of John Wesley* (various posthumous editions).

David Hume was both philosopher and historian, writing *A Treatise of Human Nature* (1739–40), *Essays concerning Human Understanding* (1748), and *An Enquiry concerning Principles of*

Morals (1751), as well as *A History of Great Britain* from Julius Caesar to the Stuarts (1754–61). William Robertson became notable with his *History of Scotland during the Reigns of Queen Mary and of James IV* (1759) and *The History of Charles V* (1769).

Sir George Anson's *Voyage Round the World* (1748), Captain James Cook's *Voyages* (1773, '79, '84), and Admiral William Bligh's *Voyage to the South Seas* (1792) were distinguished additions to the literature of discovery; and Arthur Young's *A Six Months' Tour through the North of England* (1770), *A Tour in Ireland* (1780), and *Travels in France* (1792) combine travel with political and social observation.

The *Letters to his Natural Son* (1774) by Lord Chesterfield commend a dubious morality in excellent prose, and Lady Mary Wortley Montagu's *Letters* (posthumously, 1763 and later collections) gossip delightfully about herself, her travels in the East, and her later life in Italy.

CHAPTER XIII

BOSWELL, JOHNSON, AND THE CLUB

IN the years before Boswell met him [1] Johnson had published the bulk of his literary work, and in 1762 the Civil List pension of £300 a year freed him from the need to drudge for a bare living. He already had contemporary esteem, and posterity also would doubtless have esteemed him as a worthy and industrious but somewhat eccentric person. Esteem, however, was to grow into resounding posthumous fame through the friendship between the fifty-four-year-old Englishman and a twenty-two-year-old Scot which started shakily in the back parlour of a Covent Garden bookseller on 16 May 1763.

When, by becoming his biographer, Boswell became also Johnson's virtual creator, he became in effect his own destroyer for almost a century and a half. The self-portrait which peers from his *Life of Johnson* (1791) led several generations of readers to think of Boswell as a naive, humourless, foolish, thick-skinned, fawning creature who found it delicious to play the satellite to a great man, and who even took some masochistic pleasure in subjection to the great man's rebukes and gibes. In short, Boswell was commonly assumed to have been a simpleton somehow endowed with the ability to compose a masterpiece, and this assumption lingered until the discovery in 1925 and after of extensive hoards of his private papers rehabilitated him.

James Boswell

The eldest son of Alexander Boswell, eighth Laird of Auchinleck in Ayrshire, James Boswell (1740–95) was born in Edinburgh. His father became a judge of the Scottish High Court in 1754 and in that capacity bore the title of Lord Auchinleck. Young Boswell was first taught at a private school and tutored at home in strict propriety by fledgling ministers of the Church. At Edinburgh University he became proficient in Latin and Greek and acquired a command of English prose style sufficient to arouse expectations that he would become a successful author.

[1] See above, ch. IX, p. 167 ff.

As a boy, he was timid—scared of the dark and terribly afraid of ghosts; bashful in company, priggish, and puritanical. . . . He was subject to fits of depression, and in his seventeenth year suffered a protracted illness that sounds like a nervous collapse. When he emerged from it, he seemed to have undergone a physical and mental transformation. He grew suddenly robust and . . . became vain, amorous, gregarious. He began to frequent the theatre and to dangle after actresses. . . . Before very long, besides being a wit, he emerged as a sceptic and a tireless, if somewhat grubby, man of pleasure.[1]

The father's intention that his eldest son should follow him in the law was opposed by Boswell's determination to get to London, as he did by running away from home in 1760. He became a Roman Catholic directly after, but this was kept secret and it did not restrain him from dissolute conduct. He planned to root himself in London by obtaining a commission in the Guards, and to that end sought influential support through his father's friend the Earl of Eglinton. He was called home after a few months, however, and passed the next three years in desultory legal study, occasional verse-writing, and constant self-indulgence. After partially satisfying his father by qualifying in Civil Law, he returned to London in November 1762 with an allowance of £100 a year and the same intention, never to be fulfilled, of becoming a Guards officer. His fruitless seeking of patronage to smooth the way to an army commission, his profligacy and his repentant resolutions against debauchery, his disagreements with the landlord of his Downing Street lodgings—these are detailed in the *London Journal* (discovered in 1930), together with descriptions of clothes, food, and drink, of visits to coffee-houses, theatres, and taverns, and, most important, of his introduction to Johnson and of their further meetings during the ten weeks or so before Boswell ended the *London Journal* on 3 August 1763 preparatory to going abroad. He travelled in France, Switzerland, Holland, Germany, Italy,[2] and Corsica, publishing *An Account of Corsica* (1768) and *Essays in Favour of the Brave Corsicans* (1769). He succeeded to his father's property in 1782, was called to the English bar in 1786, and was Recorder of Carlisle from 1788 to 1790.

[1] See Professor F. A. Pottle's Introduction to *Boswell's London Journal 1762–1763* (McGraw-Hill, New York; Heinemann, London: 1950).
[2] See *Boswell in Holland* (1951), and *Boswell on the Grand Tour* (1953).

Boswell 'made a careful bequest of his manuscripts to his friends Sir William Forbes, the Rev. William Temple, and Edward Malone. But it is reported that the executors did not meet—they had the excuse of being widely separated—and Forbes, who was on the spot, handed the manuscripts to the tender mercies of the Boswell family. They were at once destroyed.'[1] Almost simultaneously with the printing of that statement by one of the leading Johnson scholars of this century, the long-held belief expressed in it was being shattered by the finding on 30 June 1925 at Malahide Castle, near Dublin, of a drawer and two boxes full of unpublished manuscripts by Boswell, these having been moved from Scotland to Ireland among the belongings of a Boswell descendant when she married into an Irish family. Further manuscripts were discovered in profusion at Malahide in 1930, 1937, and 1940; while a mass of letters and other writings came to light (1930–1931) at Fettercairn House, near Aberdeen, the home of a descendant of the Sir William Forbes named above as one of Boswell's three executors. These thousands of papers were bought entire by an American collector and later (1949) were acquired by Yale University.[2]

Boswell's Johnson

Among the recovered Boswell papers is the original manuscript draft of *The Life of Dr. Samuel Johnson*, including passages excised before publication. When the full work is at length printed, more will be known about Boswell's methods of composition, and the relation between what was written and what was first published. Meanwhile the *Note Book* and the *London Journal* allow us to see something of Boswell the biographer at work.

That *Boswell's Life of Johnson* is invariably so called, rather than *The Life of Johnson* by James Boswell, is in itself a recognition that the man and his book are indivisible. Boswell did

---

[1] See R. W. Chapman's Preface to *Boswell's Note Book 1776–1777: Recording Particulars of Johnson's Early Life communicated to Him and Others in Those Years* (Humphrey Milford, London, 1925).

[2] The whole collection is in process of being edited for publication. It will fill many volumes and be spread over many years. To date (1958) the *London Journal* and four volumes relating to Boswell's Continental journeys have appeared.

more than *write about* the life of Johnson, he *lived in* the life of Johnson, not only in the years of their friendship, 1763 to 1784, but also in the earlier years, as far as he was able to gather information about that period, 1709–63, from Johnson himself and others. He absorbed the material of the life into his own being, assimilating it completely and recreating it, not merely reproducing and transcribing it. It has become a truism and also a cliché that *Boswell's Life of Johnson* is the greatest of all biographies, but *why* it is the greatest is less often considered.

From youth Boswell was fascinated by the theatre, and before he left Edinburgh had had close contacts with it and its personnel. If he had been capable of full imaginative invention he might well have turned playwright, but lacking that gift his dramatic sense was exercised through an acute ear for the nuances of conversation and a remarkable ability in the writing of dialogue. Both the *Note Book* and the *London Journal* show that Johnson's conversation as given in the *Life* is not necessarily always what Johnson actually said. Boswell's aim was to make a revealing portrait of the man; verbal accuracy was subordinate to that. The greatness of the biography consists in its being a major work of art depending for effect upon selection and arrangement. Excellent conversationalist though Johnson was agreed by his friends to have been, we may without profanation guess that there were times when he was pompously oracular, tediously pontifical, and even a dreadful bore—as, indeed, every excellent conversationalist occasionally is. There is possibly more humour in Boswell's presentation of Johnson than was allowed to come to the surface. It is, for instance, likely that Boswell was not unamused at those moments when Johnson, having expressed himself in simple terms, immediately re-expressed himself in elaborate polysyllabic Johnsonese.[1]

To what extent Boswell dramatized Johnson not only by condensing and rearranging his sayings but also by elaborating or, possibly, inventing for him good things that show some significant aspect of his character, cannot be known. In the *London Journal* he records (6 July 1763) that he found much difficulty in recollecting Johnson's conversation; it required, he said, more parts than he was master of 'to retain that strength of sentiment and perspicuity of expression for which

[1] See his remark on *The Beggar's Opera* above, p. 200.

he is remarkable.'. The *Journal* was written up (about) weekly, from brief rough notes made daily, and sent in instalments to a friend in Scotland. Under the same date (6 July) Boswell mentions briefly a conversation with Johnson about Macpherson, the writer of *Ossian*. When he comes to this conversation in the *Life*, it is fuller and closes with one of the most famous of the Johnsonian *obiter dicta*:

> I added, that the same person maintained that there was no distinction between virtue and vice. JOHNSON. '. . . if he does really think that there is no distinction between virtue and vice, why, Sir, when he leaves our houses let us count our spoons.'

Since that passage does not appear in the *London Journal* entry written within a week of the actual conversation, it may be wondered whether, as set down in the *Life* much later, it was authentically dredged up from memory though not recorded before, or was part of another conversation, or was invented as a parabolical epigram picturesquely interpreting Johnson. In the Preface to the *Note Book*, cited above, it is pointed out that the phrase attributed in the *Life* (28 July 1763) to Johnson when speaking of Thomas Sheridan's system of teaching declamation—'Sir, it is burning a farthing candle at Dover, to shew light at Calais'—was first written down by Boswell as two sentences: 'He is like a man attempting to strike the English Channel' and 'It is setting up a candle at Whitechapel to give light at Westminster.' While the later version, though entirely rephrased and effectively condensed does not distort Johnson's meaning, we may nevertheless cogitate upon the problem of how much of the *art* of Johnson's conversation was provided by Boswell.

Johnson's first important literary production after his meeting with Boswell was the edition of Shakespeare in 1765.

A modern scholar [1] has acknowledged that notwithstanding all the work done since, 'Shakespeare, as he is known in the literature, not only of our own country, but of the world, is still in the main the Shakespeare of Rowe, Pope, Theobald, and the other eighteenth-century editors.' Up to 1685, Shakespeare's plays had been printed only in the early (but

---

[1] R. B. McKerrow: *The Treatment of Shakespeare's Text by his Earlier Editors, 1709–1768* (Proceedings of the British Academy, 1933, pp. 89–122), here followed.

frequently reprinted) and mostly corrupt Quartos and in the cumbersome collective Folio editions of 1623, 1632, 1663, and 1685. In 1709 Nicholas Rowe's edition attempted for the first time, by collation of the several versions of the plays, to present an improved text. His judgement was sometimes faulty, yet his edition was as a whole superior to any produced before, and he did a good deal of tidying-up by compiling lists of the dramatis personæ, revising stage directions, and providing (though not consistently nor always acceptably) act and scene divisions. Pope's edition (1725) carried out more thoroughly some features of improved formal presentation that Rowe had left uncompleted, and endeavoured to improve on Rowe's text by preferring certain earlier readings. These preferences were not always trustworthy, however, and the edition was further disfigured by 'improvements' due to Pope's eighteenth-century taste for elegance. Lewis Theobald, a skilful editor when his premises were sound, brought out (1733) an edition which has been found more reliable by later scholars than either Rowe's or Pope's, while his footnotes 'may be said to have initiated the critical study of Shakespeare's language'. Sir Thomas Hanmer's 1743–4 edition introduced capricious personal emendations, and Bishop William Warburton's (1747) was a hotch-potch of his predecessors' work with his own notes added.

As the product of nine years' spasmodic labour, there appeared in October 1765 *The Plays of William Shakespeare, in Eight Volumes, with the Corrections and Illustrations of Various Commentators; To which are added Notes by Sam. Johnson*. The importance of Johnson's edition is less in any marked textual improvement, for in the main he followed Warburton, than in the excellence of the Preface (one of his finest pieces of prose), the notes, and the critical comments on individual plays; and in his recognition of the true principles of textual scholarship even though he did not himself apply them consistently. A later edition of Shakespeare, that of Edward Capell (1768), came to be held in higher favour as a source of textual reference.

Johnson's *Journey to the Western Islands of Scotland* came out in 1775, ten years before Boswell's *Journal of a Tour to the Hebrides with Samuel Johnson*. These deal with their visit in the months of August to November 1773, and the two books have acquired the status of literary twins; but in character they differ widely, Johnson's account being mainly a description of places, antiquities, customs, and inhabitants, whereas Boswell puts Johnson in the centre of his account, which is dated day by day and is an essential supplement to the *Life*, though it also includes much on the localities and people visited.

In 1765 Johnson became acquainted with Henry Thrale and his wife Hester Lynch Thrale who, being widowed, remarried as Mrs. Piozzi. The Thrales—he was a prosperous brewer and M.P. for Southwark—had a house there and another at Streatham on the southern outskirts of London, and a room was set apart in each for Johnson. Invited more and more frequently, he 'at last . . . became one of the family'. Mrs. Piozzi's *Anecdotes of the late Samuel Johnson* (1786) and her correspondence with him (published 1778) are important as well as entertaining contributions to Johnsonian literature, as also are her diary [1] and Fanny Burney's.[2]

Frequent reference has already been made [3] to Johnson's last work, *Lives of the Most Eminent English Poets* (1783), issued as an independent publication in the year before he died but written and first printed as introductions to an edition of *The English Poets* published co-operatively by several London booksellers for whom it became a profitable venture. Johnson's fee, named by himself, was two hundred guineas. These *Lives* and the Preface, commentaries, and notes for the edition of Shakespeare have proved the most lastingly valuable of his writings. Among the numerous personal papers destroyed by Johnson were 'two quarto volumes, containing a full, fair, and most particular account of his own life, from his earliest recollection', which Boswell (who had read them in part) speaks of as 'precious records which must ever be regretted'.

Though he had had a persistent dread of death, Johnson in his final illness insisted on hearing a true account of his state. Learning that he could not recover, he said 'Then I will take no more physick, not even my opiates; for I have prayed that

---

[1] *Thraliana: The Diary of Mrs. Hester Lynch Thrale*, edited by Katherine C. Balderston (2 vols. Clarendon Press, 1942; 2nd edn. 1951).

[2] *Diary and Letters of Madame D'Arblay* (Fanny Burney), edited by Austin Dobson (6 vols. London, 1904–5). *The Diary of Fanny Burney*, selected and edited by Lewis Gibbs (1 vol. Everyman's Library, Dent, London, 1940).

[3] See above, pp. 27, etc.

I may render up my soul to God unclouded.' He died on Monday 13 December 1784 'about seven o'clock in the evening, with so little pain that his attendants hardly perceived when his dissolution took place'. He was buried in Westminster Abbey on the Monday following.

The Club

Boswell's list of the nine original members of The Club founded early in 1764 on the proposal of Sir Joshua Reynolds and with the active approval of Johnson, includes, beside those two, Edmund Burke and Oliver Goldsmith. The remaining five were Dr. Christopher Nugent, Topham Beauclerk, Bennet Langton, and Anthony Chamier (who were not men of letters), and Sir John Hawkins (1719–89) who made no mark in literature but wrote *A General History of Music* (1776) and was Johnson's first biographer, issuing a collected edition of the works and a *Life* in 1787, four years ahead of Boswell.

At first The Club had no formal title, but in 1779 it was named The Literary Club. Its membership grew to thirty-five, taking in titled men, bishops, and politicians, as well as David Garrick, the Warton brothers, Dr. Thomas Percy, Richard Brinsley Sheridan, Adam Smith, Edward Gibbon, and Boswell himself. The Club met for supper one evening in each week for some ten years at the Turk's Head tavern in Gerrard Street, Soho.[1] At these gatherings, which usually lasted from seven o'clock 'till a pretty late hour', Johnson's conversational gifts were amply exercised and well enjoyed. The customary conviviality was occasionally disturbed by disagreements, as when Hawkins 'one evening attacked Mr. Burke, in so rude a manner, that all the company testified their displeasure; and at their next meeting his reception was such, that he never came again'. Hawkins's exit is not surprising, for he was notoriously unclubable.

Of the members not so far discussed, the most eminent as writers were Reynolds (1723–92), Adam Smith (1723–90), Burke (1729–97), and Gibbon (1737–94). To these must be added Goldsmith (1730–74), so various and many-sided, who has been considered above (p. 202 ff.) only as a playwright. The first four here named were only incidentally men of letters:

[1] The time and place of meeting were subsequently changed.

their place in literature as excellent prose-writers is secondary to their eminence in other fields—Reynolds as painter, Adam Smith as political economist, Burke as political thinker and orator, Gibbon as historian.

Reynolds's *Discourses*—his annual addresses at the Royal Academy of Art (founded in 1768 with Reynolds as first President) from 1769 to 1790—start from the proposition that 'implicit obedience to the rules of art' must be exacted from young students, and they offer a masterly exposition of eclecticism and the Grand Style which, as a portrait painter, Reynolds himself practised. But while principles, rules, and laws were to be understood and observed, he recognized that 'by knowing their general purpose and meaning, the painter will often find that he need not confine himself to the literal sense; it will be sufficient if he preserve the spirit of the law' (Eighth Discourse). Nevertheless, Reynolds had laid down in the Sixth Discourse that

> When we have had continually before us the great works of art to impregnate our minds with kindred ideas, we are then, and not till then, fit to produce something of the same species. We behold all about us with the eyes of those penetrating observers whose works we contemplate; and our minds, accustomed to think the thoughts of the noblest and brightest intellects, are prepared for the discovery and selection of all that is great and noble in nature. The greatest natural genius cannot subsist on its own stock: he who resolves never to ransack any mind but his own, will soon be reduced, from mere barrenness, to the poorest of all imitations; he will be obliged to imitate himself, and to repeat what he has before often repeated. . . . It is vain for painters or poets to endeavour to invent without materials on which the mind may work, and from which invention must originate. Nothing can come of nothing.

The prose of the *Discourses* is characterized throughout by the ease and limpidity evident in this passage. As a philosophy of art they account for that sacrifice of spontaneity in Reynolds's own paintings which dulls the impact of his noble accomplishment and culture. Yet in the penultimate Discourse, delivered soon after the death of Gainsborough, he could say of his great contemporary, whose genuis was of a different order: 'If ever this nation should produce genius sufficient to acquire to us

the honourable distinction of an English School, the name of
Gainsborough will be transmitted to posterity, in the history
of art, among the very first of that rising name.' This prophecy,
long ago fulfilled, was spoken sincerely but against the grain.
In the later part of the Discourse, commendation of Gainsborough was hedged about with warnings to students who
might imitate his 'deficiencies' and forsake the 'style which
this Academy teaches': '. . . you may be corrupted by
excellences, not so much belonging to the art, as personal and
appropriated to the artist; and become bad copies of good
painters, instead of excellent imitators of the great universal
truth of things'.

No more than passing reference need here be made to Adam
Smith's *An Inquiry into the Nature and Causes of the Wealth of
Nations* (1776), for despite its high merit as a prose work no
one will read it purely as literature. It revolutionized politico-
economic thinking by laying down the principle that the
labour of a nation is the source of 'all the necessaries and con-
veniences of life' which it annually consumes (i.e of its *wealth*),
a principle which has ruled much subsequent political and
economic thought and action.

Burke, too, belongs far more to politics than to literature,
though the eloquence and passion of his oratory often raised
his speeches to the level of creative art. His Irish temperament
and political craft did not disdain extravagance of emotion
when it came pat to his immediate purpose, but as a member
of Parliament he would not veer from the conviction that he
was his constituents' representative, not their delegate. One
of his noblest utterances was in defence of that conviction:

> Parliament is not a *congress* of ambassadors from different and
> hostile interests; which interests each must maintain, as an agent
> and advocate, against other agents and advocates; but Parliament
> is a *deliberative* assembly of *one* nation, with *one* interest, that of the
> whole; where, not local purposes, not local prejudices ought to
> guide, but the general good, resulting from the general reason
> of the whole. You choose a member indeed; but when you have
> chosen him, he is not member of Bristol, but he is a member of
> parliament.[1]
>
> [1] *Speech to the Electors of Bristol,* 1774.

Outside politics Burke wrote *A Philosophical Inquiry into the Origin of our Ideas of the Sublime and Beautiful* (1756) with an introductory dissertation on Taste. He pronounced that whatever excites ideas of pain and danger or arouses terror is *sublime* (I, vii), and that *beauty* is a social quality drawing us to others through a sense of joy and pleasure (I, x). The *Inquiry*, exhaustively and minutely conducted, is at moments humorous through its want of humour. There is some over-insistence (though the point was typical of eighteenth-century taste) on the connection between smoothness and beauty; and some absurdity in the clinical description of the effects upon the body when 'we have before us such objects as excite love and complacency': 'The head reclines something on one side; the eye-lids are more closed than usual, and the eyes roll gently with an inclination to the object. . . .'

In *Thoughts on the Cause of the Present Discontents* (1770) Burke attributed the prevailing civil dissension to 'a faction ruling by the private inclinations of a Court, against the general sense of the people'. The *Speech on American Taxation* (1777) attacked the government for refusing to repeal the tea duty, saying *inter alia*, 'The medium, the only medium, for regaining their affection and confidence, is, that you will take off something oppressive to their minds.' *Reflections on the Revolution in France* (1790) defended the English monarchy and constitution against the assertion[1] that the king owed his crown to the choice of the people and might therefore be legally dethroned by the people. Burke went on from his denial of that proposition to survey the errors and excesses of the French revolutionaries, lamenting that 'the age of chivalry is gone. That of sophisters, economists, and calculators has succeeded; and the glory of Europe is extinguished for ever.' In his last major work, *Letters on the Proposals for Peace with the Regicide Directory of France* (1796–7), Burke attacked Pitt's ministry for attempting to negotiate with the Jacobins and, in a passage saturated with contempt, declared that 'In truth, the tribe of vulgar politicians are the lowest of our species. There is no trade so vile and mechanical as government in their hands. Virtue is not their habit.'

[1] In a sermon by Dr. Richard Price to the Revolution Club in London, 4 November 1789.

Oliver Goldsmith's output was enormous and its variety astounding. Much of it was hackwork, but it was the hackwork of a genius forced by circumstance and an improvidently gentle nature to become a menial of letters. Except Johnson, no one seems to have valued him in his lifetime at the proper worth, and even Johnson assailed him with such verbal clouts as Boswell records, while Garrick's *mot*, that Goldsmith 'wrote like an angel, but talk'd like poor Poll', is remembered parrotwise.

Born somewhere in Ireland in 1730, the son of an Irish parson, Goldsmith was educated at Trinity College, Dublin. Failing to enter the Church, he studied medicine at Edinburgh and Leyden, obtained a medical degree at (possibly) Louvain, and wandered in France, Switzerland, and Italy during 1755–6. He was in London without means in 1756, earning pittances as a doctor, a school usher, and a journalist. He applied without success for a medical post in India in 1758, and published at the same date a translation from the French, *The Memoirs of a Protestant*. His first notable original work, *An Enquiry into the State of Polite Learning* (1759) surveyed the decline of learning in the countries of western Europe and deplored the want of naturalness in current English poetry. More memorable was *The Bee*, a periodical which ran for only eight weekly numbers in October and November 1759, but as reissued in volume form in that year it holds a place among the best writings of the English essayists: 'A City Night-Piece' gives a grim picture of Goldsmith's London after midnight.

He worked in particular for John Newbery, the publisher of (mainly) children's books, beginning to write for him in January 1760 the 'Chinese Letters' first printed in the *Public Ledger* and collected as *The Citizen of the World* in 1762. Presented as the comments of a Chinese philosopher in London observing a variety of English scenes and themes, they introduced two of Goldsmith's best-remembered characters, The Man in Black and Beau Tibbs.

His novel, *The Vicar of Wakefield*, did not appear until 1766, but Boswell relates that it was sold by Johnson about 1762 for £60 to prevent Goldsmith's imprisonment for debt.[1] It is a

---

[1] Another account is that Goldsmith sold a third share in that year to B. Collins, who at length printed it.

unique masterpiece which carries the novel of sentiment as far
as it can go without slopping over into cloying sentimentality,
and the story is irradiated by a luminous spirit of simple goodness, avoiding mawkishness by a hair's-breadth yet with
certainty. Sentiment and simplicity are relieved by humour
lightly, almost casually, rippling over the surface; there is a full
measure of pathos, but also a saving grace of shrewdness; and
in Olivia, the vicar's elder daughter ('I intended to call her
after her aunt Grissel; but my wife, who during her pregnancy
had been reading romances, insisted upon her being called
Olivia'), Goldsmith at least sketched a character who is more
than a betrayed innocent.

The 'forgotten' works of Goldsmith include memoirs of
Voltaire (1761), a History of Mecklenburgh (1762), an
English grammar (written 1766), a Roman history (1769), a
history of England (1771), and, in addition to much other
miscellaneous writing, *An History of the Earth and Animated
Nature*, published soon after his death in 1774.

His two poems, *The Traveller* (1764) and *The Deserted Village*
(1770) have many typical eighteenth-century mannerisms
and artificialities, but also a refreshingly a-typical simplicity
and honesty of feeling, not without an occasional douche of
chilling realism:

> Sweet was the sound, when oft at evening's close
> Up yonder hill the village murmur rose;
> There, as I pass'd with careless steps and slow,
> The mingling notes came soften'd from below;
> The swain responsive as the milk-maid sung,
> The sober herd that low'd to meet their young;
> The noisy geese that gabbl'd o'er the pool,
> The playful children just let loose from school;
> The watchdog's voice that bay'd the whisp'ring wind,
> And the loud laugh that spoke the vacant mind.

Gibbon's *The Decline and Fall of the Roman Empire* (I, 1776;
II–III, 1781; IV–VI, 1788) is in many respects the greatest
single work of the eighteenth century, as it is also the greatest
English historical work. Of Gibbon as historian nothing need
here be said; of Gibbon as literary artist little can be said in
the absence of space for analysis and quotation. No other prose

writer has marshalled so formidable a mass of material into a creation so controlled, so confident, and so unified. In its monumentality *The Decline and Fall* epitomizes the eighteenth century as the eighteenth century liked to see itself; in its scepticism it epitomizes that century as the twentieth century tends to half-see it. As a literary achievement of unmatched amplitude and power, scope and durability, it is the fit terminal of a spacious and imposing age. Contemplating the finished work and recording his own sensations, Gibbon wrote in his *Autobiography*:

> . . . The air was temperate, the sky was serene, the silver orb of the moon was reflected from the waters, and all nature was silent. I will not dissemble the first emotions of joy on the recovery of my freedom, and, perhaps, the establishment of my fame. But my pride was soon humbled, and a sober melancholy was spread over my mind, by the idea that I had taken an everlasting leave of an old agreeable companion, and that whatsoever might be the future date of my History, the life of the historian must be short and precarious.

From the almost lyrical opening of this famous passage—the temperate air, the serene sky, the reflected moon, the silence of nature—and from the passing contemplation of possible fame, Gibbon is quickly caught back to a commoner mood of the age, the mood of sober melancholy in which eighteenth-century Englishmen brooded upon the prospect of death, as the Anglo-Saxons and the seventeenth-century Metaphysicals had in their different ways brooded before, and as, possibly with more cause but assuredly with less sobriety, twentieth-century writers also brood in their fashion.

DESCRIPTIVE NOTES
TO THE ILLUSTRATIONS

Colour Plate I (cf. text p. 199)

Scene from Gay's *The Beggar's Opera*, by William Hogarth. Oil. 22 × 28½ *in.* By courtesy of the Trustees of the Tate Gallery.

The scene is from the third act and shows Macheath in prison, with Lucy and Polly pleading for his release with the Turnkey and another official. On either side of the stage are boxes for spectators. The parts were played by Mrs. Egleton as Lucy, Mr. Hall as Lockit, Mr. Walker as Macheath, Miss Lavinia Fenton (afterwards the Duchess of Bolton) as Polly, and Mr. Hippisley as Peachum. The play was produced by John Rich at his theatre in Lincoln's Inn Fields early in 1728. Among the spectators on the right are John Gay, John Rich, and the Duke of Bolton. This version of the subject was ordered for Sir Archibald Grant in 1729 but was still unfinished at the end of 1730.

Colour Plate II (cf. text pp. 89 and 131)

Jacob Tonson, by Sir Godfrey Kneller. Oil, 36 × 28 *in.* National Portrait Gallery.

Colour Plate III (cf. text p. 180)

Pamela is married, by Joseph Highmore. Oil, 24 × 29 *in.* By courtesy of the Trustees of the Tate Gallery.

This is one of a series of twelve illustrations to Richardson's *Pamela*, painted by Highmore soon after the publication of the book. They were engraved by A. Benoist and issued in 1745. The engraving of this scene bears the following description: 'The Marriage ceremony performed in Mr. B.'s own Chappel by Mr. Williams, Mr. Peters giving her away, Mrs. Jewkes waits behind Pamela and the Maid keeps the door.'

Colour Plate IV (cf. text p. 190)

A scene from Colman and Garrick's *The Clandestine Marriage*, by Johann Zoffany. Oil, 37 × 49½ *in.* Garrick Club.

The scene is from Act IV: 'Oh, thou amiable creature! Command my heart, for it is vanquished.' It shows Thomas King as Lord Ogleby, Mrs. Baddeley as Fanny Sterling, and Robert Baddeley as Canton. The play was first produced in 1766. The performers shown here were cast in these parts for the command performance at Drury Lane on 12 October 1769. The picture was painted by express command of George III.

1 (cf. text p. 8)

The Workes of Benjamin Jonson, London, 1616. Title-page engraved by William Hole. 9¾ × 6¼ *in.* From a copy in the British Museum.

238 DESCRIPTIVE NOTES TO THE ILLUSTRATIONS

2 (cf. text pp. 2 and 18)

Inigo Jones, *costume design*. Pen and wash, 10¼ × 5¾ *in.* Devonshire Collection, Chatsworth. Reproduced by permission of the Trustees of the Chatsworth Settlement.

This design was for Queen Henrietta Maria as Chloris in the masque *Chloridia* by Ben Jonson, performed on 22 February 1631. To the design is attached this inscription: *The dessigne I conceaue to bee fitt for the Inuention and if it please hir Ma^{ve} to add or alter any thinge I desier to receue his Ma^{ts} comand and the dessign againe by this bearer. The collors allso are in hir Ma^{ts} choise; but my oppinion is that seueral fresh greenes mix with gould and siluer will be most propper*. *Chloridia* was the last masque in which Inigo Jones and Ben Jonson collaborated.

3 (cf. text p. 2)

Inigo Jones, *stage design*. Pen and wash, 11 × 7¾ *in.* Burlington-Devonshire Collection, R.I.B.A. Reproduced by permission of the Trustees of the Chatsworth Settlement. The drawing is deposited with the Royal Institute of British Architects (Courtauld Institute Photograph).

The design is for the House of Fame in *The Masque of Queenes* by Ben Jonson performed on 2 February 1609. In the printed text of the masque the following description is given of the set: 'The House of *Fame*. The structure and ornament of which (as is profest before) was entirely Mr. *Jones* his iuvention, and designe. First, for the lower Columnes, he chose the *statues* of the most excellent *Poets*, as *Homer, Virgil, Lucan*, &c. as being the substantiall supporters of *Fame*. For the vpper, *Achilles, Æneas, Cæsar*, and those great *Heroes*, which the *Poets* had cele-brated. All which stood as in massy gold. Betweene the Pillars, vnder-neath, were figur'd *Land-battayles, Sea-fights, Triumphs, Loues, Sacrifices*, and all magnificent subjects of honor: in brasse, and heighten'd with siluer. In which he profest to follow that noble description, made by *Chaucer*, of the place. Above were sited the *Masquers*, ouer whose heads he deuis'd two eminêt Figures of *Honor*, and *Vertue*, for the Arch. The *Freezes*, both below, and aboue, were filld with seueral-color'd lights, like *Emeralds, Rubies, Saphyres, Carbuncles*, &c. the reflexe of which, with other lights, placed in the Concaue, upon the *Masquers* habits, was full of glory.' This gives some idea of the elaborate scenery used for these masques. There is also a description of how the upper half of the tower revolved disclosing '*Fama bona* . . . attyr'd in white, with white wings, having a collar of gold about her neck, and a heart hanging at it' while the Queens, whom she displaced, descended and entered through the great gates below in three triumphal chariots. (For a full discussion of the masque and Inigo Jones's designs, see *Walpole Society*, Vol. XII, 1924.)

4 (cf. text p. 9)

Beaumont and Fletcher, *Phylaster*, London (1620). Woodcut from title-page, 3⅜ × 4¾ *in.* From a copy in the British Museum.

The scene shows the wounded Princess Arethusa in the forest guarded by a country gentleman who has driven Phylaster away.

5 (cf. text p. 9)
Beaumont and Fletcher, *The Maids Tragedie*, London, 1622. Woodcut from the title-page, $3\frac{1}{2} \times 4\frac{1}{2}$ in. From a copy in the British Museum. This is the second edition of the play but the woodcut was used in the 1619 edition. The scene shown is the duel between Amintor and the disguised Aspatia.

6 (cf. text p. 21)
Sir Francis Bacon, after Paul van Somer. Oil, $42\frac{1}{2} \times 39\frac{1}{2}$ in. National Portrait Gallery.

7 (cf. text p. 21)
Sir Francis Bacon. B.M. MS. Sloane 972, f. 1. Approximately half-size. This is part of a letter from Sir Francis Bacon to the Lord Chancellor, Thomas Egerton, Baron Ellesmere, touching *the History of Britain*, which he proposed to write as a tribute to Queen Elizabeth. It must have been written before 1618.

8 (cf. text p. 25)
The Holy Bible, London, 1611. Title-page engraved by Cornelis Boel. $13\frac{1}{2} \times 8\frac{3}{4}$ in. From a copy in the British Museum. The title-page shows a group of apostles at the top; on the left Moses with St. Luke and on the right Aaron and St. John. Boel, who came from Antwerp, is only known to have worked, in England, in 1611.

9 (cf. text p. 40)
Robert Herrick, *Hesperides*, London, 1648. Frontispiece engraved by W. Marshall. $6\frac{3}{8} \times 3\frac{3}{4}$ in. From a copy in the British Museum. The scene behind the bust of Herrick is of the Muses contending with the daughters of Pieros, when Helicon rose heavenward with delight. Pegasus struck the mountain with his hoof, stopped its ascent, and brought out of Helicon the soul-inspiring waters of Hippocrene.

10 (cf. text p. 32)
John Donne, *Death's Duell*, London, 1632. Frontispiece engraved by Martin Droeshout. $5\frac{1}{4} \times 4\frac{1}{8}$ in. From a copy in the British Museum. *Death's Duell*, printed after Donne's death, was the last sermon he preached, on Ash Wednesday 1631. He died five weeks later. Walton describes how Donne had himself painted in his shroud, and it is from that painting, now lost, that this engraving and his effigy were done.

11 (cf. text p. 37)
Richard Crashaw, *Steps to the Temple*, London, 1648. Title-page engraved by Thomas Cross. $5\frac{3}{8} \times 2\frac{3}{4}$ in. From a copy in the British Museum.

12 (cf. text p. 44)
Thomas Browne, *Religio Medici*, London, 1645. Title-page engraved by W. Marshall. $4\frac{1}{2} \times 2\frac{3}{8}$ in. From a copy in the British Museum. This is from the second authorized edition, two editions having been 'most imperfectly and surreptitiously printed before' in 1642.

13 (cf. text p. 56)

John Milton, *Paradise Lost*, London, 1688. Illustration to Book I engraved by M. Burgesse. 11¼ × 7⅜ *in*. From a copy in the British Museum.

There were three earlier editions than this one '*adorned with sculptures*' which was published by Jacob Tonson and was the first to be illustrated. It is a magnificent folio volume with an illustration to each book, all but one by Sir John Baptist Medina. Of Spanish descent, he was born in Brussels but settled in Britain. Employed mainly as a portrait painter, he was knighted in 1707 in Scotland by the Duke of Queensberry, Lord High Commissioner in Scotland, and was the last knight made in Scotland before the Act of Union.

14 (cf. text p. 48)

John Milton, by E. Pierce. 11 *in*. high. From a plaster cast in the National Portrait Gallery.

The original of this head, which is at Christ's College, Cambridge, was made about 1656. Edward Pierce, who died in 1695, also made busts of Cromwell and of Wren for whom he worked on the City churches and St. Paul's.

15 (cf. text p. 56)

Part of the deed for sale of Copyright in *Paradise Lost*. B.M. add. MS. 18861, approximately half-size (British Museum Photograph).

These are the original Articles of Agreement, dated 27 April 1667, between John Milton, gentleman, and Samuel Symmons, printer, for the sale of the copyright of 'a Poem intituled *Paradise Lost*' the sum paid to the poet being £5 down, with three further payments of £5 each on the sale of three editions, each of 1,300 copies. It is signed *John Milton* with his seal of arms affixed.

16 (cf. text p. 61)

John Bunyan, *The Pilgrim's Progress*. Frontispiece to part I, 1679. Engraved by Robert White. 5 × 2⅞ *in*. From a copy in the British Museum.

This is from the third edition of *The Pilgrim's Progress* and shows Bunyan sleeping; behind, Christian climbs to the Celestial City.

17 (cf. text p. 61)

John Bunyan, by Robert White. Plumbago on vellum. 4¾ × 3½ *in*. British Museum.

This drawing, probably done in 1679, is the best Bunyan portrait and is the source for the sleeping figure in the title-page of *The Pilgrim's Progress* which was also designed and engraved by White, a friend of Bunyan's.

18 (cf. text p. 65 *et seq*.)

Pierre Perrin, *Ariadne on the Marriage of Bacchus*, London, 1674. Frontispiece. 7¼ × 8½ *in*. From a copy in the British Museum.

The opera 'Now put into Musick by Monsieur *Grabut*, Master of his Majesties MUSICK', was acted by the 'Royall Academy of Musick' at the Theatre Royal, Covent Garden. The engraving shows the stage set for the prologue, with a view of the river Thames and old London Bridge as backcloth. The three nymphs represent the Thames, the Tiber and the Seine.

19 (cf. text p. 66)

Thomas Killigrew, by William Shepphard. 1650. Oil. 48¾ × 38½ in. National Portrait Gallery.

Killigrew, a gentleman-usher to Charles I, is seated in front of a portrait of the King who had been beheaded a year earlier. Killigrew holds a book inscribed *Killigrew Resident for C.R. in Venice 1650*. The pile of books on the table includes *Claricilla, The Princesse, The Pilgrim, The Parson's Wedding, Thomaso or the Wanderer, Cicilia or the Revenge,* all plays by him. At the bottom of the pile is *Eikon Basilike* published ten days after the execution of Charles and, though written by Dr. Gauden, considered by the Cavaliers to contain Charles's own thoughts and feelings. It was against this book that Milton wrote his *Eikonoklastes*.

20 (cf. text p. 79)

Part of one of the bookcases in the Pepysian Library at Magdalene College, Cambridge.

When Pepys died he left his library to his nephew, John Jackson, for life and then to a college (Magdalene by preference), where it was to be kept separate and intact. The books, some three thousand, are kept in their original bookcases and the illustration shows how the smaller volumes were raised on blocks of wood ornamented in harmony with the bindings, so that the tops should be level.

21 (cf. text p. 79)

Last page of Samuel Pepys's diary, 1669. 9⅛ × 6¾ in. Magdalene College, Cambridge.

Pepys's diary was kept in shorthand. It remained unread in Magdalene College Library until, on the publication of Evelyn's diary in 1818, it was shown to Lord Grenville who deciphered a few pages and gave them to John Smith, then an undergraduate. He was employed in deciphering the rest from 1819–22, working sometimes fourteen hours a day. Pepys used the system published by Thomas Shelton in 1641. The parts 'unfit for publication' were written in French, Latin, Greek, or Spanish.

22 (cf. text p. 83 *et seq.*)

The Compleat Auctioneer. About 1700. Engraving, 9¾ × 6¾ in. From a copy in the British Museum.

The print represents a book-stall such as were erected in the open air. Among the books for sale are *Don Quixote, Poems of several Occasions* by the Earl of Rochester, *The Expert Doctors Dispensatory* by Nicholas

R

Culpepper, a *Life of Oliver Cromwell,* and Euclid. Below the print are these lines:

> Come Sirs and view this famous Library
> 'Tis pitty learning shou'd discourag'd be:
> Here's Bookes (that is, if they were but well Sold)
> I will maintain't are worth their weight in Gold
> Then bid apace, and break me out of hand:
> Ne'er cry you don't the subject understand:
> For this I'll say—howe'er the case may hit,
> Whoever buys of me—I teach 'em Wit.

23 (cf. text p. 83 *et seq.*)
Engraved advertisement for Roger Tucker, bookseller. *c.* 1700. 6¼ × 3½ *in.* From the Bagford Collection in the British Museum.

24 (cf. text p. 92)
A scene in a Coffee House. Water-colour, 5¾ × 8¾ *in.* British Museum. Though the signature and date are faked this is undoubtedly a scene from the end of the seventeenth century. The coffee is being kept warm in pots in front of the fire and the boy is collecting clay pipes. The news sheets, printed in double columns, are much in evidence.

25 (cf. text p. 102)
Daniel Defoe, *The Life and Strange Surprising Adventures of Robinson Crusoe, Mariner, of York.* London, 1719. Frontispiece engraved by Clark and Pine, 5½ × 3½ *in.* From a copy in the possession of Sir Louis Sterling, Kt.
This is the first edition and such was the success of the book that three further editions were published in the same year.

26 (cf. text p. 100)
The Whigs Medly, engraved by George Bickham, 1711. 16¾ × 14¾ *in.* From a copy in the British Museum.
This satire against the Whigs shows many prints lying one above the other. The bottom one is of *The three false Bretheren Defoe, the Devil and the Pope.* Another, *A deformed Head in the Pillory,* may also be a caricature of Defoe. Bickham did several of these medleys.

27 (cf. text p. 129)
Joseph Addison, by Michael Dahl. Oil, 40½ × 31¾ *in.* National Portrait Gallery.
This portrait was painted in 1719, the year of Addison's death.

28 (cf. text p. 107)
Jonathan Swift, by Charles Jervas. Oil, 48½ × 38¼ *in.* National Portrait Gallery.
Jervas was a successful though not a great painter. He had many literary friends including Pope, Addison, Swift, Lady Mary Wortley Montagu, and others. Pope took painting lessons from him for over a year and addressed an adulatory poem to him. Jervas also embarked on a new translation of *Don Quixote,* though he knew no Spanish and does not appear to have studied the original.

29 (cf. text p. 147)

Alexander Pope, *The Dunciad*. London, 1729. Engraved title-page, 7 × 4½ *in*. From a copy in the possession of Mr. I. A. Williams.

There were at least nine different editions or impressions of *The Dunciad* published in the first two years 1728 and 1729, but the exact order is hard to determine.

30 (cf. text p. 146)

Alexander Pope, *The Rape of the Lock*, 1714. Engraved illustration (opposite p. 19) by Michael van der Gucht. 5½ × 4⅛ *in*. From a copy in the British Museum.

The severed lock is being held up while the lady is comforted by her friends.

31 (cf. text p. 145)

A view in the garden of Pope's villa at Twickenham, by William Kent. Pen and wash, 11⅜ × 15⅝ *in*. (British Museum Photograph).

This view shows some of the many objects in the gardens at Twickenham, including a bust of Homer, a fountain with a rainbow gleaming in the spray, and a temple with an altar smoking in the centre.

32 (cf. text p. 152)

Hudibras and the Lawyer, by William Hogarth. Pen and wash. 9⅝ × 13¼ *in*. Royal Library, Windsor Castle. Reproduced by gracious permission of Her Majesty the Queen.

This is one of a series of illustrations made by Hogarth for an edition of *Hudibras* by Samuel Butler, published in 1726. As the drawing was to be engraved, it is in reverse and the clerks write with their left hands.

33 (cf. text p. 157)

Isaac Watts, by an unknown artist. Oil, 29¼ × 24½ *in*. National Portrait Gallery.

34 (cf. text p. 153)

Matthew Prior, by Jonathan Richardson. Oil, 49 × 39 *in*. National Portrait Gallery.

35 (cf. text p. 156)

John Philips, *Cyder*, London, 1708. Frontispiece engraved by Michael van der Gucht. 6¾ × 4⅛ *in*. From a copy in the possession of Mr. I. A. Williams.

This engraving shows three gardeners caring for the apple trees; two are grafting while the third digs. In the background, yet another gardener pulls a roller.

36 (cf. text p. 179)

Samuel Richardson, by Joseph Highmore. Oil, 20 × 13¾ *in*. National Portrait Gallery.

37 (cf. text p. 186)

Tobias Smollett, by an unknown artist. About 1770. Oil, 27 × 20 *in.* National Portrait Gallery.

38 (cf. text p. 187)

Laurence Sterne, by L. C. de Carmontelle. Chalk and water-colour, 10⅜ × 6⅞ *in.* National Portrait Gallery.

39 (cf. text p. 186)

Tobias Smollett, *Roderick Random*, 1780 edition. Illustration (opposite p. 142) by Robert Dodd, engraved by James Heath. 6¼ × 3⅞ *in.* From a copy in the British Museum.

The scene shown is of Roderick escorting Narcissa to the House, having saved her from Sir Timothy Thicket, who is seen lying in the background.

40 (cf. text p. 190 *et seq.*)

A Just View of the British Stage, or three Heads are better than one Scene Newgate by M D—v—to, by William Hogarth. 1725. Engraving, 7¼ × 8½ *in.* From a copy in the British Museum.

Under the engraving is this explanation: 'This print represents the rehearsing of a new Farce that will Include yᵉ two famous entertainments Dr. Faustus & Harlequin Shepherd to wᶜʰ will be added Scaramouch Jack Hall the Chimney-Sweeper's Escape from Newgate through yᵉ Privy, with yᵉ comical Humours of Ben Jonson's Ghost, Concluding wᵗʰ the Hay-Dance Perform'd in yᵉ Air by yᵉ figures A. B. C. assisted by Ropes from yᵉ Muses.' The three figures are Wilks, Cibber, and Booth. The paper hung over the privy consists of torn leaves from *The Way of the World, Hamlet, Macbeth* and *Julius Cæsar.* M D—v—to in the title was Devoto, a scene painter at various theatres.

41 (cf. text p. 190 *et seq.*)

The Rival Printers. 1728. Engraving, 7¼ × 12¼ *in.* From a copy in the British Museum.

In the centre Shakespeare (*E*) is rising from the ground, to the left Walker (*B*) is pouring out a bag of WALKER'S PLAYS, i.e. his edition of Shakespeare, and is about to be arrested by a bailiff (*C*). To the right Tonson (*A*) pours out his edition, and on either side of him are Pope (*D*) weeping, and Theobald (*D*) pointing to THEOBALD'S RESTOR'D SHAKSPEARE. All are upset by the lack of demand for their editions of Shakespeare's Works. The object of the print is to ridicule the rival printers for selling cheap plays and also the general public for its taste for dancing dogs, tumblers, and singers, to the neglect of Shakespeare.

42 (cf. text p. 190 *et seq.*)

Rich's Glory on his Triumphant Entry into Covent-Garden, by William Hogarth. Engraving. 6½ × 12 *in.* (size of sheet). From a copy in the Victoria and Albert Museum (Crown Copyright Reserved).

This print refers to the opening of Covent Garden Theatre on 18 December 1732, when John Rich removed there from the Playhouse in Lincoln's Inn Fields.

43 (cf. text pp. 67 and 193)
Colley Cibber, by Giuseppe Grisoni. Oil, 49½ × 39¼ in. Garrick Club. Colley Cibber is shown as Lord Foppington in *The Relapse* by Vanbrugh.

44 (cf. text p. 203)
Mr. SHUTER, Mr. QUICK, & Mrs. GREEN in the Characters of HARDCASTLE, TONY LUMPKIN, and Mrs. HARDCASTLE. 1776. Mezzotint engraving by R. Laurie, after Thomas Parkinson, 9⅞ × 13⅞ in. From a copy in the Victoria and Albert Museum (Crown Copyright Reserved). This scene from *She Stoops to Conquer* shows Mrs. Hardcastle begging for her life from Hardcastle, who looks at her in astonishment, while Tony Lumpkin enjoys the success of his scheme. The three performers appeared as these characters in the original production at Covent Garden in 1773.

45 (cf. text p. 200)
The Baboon and the Poultry, by H. Gravelot. 1738. Pen and wash, 6⅞ × 3⅛ in. In the British Museum.
The second volume of Gay's *Fables* is one of the most beautiful books published in England. The illustrations, for which the majority of the original drawings are in the British Museum, were made by Gravelot, a French artist who worked in England from 1732 to 1754. He also made a series of illustrations for the second edition of Theobald's edition of Shakespeare and (with Francis Hayman) some of the plates for Richardson's *Pamela*.

46 (cf. text p. 215)
Horace Walpole, *The Description of Strawberry Hill*. 1784. View of the Library. Engraving, 7 × 10½ in. From a copy in the British Museum. The decoration of the Library and the picturesque disarray of the books are in complete contrast to Pepys's Library of a century earlier.

47 (cf. text p. 235)
Oliver Goldsmith, *The Deserted Village*. 1770. Vignette from the title-page, designed and engraved by Isaac Taylor, 3 × 5 in. From a copy in the possession of Mr. I. A. Williams.
This attractive engraving shows 'the sad historian of the pensive plain' against a view of the deserted village.

48 (cf. text p. 217)
Despair offering a bowl of poison to Thomas Chatterton, attributed to John Flaxman, R.A. Pencil, 7½ × 9 in. Mr. I. A. Williams.
Flaxman, who lived from 1755 to 1826, was equally eminent as a draughtsman and as a sculptor. This drawing must have been made a few years after Chatterton's death. The initials J. W. stand for James Ward and are later additions. Another drawing of the same subject by the same hand is in the British Museum.

49 (cf. text p. 218)

Designs by Mr. R. Bentley for six poems by Mr. T. Gray. 1753 (p. 7). Engraving, 4½ × 6¼ *in.* From a copy in the British Museum.

This tailpiece to the 'Ode on the Death of a Favourite Cat' shows Charon poling the cat over the Styx to the Underworld, while Cerberus, the three-headed dog barks at it.

50 (cf. text p. 219)

Christopher Smart, *Poems on Several Occasions.* 1752. Frontispiece by Francis Hayman, engraved by C. Grignion, 9 × 7 *in.* From a copy in the possession of Mr. I. A. Williams.

Francis Hayman was one of the original members of the Royal Academy. The illustration is to 'The Hop Garden' and gives a lively picture of rustic sport among the hop-pickers.

51 (cf. text p. 232)

Edmund Burke, by Sir Joshua Reynolds. Oil, 29½ × 24½ *in.* Reproduced by permission of the Board of Governors and Guardians of the National Gallery of Ireland.

This portrait is probably the one exhibited in the Royal Academy in 1774. Reynolds exhibited regularly at the Academy from its foundation in 1768 and was its first President.

52 (cf. text p. 230)

Sir Joshua Reynolds, by himself. Oil, 29½ × 24½ *in.* From the painting at Althorp by permission of Earl Spencer.

This is one of many self-portraits by Reynolds and was exhibited in the Royal Academy, 1773.

53 (cf. text p. 223)

Dr. Samuel Johnson, by Sir Joshua Reynolds. 1756/7. Oil, 48½ × 43 *in.* National Portrait Gallery.

54 (cf. text p. 190)

David Garrick, by Sir Joshua Reynolds. Oil, 29½ × 24½ *in.* Reproduced by gracious permission of Her Majesty the Queen.

Garrick appeared as Kitely in Ben Jonson's *Every Man in His Humour* in 1751. He sat for this portrait in 1767 and it was given by Reynolds to Burke.

Reynolds painted at least ten of his fellow members of The Club, several of them many times.

55 (cf. text p. 224)

James Boswell as a Corsican Chief, by Samuel Wale. Engraved by I. Miller. 6¼ × 3⅞ *in.* From a copy in the British Museum.

The engraving shows Boswell in the dress of an armed Corsican chief, as he appeared at the Shakespeare Jubilee celebrations at Stratford-upon-Avon in September 1769.

56 (cf. text p. 225)

Dr. Johnson and Boswell, by Samuel Collings. Pencil, 8½ × 10¼ *in*. Victoria and Albert Museum.

This is one of the original drawings for *The Picturesque Beauties of Boswell* published in 1786. It shows Boswell and Johnson walking up a street in Edinburgh, deep in discussion.

Text illustration, p. 40

Robert Herrick, *Hesperides*, 1648, p. 18. Same size. From a copy in the British Museum.

This is perhaps the best known of all Herrick's poems.

Text illustration, p. 78

Izaak Walton, *The Compleat Angler*, 1653, p. 168. Same size. From a copy in the British Museum.

This is one of the many charming engravings of fish in the first edition.

Text illustration, p. 90

B.M. MS. Egerton 2869. Same size.

This is the first page of a letter from Dryden to Jacob Tonson on Lady Chudleigh's verses which 'are better than any wch are printed before the Book' (the translation of Virgil, now preparing for the second edition, 1698); on the reception of *Alexander's Feast* which was most favourable, on the dangerous fall of his son Charles in Rome, and other subjects. It was written about December 1697.

Text illustration, p. 112

B.M. Add. MS. 39839. Slightly reduced.

This is one of the series of letters to Vanessa (Esther Vanhomrigh), from Swift. These, and drafts of her letters to him, were long supposed to have been destroyed, but were rediscovered in the early years of this century. They belong to the period 1711–22.

Text illustration, p. 134

The Tatler, No. 104, December 6–December 8, 1709. About half-size. From a copy in the British Museum.

This is the first side of a representative issue of *The Tatler*.

Text illustration, p. 136

The Female Tatler, September 1709; *The Observator*, February 1711; *The Grouler*, February 1711. Each approximately half-size. From copies in the British Museum.

These are typical examples of early eighteenth-century news-sheets.

Text illustration, p. 138

B.M. Add. M.S. 21110. Half-size.

This is the agreement by Joseph Addison and Richard Steele to sell to Samuel Buckley for £575 their half-share in the seven volumes of the collected edition of *The Spectator*, dated at the Fountain tavern in the Strand, 10 Nov, 1712. On the back is Buckley's assigment to Jacob Tonson for £500 in 1714.

Text illustration, p. 146
  Subscription ticket for Alexander Pope's translation of *The Iliad*.
  Two-thirds size. From a copy in the British Museum.

Text illustration, p. 171
  Samuel Johnson, *A Dictionary of the English Language*, 3rd ed. 1765.
  Three-quarters size. From the copy in the British Museum.
  This was Johnson's own interleaved copy which he corrected for the
  fourth edition published in 1773. Altogether five editions of the
  Dictionary were published in Johnson's lifetime.

Text illustration, p. 174 (see also text p. 91)
  Samuel Johnson, Letter to Thomas Longman. Slightly reduced.
  Reproduced by permission of the Huntington Library, San Marino,
  California.
  In this letter Johnson invites the booksellers who were to publish his
  Dictionary to breakfast, so that the contract might be signed. The
  booksellers concerned were Robert Dodsley, Charles Hitch, Andrew
  Millar, Thomas Longman, and John and Paul Knaptons. The contract
  was signed on 18 June 1746 and the price stipulated was £1,575.
  Thomas Longman, founder of the present firm of publishers, died soon
  after the publication of the *Dictionary* in 1755.

Text illustration, p. 206
  Playbill for the first performance of *The School for Scandal* by Richard
  Brinsley Sheridan at the Theatre Royal, Drury Lane on 9 May 1777.
  Much reduced. From a copy in the Victoria and Albert Museum
  (Crown Copyright Reserved).
  The first performance was, in fact, on 8 May, and the anticipation
  was possibly decided on at the last moment. 'Performed but once'
  suggests that the play was put on, at first, for but a single night, which
  was a common practice. *The School for Scandal* was played, however,
  with the exception of a Benefit, for fifteen consecutive nights and continued to be performed two or three times a week for the next two
  seasons.

Text illustration, p. 236
  This woodcut is the heading to Discourse No. 10 given at the Royal
  Academy, in December 1782 by Sir Joshua Reynolds. Slightly reduced.
  From a copy in the British Museum.

INDEX